Da Capo al Fine

A LIFE IN MUSIC

ALEXANDER FARIS

Da Capo al Fine

A LIFE IN MUSIC

Matador
5 Weir Road
Kibworth Beauchamp
Leicester LE8 0LQ, UK
Tel: (+44) 116 279 2299
Email: books@troubador.co.uk
Web: www.troubador.co.uk/matador

ISBN 978 1848761 131

British Library Cataloguing in Publication Data.
A catalogue record for this book is available from the British Library.

Typeset in 12pt Perpetua by Troubador Publishing Ltd, Leicester, UK

Matador is an imprint of Troubador Publishing Ltd

Printed in Great Britain by the MPG Books Group, Bodmin and King's Lynn

For John and Harriet
and in memory of Katharine
With my love

CONTENTS

APPENDICES

Preface

On a sheet of music, *Da Capo Al Fine* means 'repeat from beginning to end' or, rather, 'to the *point* marked END'. There may still be a Coda, a tail. An autobiography.

My teenage ambition was to become a conductor. *A Life in Music* is about the journey as much as the destinations.

Acknowledgments

I am indebted to David Llewellyn and Carlo Ardito for constant encouragement and scrupulous editing; to Alan Cooper for weekly reminders of forgotten events and for an impeccable typescript; to Ann Melsom for the generosity of her labour in contributing the index; and to the multitude of others who have been my friends and colleagues *da capo al fine*.

The Author
Da Capo…

North of the Border

he first time I heard the *Enigma Variations* the work was conducted by Sir Edward Elgar in the Ulster Hall, Belfast. He had a mane of silver hair, and sat in a handsome mahogany chair to conduct. In less than a month he was dead.

It was January, 1934. By the end of the year Holst and Delius had died too, and what we thought of as modern music seemed to have come to a standstill.

To an Irish thirteen–year–old *Enigma* seemed strange and modern. What would I have thought of *Petrouchka, The Firebird, The Rite of Spring?* I knew nothing of Stravinsky's early (c.1930) recordings, nor had these works reached our local theatre or concert platforms. Musical education was based on 'the three B's', (Bach, Beethoven and Brahms), with a smattering of Haydn and Mozart, and a note–for–note, cover–to–cover knowledge of *The Messiah.* For the exams of the Royal Schools of Music we had to learn graded short pieces composed for the purpose by eminent professors. I remember that, at six, my talent was stretched by a piece called *A–Sailing.* I hope the composer made a royalty from the copy my mother paid for.

Born in Caledon, Co. Tyrone, a mile north of the three week-old border between North and South, I was a British subject. I am Irish by temperament, but owe my professional career to England and my love of London.

The village of Caledon encircled the Caledon estate, seat of the Earl of Caledon, father of the young Harold Alexander, the future Field Marshal. The latter served as a young officer in the Irish Guards during the Great War. On one occasion there was to be a Christmas concert in honour of the young soldiers on leave from the front. For the occasion mother composed a series of verses to be sung by local children. At the last minute it was heard that Harold Alexander was to be present. In the consequent excitement mother wrote a new verse in honour of this special hero, in whose footsteps I was to follow twenty-five years later as a lieutenant in the Irish Guards.

A major catastrophe occurred during my infancy in Caledon. One fine afternoon the baker drove up the drive to our pretty Italianate manse, in his scarlet

Katharine   Sandy   Harriet   John

John, Katherine, Sandy and Harriet

horse–drawn van. My mother took Katharine, my elder sister and me to see the fun. Mother, ("Mammy"), bought the week's bread, and then, as a special treat, bought both of us penny buns with white sugar–icing. Katharine and I went round to the back yard where we kept hens. I walked with my left hand in Katharine's and my right hand hanging by my side. Suddenly a bold hen, realising that this was her lucky day, plucked the bun from my hand. Floods of tears.

I was seventy–five years old before I found it in me to forgive that hen, it never having occurred to me that we had probably long since eaten her for Sunday lunch. Dinner, we called it.

My father was Minister of the Caledon Presbyterian Church until we moved in 1924 to Coagh, on the borders of Loch Neagh, for a sadly short period. Daddy developed pernicious anaemia, then incurable, and died in September 1925. Had he lived for one more year he would have survived; doctors had by then discovered the liver cure for that hitherto mortal disease.

My father's death transformed the entire history of our family. We moved to a city life in Belfast. Mother returned to her former post as a teacher in Victoria College, Ulster's principal girls' school, of which she later became headmistress. John, my elder brother, eight years my senior, was withdrawn from the Royal School, Dungannon, where he had been a boarder, and sent as a day boy to "Inst", (the Royal Belfast Academical Institution). Katharine, my elder sister, attended Victoria College, where I was enrolled, at the age of four, into the kindergarten.

I proceeded to "Inchmarlo", the institution's preparatory school, where I twice took leading roles in Gilbert and Sullivan operas, first as Katisha in *The Mikado*, later as the Duchess of Plaza–Toro in *The Gondoliers*. I should have played Iolanthe in *Iolanthe*, but came down, as did John and my younger sister Harriet, with diphtheria. A major epidemic smote Belfast's children. Many died.

The epidemic affected John in more ways than one. He had just been promoted to play Rugby in the school's 1st XV, but was still in hospital on the relevant date — however, his academic career was resumed with considerable élan. He went on to become head boy of the school before winning a scholarship to Worcester College, Oxford.

Eight years later, Sandy, not his brother's match as an academic, also reached the dizzy heights of head boy, after a year as a probably priggish prefect, (they taught us about alliteration), and proceeded on his musical career with reasonable success.

The Royal Belfast Academical Institution is Ulster's major boys' school. Founded in 1810, with sponsorship from the Duke of Wellington, who corresponded from the field while he was engaged in the Peninsular War, concerning the foundation of Inst. The school is housed in a building of simple classic elegance, designed by Sir John Soane.

My best friend at school, beside whom I sat through most classes, was Charles Monteith. "Charlie" was later seriously wounded in Burma during the second World War. He returned to London and eventually became chairman of Faber and Faber.

R.B.A.I
Sir John Soane's elegant design dwarfed by Belfast Victoriana

We had a happy home. It was also, in a sense, a happy second school, for my loving mother was an amazing polymath who could teach anybody anything, making even difficult subjects seem easy to the dullest brain. Not that any of us was exactly dull, but we sometimes had our own problems, particularly if we, (I speak of myself), had been inattentive in school:

'Mammy, I don't understand quadratic equations!'
'Oh, they're beautiful! How are you told to do them?'
so—and—so
'Well, you can leave out that line and it will all come out right; but don't tell Mr McKenna I told you.'

And so on. It might be Greek or Geometry — anything. Mother could help you pass your exams.

When it came to music, I started teaching myself. Mother was musical, but, having a right hand injured in infancy, she could not play the piano. She was a good singer and violinist. John and Katharine were not musical. Harriet played piano and cello rather well. And Sandy?

When we came home from church on Sunday morning, I would go straight to our upright Chappell piano, and, standing with the keyboard at eye—level, pick out the hymn tunes, often getting them wrong at first, then correcting my errors. Mother began to suspect a musical talent and called in her school's music teacher, Miss Winifred S. Bell, to give me the once—over. Miss Bell had no doubts; I had my first piano lesson before my fifth birthday.

Before moving to the headmistress' house in the grounds of Drumglass, where a former Victorian mansion had become the boarders' residence and kindergarten for Victoria College, we lived in a nearby house called Rosebank.

Our household was dominated, if not actually ruled over, by Lily Law, our very Irish, very Catholic maid, or cook—general, as a domestic agent would then have described her. She was amusing, but had a fierce tongue.

On one occasion two cousins called in for a meal. So far, so good. But the next day my mother invited one of her teaching colleagues to afternoon tea. This involved Lily placing one extra cup and saucer on the tea—tray. A thunderous tirade issued from the kitchen: 'This house has gone ENTERTAINING MAD!'

I used to visit that kitchen of an evening just for the pleasure of hearing Lily's witty conversation, including some near—libellous anecdotes. Lily had previously worked for two mistresses; Mrs Moore—Brabazon and a Mrs Turnbull. Mrs M—B had once rebuked Lily for helping one of the servants by lifting a bucket. According to

Lily, she said, "PUT YOU DOWN THAT BUCKET, Lily, and never let me see you helping the other servants."

Lily's sole duty was supposedly that of lady's maid.

Later in Belfast, when Lily was working for Mrs Turnbull, she found her mistress sitting on the stairs in tears, 'Oh, Lily, he's gone', (referring to her husband's death).

"'Gone where?" says I.' (Knowing perfectly well what she meant.)

In my teens I founded a home orchestra. With more than a dozen players, it was really a chamber group, but with a touch of *folie de grandeur* I named it "The Nutcracker Orchestra". It was made up of a family group: myself as conductor, mother on viola, and Harriet, (still known as "Hilary"); and a group of school friends, including Denis Harriman, violin and leader; Geoffrey Simmons, a fine, young violinist, who was later killed in the Belfast blitz; "The Moss Bros", Ian Moss on piano and his brother Clifford on oboe; plus a variable number of others from time to time. We rehearsed at home, mother giving us sandwiches in our break. We played at various genteel functions such as fêtes and sales. On one occasion mother persuaded Captain Corrin, a "man from the ministry", with some responsibility for the city's music, to attend one of our rehearsals. He gave an approving verdict, and was complimentary about my conducting, perhaps out of politeness to my mother, his hostess.

In June 1939 our little orchestra auditioned for B. Walton O'Donnell, musical director of BBC Northern Ireland. After some friendly encouragement we were promised a further hearing, which never took place because of the outbreak of war.

I was by then attending symphony concerts in the Ulster Hall or the Albert Hall, the two popular venues for music lovers, (and politicians).

I was taught piano by the aforementioned Miss Bell, a musical spirit whose sensitivity of phrasing lives with me to this day; and harmony and counterpoint by one George Smith, an ebullient widely–read man with whom I played piano duet versions of Beethoven and Mozart Symphonies. That was how we learnt the classics then – at the piano. To hear the orchestration we had to wait until someone had 78s of the great works, or until they appeared in the programmes of symphony concerts in the city.

Then came moments of epiphany. I was taken to a rehearsal of the Beethoven G major piano concerto, played by Wilhelm Backhaus, conducted by Adrian Boult. I had never heard the piece. I cannot be the only one to find the string chord of B major after the piano opening one of the most beguiling surprises in music; but it was the way the great pianist brought his second entry to its conclusion that had me sweating. My steel–framed glasses steamed up with excitement (it happens sometimes nowadays). I still have autographs of Backhaus, Szigeti, Henry Wood, Conchita Supervia, Albert Coates, and many others, including half that of Sir Arthur Bliss. (He had been conducting his film music for H.G. Wells' *Things to Come*. My pen ran out of ink, and he was late for a plane).

Coates, the Great Panjandrum of the Bolshoi, conducted my first hearing of Tchaikovsky's 6th Symphony. It concluded the first half of a concert, and affected me so strongly that I asked to be taken home, not wanting to spoil the effect by the intrusion of other music. My understanding mother complied, and we went home on the Malone Road tram.

Coates kindly gave me his autograph in the interval before we left. He was wearing only his underpants, his sweat dripping onto the carpet. He was the fattest man I had ever seen.

Twenty years later I learned the meaning of *bathos*. In an aqua–show at the Wembley Pool the star Esther Williams made her spectacular first entrance swimming on her back to the theme of the 2nd subject of the Pathetic Symphony. It was a time when melody was running short in popular music, and the classics were being plundered for good tunes. I didn't realise that I was listening to a hit called *This is the Story of a Starry Night*.

We had yearly visits from the D'Oyly Carte Opera Company, with Sir Henry Lytton, Bertha Lewis, Darrell Fancourt, Sydney Granville *et al.* These shows were immensely popular, though members of the musical intelligentsia did not like to be caught uttering words of too much respect about this aspect of Sullivan's music.

In 1986, in the company of other local boys and girls, (elderly ladies and gentleman made good), I conducted a concert in that Ulster Hall where I heard my first orchestral music, in celebration if the BBC's 60th anniversary of broadcasting in Northern Ireland.

'Why are they celebrating the *sixtieth* anniversary?' asked someone.

'Because,' replied a bomb–weary cynic, 'there will be no seventieth.'

In 1937, at the age of sixteen, I was becoming more and more interested in music, and the possibility of a musical career came into question. I wanted to be a conductor, and was greatly impressed by a cartoon of Dr Malcolm Sargent in the *Strand Magazine*. My mother, perceptive and ever helpful, arranged for me to be musically vetted by Norman Hay, a distinguished Ulster composer and critic. He put me through my paces and delivered a written verdict. "Sandy," he wrote in a most kindly letter, "has the ability to be a professional musician, but you must warn him, [he advised my mother], that if he takes up such a career, he will be in for some bad times." It was a wise prophecy. In the course of my career I suffered periods of unemployment lasting as long as eighteen months, with the concomitant financial distress.

But I was consistent in my ambition, and my mother with her encouragement. Eventually I ended up at Oxford with a Kitchener Scholarship, not the product of my own talent so much as the heritage of my late father's service in the Great War. We didn't say "World War I" then. In those days it was frequently referred to as "the war to end wars".

My last year at school was memorable for a unique summer holiday. My distinguished uncle Jim, (later Sir James Acheson), on furlough from the Indian Political Service, entertained three families of cousins to a holiday in Co. Mayo*. He rented a beautiful old Georgian house in Newport, where our united family experienced the last days before the outbreak of World War II.

---

* See Paradise In Mayo

Portballintrae

*P*ortballintrae is a seaside village lying between the Giant's Causeway and Dunluce Castle on the north coast of Co. Antrim. Behind the village, what is allegedly the world's oldest electric tramway runs along the cliffs, passing, first, the Bushmills whiskey distillery, then the long Runkerry Sands.

In Portballintrae, James Crawford, my mother's cousin, owned two semi–detached verandah-fronted houses on the sea front. "Cousin Jimmy", as we knew him, was the chairman of the York Street Linen Factory, which made sheets for King George V. My grandfather on the other side of the family created his own linen factory in Portadown, from which the products were conveyed to Belfast in barges bearing the names of his daughters, my mother Grace, Emily, Mary and Anne, my aunts.

Cousin Jimmy, a great Christian and the most generous of men, lent my mother one of his houses every July and August for our family. We only had to cross the road to reach a safe children's beach surrounded by easily climbable rocks with a bathing pool where we all learned to swim as children, ('*Mammy, watch me dive backwards!*')

At the end of the beach there was a rocky inlet, used by the fishermen to moor their coble, (pronounced *cobble*), a flat–bottomed boat on which they piled their nets to go out fishing for salmon twice a day. In between their sailings they would allow children to use the boat as a playground. Boarding it was an easy jump from the rocks, and if you misjudged the distance, the water was shallow and did no harm other than to wet our already splashed clothes. There we would play for hours until a high tide brought the fishermen back to set out for their next haul.

Cousin Jimmy also had a talent for making model yachts, and sister Harriet and I used to race our yachts across one of the smaller ponds, which was fine until, when I was a little older, I was given a clockwork motor–boat and I would consistently beat Harriet. One or two tears were shed.

Cousin Jimmy, the devout Christian, would read to the family on Sundays, either from a bible or from a religious book such as *Pilgrim's Progress* before we all went to church in Dunluce Presbyterian Church, near Bushmills. The nearby distillery had been closed for several years, but, as my family were strict teetotallers, this posed no threat. If we were not lucky enough to be offered a lift in cousin Jimmy's car, we had to walk over a mile there and back before lunch.

I love the sea. In the early 1920s, at the age of one? two? three? I can't tell, except that I was sooner or later able to paddle from the friendly beach. At times I was in the care of my Aunt Molly, while my mother stayed at home in Coagh to care for my father, who was already showing the symptoms of the pernicious anaemia which led to his death in 1925. From then on, for many years, we spent every summer, sometimes for the whole of July and August, in cousin Jimmy's house, *Blairbank*; but come the pre—war summer of 1939, we had the splendid holiday in Co. Mayo, which I recall in the next chapter.

The war intervened. By the time I had completed my service in the Irish Guards, including a two—year spell in peacetime Germany, and had become a student at the Royal College of Music, my mother had acquired a cliffside house in Portmoon, a few miles east of the Causeway. This became our holiday home and a resort for family and friends for several years.

Paradise in Mayo

Dramatis Personæ

James Acheson, (50), "Uncle Jim", our host. Diplomat in the Indian Political Service; currently Political Resident on the North West Frontier.
Violet Acheson, (45), "Auntie Vio", his wife, née Field.

Their Children:

Janet, (21), Later Janey Ironside, Professor of Fashion Design at the Royal College of Art, Knightsbridge.
James, (19), "Jimmy". Undergraduate, Christ Church, Oxford.
Anthony, (17), Schoolboy, Wellington College. Later in the Royal Engineers, then farmer/fruit–grower.
Kitty, (15), Schoolgirl, Victoria College, Belfast.
Anne Acheson, (57), later "Nan" or "Auntie Nan". Sculptor, sister of James senior.
Grace Faris, (53), née Acheson. Widow of the Rev. George Faris; sister of James senior; Headmistress of Victoria College, Belfast.

Her Children

John, (26), Oxford philosophy graduate. Later Professor of Metaphysics at Queen's University, Belfast.
Katharine, (23). School teacher.
Alexander, (18), "Sandy". Schoolboy at 'Inst', (The Royal Belfast Academical Institution). Author of this memoir.
Harriet, (15), Schoolgirl, Victoria College, Belfast.
Edgar Acheson, (48), "Uncle Edgar". Chairman, Bannview Weaving Factory, Portadown. Brother of James senior;

Peter Williams*, (17). Nephew of Violet Acheson.*

Evelyn Williams, (12), "Eve". Niece of Violet Acheson, later "Muffet" Durnford.

Roma Holmes, (19). Belfast girlfriend of Jimmy's.

Christopher Ironside, (27). Artist; Janet's fiancé.

Michael Patton–Bethune, Oxford friend of Jimmy's.

The Staff

May, Caretaker and Housekeeper.

Michael Lavelle, Ghillie.

John Meaney, Boat Hand.

The Cars

Uncle Jim's grand new Wolseley 21.
The Faris family's modest new Morris 8.
"Baby", Jimmy's beloved ancient Lancia.
Uncle Edgar's Ford 10 (?)

Characters in the Wings

Adolf Hitler　　**Neville Chamberlain**

Newport House, a large lovable Georgian Irish country house, festooned in Virginia creeper, was destined, in the summer of 1939, through the generosity of my Uncle Jim, to be the setting of a happy holiday for three families of cousins and their friends; an idyll planned to last for two months, fated to be curtailed only in its last days by the outbreak of war.

---

* Peter and Eve WILLIAMS: son and daughter of Betty, (née FIELD), and Arthur WILLIAMS. Betty was the younger sister of Violet ACHESON. Joan, older sister of Peter and Eve, was not present. Eve, ("Muffet"), also remembers the presence of Arnold POTTER, a favourite schoolmaster, ("Usher"), of Jimmy and Anthony at Wellington College, and Rev. William, (Billy), KEMP, brother of "Madre" FIELD, (mother of Violet and Betty).

Newport House: 'The Ball Game'

The house, when full – which was most of the time – slept sixteen people, but things began with an advance party consisting of Uncle Jim, Auntie Vio, Harriet and Kitty, who did the donkey–work of preparing for the forthcoming invasion of family and friends. They were followed within days, to the thrill of the teenage girls, by Jimmy and his Oxford friend Michael.

The full party eventually consisted of two groups: on the one hand the elders, on the other the teenagers and early twenty–year–olds. Those of different ages could engage in their separate interests, but there was also much united activity in the form of picnics, games and expeditions. There were no infants. More than a decade earlier the present teenagers had enjoyed many childhood holidays together, mainly at Portballintrae in Co. Antrim. In the present situation it may have been a relief for the elders not to have to bathe, dress and put to bed very young children. A new generation was still to come; the parents, aunts and uncles could enjoy a sabbatical before they became grandparents, great–aunts and great–uncles. They now worked hard enough, bless them, to create for our band of carefree teenagers a never–to–be–repeated sojourn in a kind of paradise.

The town of Newport stands at the north–east corner of Clew Bay, an archipelago, it is said, of 365 islands (366 in a leap year, joke the locals). Some of these islands are merely rocks peeping above the water at low tide, but many are big enough to land on and explore, and parties of us would set sail in our fishing boat – the *Tope Queen* – provided with picnic hampers prepared by Mother and Aunt Vio, to land on Inishu or Inishturk, à la Treasure Island or Robinson Crusoe, as though we were hoping to find gold or Man Friday. Beyond the bay, to the south, rose the gentle curve of Croagh Patrick, the holy mountain; where recently gold has indeed been discovered and mined, but which then was the goal of spiritual rather than commercial pilgrimage.

Apart from one oddity Newport House still boasted its original classical entrance, with a large front doorway flanked by narrow side windows and surmounted by a Palladian pediment. All this was still there except for the door itself. This had been replaced by a couple of ramshackle contraptions which would not have been out of place in Cold Comfort Farm. At the base, stable–like, were double wooden half–doors less than two feet high. The space above was filled by a large sash window. When the lower section of this was raised to its full extent the space for entrance and egress was no more than 5ft.6in. high. We regularly bumped our heads until someone fixed two fluttering pieces of rag, warning one to duck,

Outside, in front of this eccentric Irish portal, there was a flagged terrace, about 15ft by 8ft, with a flat–topped low wall at either end and a short flight of steps leading down to the gravel drive and an expanse of unkempt grass, beyond which stood the belt of trees that hid the house from the town.

The terrace and its dimensions assumed great importance, in that it became the arena for one of our favourite pastimes. The Ball Game, inspired brainchild of Kitty and Harriet, was a kind of outdoor ping–pong played with a tennis ball. There was no net, the bats were the palms of our hands. One player sat on each terrace wall, (or there could be doubles). Legs must dangle, feet must not touch the ground. The ball was bounced from wall to wall, under rules which, easier to observe than to enumerate, engendered mounting tension as play went on. This game, demanding, as it did, no little skill, gave hours of pleasure to all the family.

The indoor counterpart to the Ball Game was Flying Demon, (or Racing Demon), which we played at a large round table after supper. It aroused competitive high spirits and not a few arguments, and gave rise to a catch–phrase, 'I'm sacrificing myself for the common cause', called out by a player who gave up precious time, (the game depended on speed), to tidy up the muddled piles of cards in the centre of the table. The phrase came into common usage in the course of other holiday activities.

At a smaller table in the same room the elders would be playing bridge. The evening's games ended when oil lamps and candles were brought in to herald the approach of bedtime. Trimming the wicks of the lamps was one of my duties – a skill of which I was rather proud.

Away from the house and its grounds our favourite occupation was fishing, in this case trailing lines with spinning rubber eels to catch tope. A tope is a white edible dogfish looking like a baby shark and tasting like cod. Another seafood, which we gathered from the rocks, was carrageen moss. This seaweed was widely used elsewhere for its curative properties – I think it contained iodine – but could be made with milk into forms of rennet, (junket), which were delicious, well, quite palatable, to eat with fruit.

Uncle Jim supervised our first sailing trips in the *Tope Queen*, then left us to our own devices while he took to his preferred sport of angling. He would go off for a day with Michael the ghillie, sometimes joined by Uncle Edgar on one of his occasional visits.

The *Tope Queen* gave me my introduction to sailing. If there is a technical name for this type of vessel I do not know it. She had no deck, but boasted a mainsail and a jib, I suppose she must also have had a keel. She was rounded and hollow and held twelve of us. My cousins Jimmy and Anthony were already competent sailors. My first lesson, painfully learnt, was to duck when the boat put about, (to the shout of "Lee–O!"), in order not to be clonked on the head by the boom.

Roma, Jimmy's girlfriend, was the decorative member of the crew, closely rivalled by Harriet and Kitty, who still had something of the tomboy about them. Anthony and I were good friends in a no–nonsense way. He had sometimes stayed in our Belfast house when his parents were in India. He already showed promise as an entrepreneur. When the rest of us were broke at the end of the holidays Anthony would somehow have become rich. By quite legitimate means, of course, ('I'll develop your photos for sixpence!' – that sort of thing).

Jimmy won all hearts; he had glamour. At Wellington, which he hated, he had been a rebel, (idealist, anti–military in that temple of military tradition). Shock waves rose in the family when he was not appointed a prefect at the due time. Aunt Vio came down like a wolf on the fold, interviewed the Headmaster, and put things right. Mrs Acheson took no prisoners.

In spite of, or perhaps because of, our difference in age and temperament, Jimmy and I formed a friendship which expressed itself in correspondence even when the holiday was over, our exchange of letters continuing until Jimmy was killed in an aircraft of Coastal Command.

As time went on others joined our party, including Peter and Evelyn Williams, nephew and niece of Auntie Vio's. Peter was my age, quiet, athletic and charming – a future doctor. Eve was only twelve, by far the youngest member of the community. Peter and Harriet fell in love, (I learned later), an attachment which lasted for some time; but eventually geographical separation led them to find other loves, and, eventually, spouses.

The arrival of Janet, (later "Janey"), and her would–be fiancé Christopher caused rather a stir. To me Christopher seemed rather exotic against our Irish family background. I felt that Uncle Jim was slightly suspicious of him. In dress and demeanour the two men typified the diplomat and the artist respectively. But Uncle Jim was no philistine, was in fact a considerable scholar. Moreover, he was a kind man. Perhaps his attitude was merely that of an over—cautious father towards a prospective son—in—law.

Expeditions to beauty spots — Galway, Connemara, Achill Island — were planned with military precision, but, as with military exercises, sometimes suffered from too many planners, and things could become mildly chaotic. A fine convoy of cars would set out in the morning — the Wolseley, the Morris 8, Jimmy's Lancia — only to become separated before long. Maps were misread, drivers took the wrong side roads, rendezvous were missed, tempers frayed. Perhaps I exaggerate, perhaps that only happened once.

Concerning one activity my mind is a blank. Harriet reminds me that there were surfing expeditions to nearby beaches, efficiently marshalled by Jimmy. I must have gone on more than one of these, for I was fond of surfing from Portballintrae days; but after nearly sixty years this is an unexplained blind spot in my Newport memories.

We never ate in tourist hotels or restaurants. The commissariat was based in the kitchens of Newport House, presided over by Mother and Auntie Vio. Because Newport was little more than a village the main supplies of groceries were obtained on weekly trips to the larger Westport. Picnics, like our substantial main meals, (notably the extensive Irish breakfasts), were prepared in the large kitchens of Newport House by Mother and Auntie Vio. Harriet maintains that Vio, though the most generous of women, tended to underestimate the appetites of voracious teenagers, and that, for picnics, Mother would sneak in extra baskets of goodies. On the whole we were lucky with weather, but once or twice rain led us to return early to our evening card battles at the round table.

Anne Acheson, ("Auntie Nan"), was the most distinguished of the house guests, She was a well—known sculptor, later to be elected the first woman Fellow of The Royal British Society of Sculptors. She had been awarded the CBE for her invention of the plaster cast, developed originally in papier maché when she worked with orthopaedic casualties during the first world war.

We had few outside visitors, but one such was Canon Shea, Rector of the little Church of Ireland which stood in the grounds, where we would attend Matins, with Uncle Jim reading the lessons. The Canon discovered that Mother was an expert in mathematical puzzles; she subscribed to a Belgian magazine, Le Sphinx, whose abstruse posers she used to solve. As a fellow enthusiast the good Canon made all too frequent calls upon Mother's time. On one occasion the ladies of our party were invited to tea at the rectory. It appeared that Mrs Shea had poor sight, for the best china, produced for the occasion, was thick with dust.

Throughout the summer the threat of war was mounting. Finally, at the end of August, Uncle Jim was recalled from his furlough. The party dispersed, the Faris contingent returning to Belfast. On Sunday 3rd September the Morning Service was postponed for fifteen minutes while Neville Chamberlain told the nation that we were at war with Germany.

On my next visit to London I tried to phone Jimmy's friend Michael Patton–Bethune. A member of his family answered, 'Oh, didn't you know, Michael was killed.'

The Paradise had ended. We gave our attention to the War.

Appendicitis and Photography in Cork

*I*n 1936, when I was fifteen, I was invited to stay in Cork with my Uncle Sam and auntie Molly, a childless couple who lived in a beautiful secluded house called Cittadella on the Blackrock Road.

Uncle Sam, (I am Samuel Alexander, his namesake), was a deeply religious man, and a leading light in the Boy's Brigade. He took over my grandfather's business as a tea merchant in what became known as Washington Street; its previous name, Great George's Street, having been banned by the Southern Irish anti–royalist fraternity.

In 1956 Uncle Sam came to stay with me in South Kensington, but he had a heart attack on the journey. I called my doctor and he was taken to St Mary's hospital where I visited him for a few days; this was the best I could do because in the evening I was conducting *Wedding In Paris* at the London Hippodrome. Sadly, my uncle died within a few days, whereupon I had the responsibility of arranging for Uncle Sam's body to be transported back to Ireland. In an interview with the Coroner's official, I was informed that I would have to pay 4s/7d for the cost of exporting a corpse to Ireland.

Auntie Molly thanked me profusely for my handling of the situation, whereas I was suffering guilt for not having met uncle Sam on his arrival at the station.

1936. After a few days of stomach pain, a lady doctor came and diagnosed appendicitis, whereupon I was rushed to the Victoria Hospital and operated on that same night. The surgeon, Doctor Mary Hearn, was married to the Protestant Bishop of Cork. This gave rise to a limerick by my late, great friend, George Cernoch:

The Protestant Bishop of Cork
Had a violent hatred of pork.
So strong this aversion,
It caused his conversion;
He's now the Chief Rabbi of York

This limerick, be it said, had no basis in truth.

I awoke from the operation to find myself the winner of a photography prize in the *Irish Press*. The subject of the photograph was the *Moshulu*, the last large grain ship, which was moored close to a modern grain silo. The newspaper published it under the title *The Old and the New*. The photograph was taken on a quarter plate camera, on glass, a format which is now history.

Meanwhile, telephone wires buzzed between Cork and Portballintrae, where my mother was on holiday with the rest of the family. My aunt Hazel drove to Cork and drove me back via Waterford and Dublin to Portballintrae where mother and the rest of the family were staying in an unfamiliar house called *Alt—na—Craig*. There we spent the rest of the holiday, enjoying the beauties of the river Bush, Runkerry Sands, Dunluce Castle, (of Spanish Armada fame), and The Giant's Causeway.

Moshulu, last of the grain ships
Sandy's prize-winning photo Cork 1936

Oxford

hrist Church, Oxford, had for centuries had a reputation as a place of learning for the aristocracy. Its history is littered with the names of the nobility and gentry. After the Great War, however, this image was regarded generally with some disapproval, and in the course of the 1930s, 'The House', as it was known from its ecclesiastical title, *Aedes Christi*, began to accept pupils from all classes. This was explained to me on my arrival by the Senior Censor, the don or Student as he was entitled, who was in charge of the allotment of rooms to newcomers. In The House, dons were known as Students; undergraduates, reasonably enough, as undergraduates.

In the interests of this process of democratisation, a new undergraduate might find himself paired with a room–mate from a widely different background. Hence, as the Censor informed me, I had been placed in company with Mr P. F. Kerr, cousin of a marquess. The latent snob in me had no objection to this. (I had no choice anyway).

I met Peter Kerr, a quiet, kind, devout Catholic, with a fondness for jazz and the popular light music of the day. We became life–long friends. Peter's cousin, The Marquess of Lothian, was at this time Ambassador to America. After my first year sharing with Peter, Lord Lothian died in Washington of food poisoning contracted at a public banquet. Though from a Catholic family, he had become a Christian Scientist, and refused to have a doctor.

Peter inherited the title. I was now sharing rooms with a marquess.

I came to Oxford hoping to find training as a conductor – there was no such thing. Oxford's musical education was firmly allied to the great tradition of English church music. The pundits thought in terms of cathedrals and church organists, not of conductors and orchestras, nor of the theatre and concert halls. Such things were not, of course, condemned outright, they were simply not Oxford's speciality. In one sense only I was in the wrong place. We concentrated on counterpoint, harmony and history of music, I managed reasonably well, and at the end of a first year passed my 1st B. Mus. At the end of the second year I failed part of my 2nd B. Mus., and had to ring my mother on my twenty–first birthday to tell her so. It involved staying on for a further term, partly at my mother's expense. In the end I made good, and all came well, leaving me free to volunteer for the army. My contemporaries had nearly all been conscripted, but there was no conscription in Ulster, Winston Churchill having made a deal with Eamonn De Valera, the Prime Minister of Eire: no conscription in Ulster, and England could keep control of her three Irish ports, (the Treaty Ports); Berehaven, Lough Swilley and Queenstown, (now Cobh), which were of enormous strategic importance.

My examination failure had its roots in problems common to many a nineteen–year–old. I was inhibited about sex, although in my early teens I had fallen passionately in love, at different times, with three girls: Mary Plenderleith, Betty Kane and, in particular, the redhead Joan Robinson with whom I used to play piano duets, winning more than one award at the Belfast annual music festival.

I was inhibited, too, in self–expression. I could not compose – not, that is to say, anything I could consider as serious music. Trying to write music became a form of torture. I was beset, too, by a whole menagerie of obsessions and rituals, which led eventually to a psychiatrist's couch. A fairly ordinary story, such as may be expected of a fatherless teenager, but to me a long, drawn–out, painful experience.

BUT: What I *could* do was to invent light melodies, a talent of no use to me in Oxford, but one that has since earned me an old-ager's income.

One further unhappy incident before I tell of a success or two. Shortly after I came up, I was persuaded to play the organ on Sundays for the Oxford Presbyterian Church. I struggled manfully for a while, but, frankly, was not the best man for the job. Eventually the Minister, as gently and kindly as he could, bless him, gave me a handsome present and the sack. I was probably wrong to feel seriously hurt by this, but I still sometimes wake at night with a pang of humiliation at the memory.

On the conducting front I fought my own fight. I founded the Oxford Musicians' Club, (successor to the temporarily defunct Oxford Musical Club and Union). With this unit I conducted a classical concert, and later a production of *HMS Pinafore*. Two successes. After the concert I telephoned my mother, saying, "Now I know I can conduct." I hope she felt that her unceasing encouragement had been worthwhile.

The classical concert took place in St John's College. I conducted, among other works, a Mozart symphony. At that college I found a new friend, Bruce Montgomery, the College Organist and Choir Master. Bruce composed organ and choir music including *An Oxford Requiem* and later turned to film music, including, notably, the *Carry On* series. He became a crime writer under the name Edmund Crispin, his novels featuring the Oxford Don Gervais Fen, pre–dating Colin Dexter's Inspector Morse.

The 'phoney war' was proceeding. Hundreds of troops were stationed in

Northern Ireland, many in a camp at Ballykinlar near Newcastle, Co. Down ('where the mountains of Mourne sweep down to the sea'). In a summer vacation I joined ENSA, the Entertainments National Service Association. Concert parties would be sent there to entertain the troops. I would be employed as piano accompanist, turning up proudly displaying my triangular ENSA badge, never dreaming that I would one day be a Guards officer.

In an unexpected escape from Academia, I enjoyed an unusual honour, shared, I believe, with only one other individual: I played the piano for the late Queen Mary. She had been evacuated to Badminton, (The Duke of Beaufort's pad, as I had heard it called), where she periodically entertained the troops stationed nearby to a film show. To break the ice there was a sing–song before the film, usually accompanied at the piano by the music master of Radley School. He was ill and I was called in. The request came from a Captain Something–or–Other, Entertainments Officer for the South Midlands District. After a good lunch on a drive across the Cotswolds, I played wartime and other popular songs in the Great Hall, and the troops joined in lustily. I was good at this, playing, let's face it,

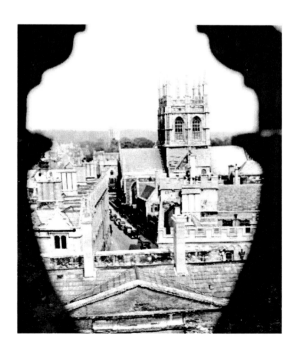

Oxford, 1941
A firewatcher's dawn view

songs my mother taught me, (*Tipperary*, etc). We then saw a preview of the film *Rebecca*, (Joan Fontaine, Laurence Olivier), after which Her Majesty thanked me, and we were entertained to sherry and Benson and Hedges cigarettes. I pocketed a few of these to show off to my friends. There was a red warning and we drove back to Oxford in a blackout, guided along the drive at Badminton by a corporal's lighted cigarette, while German aircraft flew over on the way to bomb who knows what western city.

In addition to my room–mate who was to become a life–long friend, I found another friend in Mervyn Wingfield, who introduced me to his family, the owners of Barrington Park near Burford in the Cotswolds, a handsome mansion with a river running below and a deer herd in the large estate.

On one occasion, Mervyn and I decided to go to London for the day; why, I cannot remember. At the end of the day the two of us decided to hitch–hike back to Barrington. Our attempt at hitch–hiking was a total failure and we spent the night on various roads in between. The adventure was a disaster: on the next morning Mervyn proved to have a bad sore throat, his mother was furious with both of us. The row blew over and it wasn't many months before Mervyn joined the Air Force and went to Canada where he died in an air crash.

The Gowns across Peck
Last night of Trinity term, 1942

Subsequently, when I was serving with the Irish Guards in North West Europe, I heard one night that Mervyn's brother Charles, who was in the Coldstream Guards, had been shot in the head. By a miracle of luck and surgery he survived and became the head of the Wingfield family at Barrington, who have remained my good friends.

The Germans didn't bomb Oxford.

In 1942 they bombed Exeter, Bath, Norwich, York, Canterbury, Bury St. Edmunds and Cambridge. These were the "Baedeker Raids", the Germans' reprisals for our bombing of German cities of historic beauty.

Oxford was therefore right to be apprehensive. Hence it was that dons and undergraduates alike shared firewatching duties; I found myself more than once spending two hours on the roof of the library of Christ Church. On more than one occasion I had the breathtaking experience of seeing the dawn arise over the city's dreaming spires.

A nocturnal event of a different nature occurred on the last night of Trinity term 1942. I was one of a mischievous group of students engaged on a somewhat childish prank. Late at night we pinched gowns from the rooms of our fellows, strung them together and hung the chain across Peckwater quad. This caused chaos the next morning when the gownless students were due to attend the official end of term interviews wearing gowns. Most of my friends were leaving that day for the summer vacation. I, being the scapegoat, was hauled up by the Junior Censor, the disciplinary don. I was lucky that he was a friendly being; otherwise I might have been sent down.

I am still proud of my impressive photograph of the scene. Boys will be boys.

The Oxford friends who preceded me into the army were mostly public school boys from Ampleforth or Downside, some of them titled, but all earmarked for entry into the Brigade of Guards. Though I was doubtful of my acceptance, I was interviewed by the Lieutenant–Colonel of the Irish Guards. He seemed a nice man, but I had the feeling that he thought I was Not His Kind of Person. However, I scraped through, and ended up as a humble guardsman at Pirbright Camp.

After six months, including time as a guardsman at Pirbright then an Officer/Cadet at Sandhurst, I ended up as a 2nd Lieutenant in the Irish Guards Training Battalion at Lingfield. Here there were some ancient peace–time senior officers who occasionally glanced at me askance as though I were Not Their Kind of Person either, but my contemporaries were all good companions, and when I first ventured to play the Mess piano I became everybody's friend.

From then on, throughout the Northwest European campaign and long afterwards I was *persona grata* in the Regiment. Music had become my passport to social acceptance.

From Lingfield we were regularly allowed 36-hour weekend leave in London. One had to behave carefully. Officers in the Brigade of Guards were not expected 1) to carry a parcel in public and 2) to be seen arm-in-arm with a woman, unless she was one's elderly mother.

Incidental

Chords

The Last Chord of Madam Butterfly
  In a letter to The Listener, (4th February 1982), Dr Mosco Carner, referring to an article by Leslie Gardiner, wrote:
  '... finally, it is puzzling that Mr Gardiner should find the closing chord of the opera 'enigmatic'... it is simply a G major chord which, crashing in after a B minor tonality, suggests the shattering effect Butterfly's suicide has on Pinkerton and Sharpless.'
  I replied:
  'Sir: Dr Mosco Carner too easily dismisses the final chord of Madam Butterfly as "simply a G major chord". On the page and at the piano it is manifestly G major. In orchestration, however, Puccini endows the chord with powerful dissonance by three means:
  One: He states the chord in its first inversion.
  Two: The bass note, B, is so heavily doubled in the three octaves below middle C, (on bass clarinet, two bassoons, horn, two trombones, timpani, violas, cellos and double–basses), that the listener senses the presence of F sharp as a harmonic, clashing with the tonic G. The chord takes on the colour of B minor with an added minor sixth.
  Three: A loud stroke on the tam–tam, with its confusion of harmonics, further shatters the tonality. Not only does this chord, played *tutta forza*, come as a shock, but its dissonance – avoiding finality – and its tonal ambivalence leave the audience with a sense of unease. I am not surprised that Leslie Gardiner finds it "enigmatic".'
  Reading these letters after some years, I tend to the view that the chord is B minor, with the fifth heard only as a harmonic, and a minor sixth as the strong melody note. These thoughts lead me to:
  The First Chord of the *Emperor Concerto* – E flat major? No one would seriously question that. But observe that the fifth is missing. There is no B flat until the piano

arpeggio begins. One might therefore argue – this time with tongue in cheek – that it is the first inversion of C minor, with the tonic omitted.

For some time I concluded that Beethoven wanted to give the piano the opportunity of completing and enriching the incomplete opening chord; but it was pointed out to me that the last chord of the first movement of the *Eroica* symphony is also without a fifth – no B flat.

It seems that Beethoven regarded the fifth as unnecessary – or even intrusive – in a root position major chord. The fifth occurs twice early in the harmonic series, making its presence felt even if it is not actually played. If it is sounded on an instrument it creates its own, unwanted harmonics.

Is the omission of the fifth common practice among 18th and 19th century composers? The quest is on!

Battle Music

The Way You Look Tonight was my personal war music. Not *We'll Meet Again*, or the *White Cliffs of Dover*, or even *We're Gonna Hang Out the Washing on the Siegfried Line*; it was *TWYLT* that I played wherever there was a piano in a billet, from the Falaise gap to the Elbe; in Nijmegen, Eindhoven, Maastricht and Gummersbach. I must have played this, the Commanding Officer's favourite tune, at least 500 times; on one occasion the Adjutant, 'Tinker' Taylor, was dispatched to summon me from my bed to play it in my pyjamas, with an Irish Guards battle–dress top.

Lt. Col Giles Vandeleur – 'Colonel Giles' – loved music. When the 2nd Battalion was pulled back to rest for a few days, Giles would insist on a piano in the Officers' Mess and the evenings became a series of *soirées musicales*. The obligatory item was always *TWYLT*, (usually repeated many times), but Giles's tastes were eclectic. From my limited remembered repertoire he would often choose Bach's *Sheep May Safely*

Author at ease

Officer's Mess, Gummersbach

Graze, whereas John Haslewood, his second–in–command, another music lover, favoured *Jesu, Joy of Man's Desiring*, and in those days I could get my fingers round the Chopin *Fantaisie–Impromptu* in C# minor, (the slow middle section of which was nicked for the popular song *I'm Always Chasing Rainbows*).

There was entertainment of a lower order. Now and again some of us would write our own songs, usually rude. I confess to being the principal offender, but 'Rip', our Medical Officer, was a fine contributor.

One such song came into being as follows: At that time the possibility of creating a test tube baby was being aired. Few took the idea seriously, regarding it as the fantasy of mad scientists, but I saw its potential as a cabaret number. The first lines may indicate something of its content:

> *In olden days the British nation*
> *Got their sons by copulation...*

Most of the rest cannot be printed here, being too explicitly carnal, but the words were sung then with frank and gleeful innocence by lonely young men whose womenfolk were too far away to be shocked, although many of them would no doubt merely have giggled. (For those interested, please e-mail the author for the full uncensored version). The refrain, however, was harmless enough. Over a boogie–woogie bass, it ran:

TEST TUBE BABY!
Maybe I love you, but maybe
My devotion would be greater far
If you had a granny or a grand–pa–pa.

Life was not all music. I sometimes wondered how I came to have a commission in the Micks. As a schoolboy I was certainly not militarily minded. However, the war came, it was unthinkable not to join up (at Churchill's insistence there was no conscription in Northern Ireland), my Oxford friends were going into the Brigade. I decided to have a go, and they took me. I remember my surprise when, on my medical inspection at a recruiting office, (in North Acton on a wet Monday), the doctor looked at me and said "Good physique". I had always thought of myself as rather a weedy specimen.

It was the beginning of a growth of physical and mental self–confidence. Before long I was succeeding in feats which I would have deemed impossible a year earlier, such as crossing a river hanging upside down from a stretched wire in full battle

'Rip' Medical Officer

order. (A piece of cake, really). Thanks to the army, when I was demobilised in January 1947, I entered the Royal College of Music a fit man.

At Bovington Camp, whither I was sent on a Signal Officer's course, we swanned around the Dorset byways, (Puddletown! Piddletrenthide!), in little pickup trucks which were kitted out with the same mark of wireless sets as those we would eventually find in our tanks. The great dodge was to discover the best caffs for char–and–a–wad, then to call up the sergeant instructor giving him a false map reference for our location, and giving us a longer tea–break. Unfortunately the sergeant was wise to the same pull–ups for car–men, and usually found us pretty soon. This sort of hanky–panky apart, the course was impeccably planned and the instructors excellent. I came out top – I think.

12th August 1944. After a cross–channel flight in an ancient Dakota (DC3), a group of us landed on a sunny summer's day in a Normandy cornfield, reinforcements to the 5th Guards Armoured Brigade. The next day I was made Battalion Signal Officer, replacing a wounded predecessor, and held that position until well after the end of the war. The army had sussed me out pretty well. I was no tactician, and would have made a lousy troop commander.

I was introduced to Sergeant Flynn, ('Porky Flynn'), the Battalion Signal Sergeant. I was conscious of being a green young officer. No doubt Sgt. Flynn was aware of this. With tact and understanding this wise and experienced non–commissioned officer guided me in the ways of a fighting unit. This was, at least in our battalion, a typical officer/NCO relationship. While discipline was no less, the formalities of the parade ground were relaxed in favour of the immediate demands of war. The sergeant, nominally my junior in rank, became my guide and mentor, while I contributed the skills I had learnt.

We had support in our signal team by a corporal in the Royal Corps of Signals, a boffin of higher technical skills than our own. If a faulty wireless set proved beyond repair, Corporal Gray would replace it with a new set and remove the offending instrument to some sort of intensive care unit. His higher technical skill backed us up on many occasions.

To begin with I had to control the battalion wireless network, (80 tanks, scout cars etc, each with a wireless), from a seat inside the turret of the Commanding Officer's Sherman tank, while he stood with his head in the fresh air. The petrol fumes used to make me feel sick. Before long, however, Colonel Giles took to commanding the Battalion from a scout car, and I became the commander of that particular Sherman tank, standing with my head outside, thank goodness.

The tank was named St. Patrick. It was one of a group of vehicles later ambushed by the Germans the day after our leading tanks had captured the bridge leading over the Escaut Canal into Holland – 'Joe's Bridge', as it is still known, (after

Lt. Col. J.O.E. Vandeleur, who commanded the operation). 'St. Patrick' was hit, and began to brew up, with black smoke billowing from it. The hull gunner, Guardsman Keefe, escaped to safety, then, realising that his mate, the driver, was trapped, (because the turret gun was traversed over his escape hatch), Keefe, returning from safety to danger, climbed in the turret and traversed the gun, (an agonisingly slow process), enabling the driver, Sergeant Gorton, to be rescued, unconscious, but alive. Seconds later the tank exploded.

During this action I was 500 yards away, with Col. Giles, at Brigade Headquarters. I wonder how I would have coped had I been in the action, but God did not pose that question.

Six days later we advanced northwards towards Valkenswaard. As dusk fell the far end of the town was ablaze; we learnt later that the Germans had set fire to a cigar factory. (I thought there was rather an expensive smell).

We parked our Headquarters Squadron tanks on both sides of a street in the centre of the town. Because it was believed that all the Germans had gone, the tank crews were dismissed and welcomed by the townsfolk into billets in the local apartments. Battalion Headquarters was set up in a block of flats. My tank was outside that building.

Sandy and 'St Patrick'

We were given permission to close down our wireless network, apart from maintaining a radio link to Brigade Headquarters. As Signal Officer it was my duty to ensure that this was properly carried out. Thus I was the last person left on board any tank. I was just about to dismount when a German vehicle, armoured, but open–topped like one of our own Bren–gun carriers, drove up the road towards me at speed. The driver was making a bid for escape. When he was less than twenty metres away his vehicle hit a tank on my side of the road, off which it ricocheted, crashing heavily into a tank across the way. The driver jumped out. There were no others. He ran towards me. It may be that he was trying to hide and didn't see me. I drew my revolver, which had not been fired since I was in training, and, in my fluent German, shouted "Halt!", and 'halt' he did. The lad was courteous, but I suppose he had no alternative. He handed me his pistol, a beautifully engineered Walter P38.

We faced each other in silence. Knowing no more German words (except *Hitler kaputt!*), I gestured to him to go into our Battalion Headquarters, where he would be processed as a prisoner of war. He wouldn't go. I didn't know what to do, not being used to this kind of social situation. The revolver in my hand was meaningless, since I had no intention of firing it.

Eventually I realised that he was trying to tell me something. He was pointing to his belt (with some difficulty, since he had his hands up). It turned out that he had there a stick grenade which he wanted to give me. He was rightly afraid of being accused of hiding it, which would have got him in terrible trouble – but nothing to the trouble I would have been in had I allowed him to enter headquarters with this weapon on his person.

I took it from him and escorted him inside. I have often wondered what happened to him. He was the first German I had ever met. He was, I suppose, nineteen. I was twenty–three. He is probably a grandfather by now, maybe someone famous. Perhaps he is Helmut Kohl.

One of our heaviest days of casualties occurred at Elst, a few miles north of Nijmegen. The Germans had built up a strong defence, and were using flame throwers for the first time. There was some bitter close–quarters fighting, resulting in many deaths. At the end of the day Brigadier Norman Gwatkin visited the battalion to sympathise and to review the situation. As he was talking to the Commanding Officer and surveying the carnage, two guardsmen passed by carrying a stretcher on which was a body covered by a blanket. The officers were nodding gravely when the blanket caught on a thorn in the hedge, falling off to reveal an old dead pig – one of the day's casualties – which the two Micks were smuggling back for supper; a tough and potentially unhygienic meal, one would have thought.

The laughter provoked by such a prank at the end of a tragic day possibly

Joe's Bridge
(By permission of the Irish Guards)

provided a safety–valve, a therapy, for the unspoken private grief of those who had lost their comrades. Which was all of us.

We entered Douai in September 1944. Battalion headquarters was set up in the large central square of the town. The local residents were there welcoming us with fruit and flowers. It was a hot summer's afternoon. Suddenly there was a commotion in the corner of the square. A hostile crowd had gathered round a young woman. It transpired that she was a prostitute — which was not the cause of the trouble — she was a collaborator. Someone was cutting off her hair to the jeers of the onlookers. It was an unpleasant moment, but one could understand the deep hatred felt by the crowd.

That evening, or the next, we made our lightning advance to Brussels. The division moved fifty miles overnight. This was said by someone to be the fastest advance in the history of war. Said to be.

More of Brussels later, but I digress with a leap to the day fifty years later on a celebratory visit to Douai. Tinker Taylor, who better, was in charge of our party, a bus–load of WWII Irish Guards veterans. We were royally entertained, and returned this hospitality with a party in the Town Hall.

On this occasion I had to make a speech of welcome in French. I had put immense labour into writing this speech, had had it checked by a French neighbour, and learned it by heart as I walked round Primrose Hill. After the speech I was conversing with a French general (as one does):

'Was my French all right?' I asked.

'Excellent! Vous pourrez avoir addressé la Chambre des députés!'

I glowed with pride.

Christmas, 1944. We were relaxing in Maastricht when we were suddenly summoned to the Ardennes to support the Americans in resisting Von Runstedt's new offensive. Here the 2nd Battalion had a lucky break: the tanks were grounded in deep snow, while the 3rd Battalion infantry had to go and help the Yanks.

2nd Battalion HQ was in Landen, a village between Louvain and Liege. We were billeted in a gentleman's farmhouse, vast and gaunt, home of the burgomaster and three generations of his family. The main rooms of the house were warm, but the bedrooms were so cold that John Yerburgh, our Technical Officer, and I could scrape ice off our bedroom walls in the morning. The duck pond in front of the house was frozen over, so we skated on it. It wasn't really big enough for skating; one had to be very good at stopping and turning. Then, sure enough, came the thaw, and some idiot fell through; it had to happen.

The old grandmother, matriarch of the family, was bedridden with angina. It was said that she had not long to live. She was grateful for Rip's assiduous medical attention, and lucky to have it. The house was run by her middle–aged daughter, who treated us with polite respect.

John Yerburgh

We had our customary musical evenings until, one day, the daughter told Colonel Giles that the old lady had taken a turn for the worse. Would we, she asked, be so kind as not to have music in the evenings, we naturally agreed. But one night – I think it was Christmas Eve – Brigadier Norman came to dinner, and Giles said, "Sandy, I'm sure it wouldn't matter if you played a little quiet classical music; we won't have any singing." So I played the up–market end of my repertoire.

The grandmother died during the night. I had bumped her off!

I was terrified of meeting the daughter, who was more than a little awesome, but I ran into her on the stairs. "Oh, Lieutenant Faris!", she exclaimed, "I must tell you! Mother's last words were 'What beautiful music!'" I blessed that old lady from my heart. With her dying words she had got me off the hook!

Brussels

At midnight on 3rd September 1944, the fifth anniversary of the declaration of war, we rode into Brussels in our Sherman tanks after our lightning 50–mile run from Douai.

The Shermans were certainly mechanically reliable; when hit by a German shell they might blow up, (mine once did, fortunately in my absence), but they never broke down. On one occasion a guardsman, replying to a query from the visiting War Minister, said, 'Well sir, the Germans call them Tommy cookers and we call them Ronson lighters.'

But they never broke down, so we made our triumphal entry into the Belgian capital to the rapturous applause and heartfelt greetings from the Belgian people. We were welcomed into their houses; I was received into a comfortable flat by two ladies who made up a bed with sparkling white sheets. Oh, what joy after nights in the mud or under a parked tank! The other residents on the block had joined together to establish a communal dormitory in the basement, giving up their flats to us, their liberators.

My two hostesses chatted with me in the high stairwell of the building which was lit by a light that was turned on by a passenger as required, then went off automatically after a minute or so. My ladies were in tearful and talkative mood:

'Oh, we knew you would come! Ah! Les misères qui sont passées…'

Lights off.

Lights on again…

'Cinq années de souffrances! Les misères qui sont passées…'

Lights off.

Lights on again…

'Cinq années de souffrances!…'

The Anglo–Belgian outpouring was repetitive; first one lady, then the other. Then to bed, to wake up early to music from a street band. It was a tear–jerker; they were playing *We're Going To Hang Out The Washing On The Siegfried Line*; a song we hadn't heard while the Germans were in the ascendant.

Children followed the band in a percussion section of drums, cymbals, saucepans etc. Not a German in sight.

A few months later, when we were safely established in Germany, it became possible to allow short (48 hour) leave to all ranks, small groups at a time. Officers had the use of the Eye Club, a name based on the open eye symbol of the Guards Armoured Division, situated in a hotel on a central boulevard of Brussels.

This small hotel was taken over by the Division, either funded by the army or maybe (I don't know) a free loan from the city of Brussels, a gesture of gratitude for the liberation. On one visit I spent two hours of my first morning in a music shop, playing the piano in an upstairs studio. When I came down asking to pay I was told, 'Oh non, monsieur, c'est pour la libération!' We were given many things on that basis including free drinks and meals etc from grateful *Bruxellois*. The Belgian Opera was in the course of revival at the renowned Théâtre de la Monnaie, where in later peacetime years I was to conduct a performance of the Sadler's Wells production of Gilbert and Sullivan's *Iolanthe*.

The hordes of back–up troops, American and British, who descended upon Brussels, were, to say the least, less popular than the much loved liberators — Ourselves.

There was an end–of–war victory parade. The succeeding socialising included a grand ball in the hôtel–de–ville, scene of the Duchess of Richmond's ball on the eve of Waterloo, recounted in Thackeray's *Vanity Fair*.

Farewell to Armour

The Finale in Gummersbach

*W*hen Giles Vandeleur, our Commanding Officer, was wounded in April 1945, John Haslewood took over, and led us with skill and confidence through some bad times toward the happy ending on the Elbe. I was on leave in Belfast on VE Day, but started back that night. From Stranraer on the Scottish coast all the way to London there was a victory beacon on every hilltop. I was too excited to sleep.

A happy ending, but with a sad sequel: we were deprived of our armour, to become infantrymen again; an army at peace in a foreign country. At the Farewell to Armour parade at Rotenburg airfield on 9 June 1944 — just one month after VE Day — we said goodbye to the tanks which for years had been our friends, our protection and part of our consciousness.

As the war ended the 2nd Battalion Irish Guards was stationed in a village north of Hamburg. I had a pleasant room on the pretty village street, where I lay by an open window in the sunny May days, listening to the columns of demobilised German troops marching and singing on their way to wherever the Allied Control Commission had decided was to be their peacetime destination. I spent much of my time writing the words and music of songs, sometimes lubricious, e.g. Test Tube Baby, (see Battle Music), to be sung in the officer's mess, which was situated in the grand house of the village.

The 2nd Battalion was posted to Gummersbach, a small town lying in a pretty valley about forty miles east of Cologne. We were there for several months before moving north again. There was a danger of idleness; we had to find things for people to do, although one or another squadron was always engaged on the unenviable task of supervising camps of displaced persons. There was a multitude of these DPs — Russians, Italians, Poles — who had been assembled together in our charge, and among them there were some very hard characters. Gangs would sometimes break out of camp at night to loot, rape and murder in the nearby villages. Adequate policing of such numbers was virtually impossible. One ruffian with a stolen gun took a casual pot–shot at Peter Agnew, our Intelligence Officer. Eventually troublemakers and all were going to have to be repatriated, of which more later.

Irish Guardsman Roger Keyes recalls less violent moments:

"The pipes and drums beat Retreat regularly, and this was very popular with the local Germans, who came from miles around to see the ceremony, and always applauded.

"At the same time there was opportunity for leisure and entertainments of various kinds. In Gummersbach there was a cinema which doubled as a theatre. Local German labour was used to spruce this place up, and I may say this was done with the usual German efficiency. One touch of class was the carving in wood, and subsequent painting in colour, of a large Mick capstar which was then fixed to the proscenium arch above the stage.

"Then there was the Boxing Day football match between officers and sergeants — more in the nature of a rag than anything. The Germans could not understand this at all, shaking their heads and saying how bad for discipline this must be. The concept of the camaraderie which existed in the Micks alongside tough discipline quite escaped them."

For those who were idle Colonel Giles, (back amongst us with his wounds healed), decreed company marches. (We were now companies rather than squadrons). I was seconded to Stephen Langton's company. I didn't march a step. Stephen having given me the cushy job of recce officer, I drove ahead in a jeep to find billets for each night. Our destination was Paris. How we got away with that I'll never know, (except that Giles had a sense of humour and approved of the good life), but we ended up one night at the Bal Tabarin. Some company march!

Some Company March!
Stephen Langton at Longchamps, 1945

Back in Gummersbach it was showtime. Tony de Lotbiniere and I concocted *Danger, Men at Play!*, an all–ranks revue which became a smash hit. The cast included John Gorman, ('the Blockhead'), who gallantly went on in spite of a severe attack of pleurisy. Guardsman Tinsley, who sang *Shine Through My Dreams*, earning himself the affectionate nickname of 'Shiner', and James Osborne, ('The Gangler'), who wandered on stage from time to time, on each occasion with a larger watering can, (pantomime cans designed in painted plywood, identical except in size, which ranged from the miniscule to the gigantic). To the question "What are you doing here?", he would reply with the catch phrase, "I'm carrying the can back!"[2], which had the audience in laughter, applauding an officer who was a good enough sport to make a fool of himself. For Gangler's final entrance he descended from the flies on a rope, wrestling with the largest can of all — not to land on the floor, but, instead, to go straight through it by way of a concealed trap–door. This brought the house down. An already popular officer became more popular still. A star was born.

Footnote: there wasn't a single F–word in the show, and nobody noticed.

In due course the DP problem was settled by international agreement. Hence, on a muggy dark night I found myself in command of a small convoy of three–tonners loaded with convicted Russian criminals from the DP camps. Our destination was Krefeld, a railway junction in the Ruhr. For five minutes in every hour we halted for bodily functions. The convicts were not allowed to dismount, but had to urinate in relays over the tailboards.

What took place on the station platform at Krefeld disturbed me and my accompanying NCOs. There were other contingents similar to ours. A long cattle–train was drawn up at the platform. When the order was given, the men were herded like veal calves into the train. The doors clanged shut and were wired and padlocked, presumably to remain so until arrival in Russia.

I am ashamed to say that we joked at the predicament of these human beings, although the joking arose, I dare say, from the need to cover up our sense of disquiet.

"I wouldn't like to be these geezers when they get to the other end" (ha–ha!) "Salt mines in Siberia, most likely" (ha–ha!) I thought: "That or the firing squad". I still feel uncomfortable about the whole episode, a nasty little example of post–war political cruelty. Yes, they were criminals, but . . . But I no longer have the stomach to joke about it.

With that one grim exception, the eighteen months I spent in Germany after the war were idyllic. I think of those days, paradoxically, as time profitably wasted.

Fraternising with Germans was strictly forbidden but musicians got away with it. We were officially encouraged to help the Germans get their operas going again.

---

2 'To carry the can back', Army lingo: 'To shoulder the blame.'

The author and John Gorman

We were for ever signing chits enabling them to transport artists and scenery from one place to another, and to get on with the task of rebuilding their ruined opera houses. The State Opera in Cologne had been razed; there was grass growing in the footlights. In Hamburg, where the 2nd Battalion was soon to be posted, the auditorium of the State Opera had been destroyed but the stage had survived. A wall was built where the safety curtain had been. The remaining space on the old stage was converted into a new auditorium. There was no foyer. The former stage door became the only entrance for audience and artists alike. On a fine evening, in the interval, we would stand outside on the pavement, smoking. If one dropped a fag–end to stamp it out, a child would snatch it, crying "Zigarette für Papa!" A single cigarette was worth half–a–crown. Hundreds of thousands of cigarettes were stolen from the Hamburg docks to find their way onto the black market, together with much chocolate, coffee and soap.

The greatest German singers were eager to perform in this house; it was there that I had my introduction to opera performances of the highest international standard. It was through that stage door, too, that I entered the rebuilt opera house twenty years later, as a conductor of Sadler's Wells Opera. Everybody addressed me as 'Maestro'. Nobody ever called me that in England. No respect.

Danger Men at Play! was succeeded by another revue, *Easy on the Eyes*, to produce which I was posted to Bad Godesberg on the Rhine, the spa town where Chamberlain had once conferred with Hitler. The new revue was performed in our Divisional

'The Gangler'
James Osborne

College in Bonn, a building which later housed the West German Parliament, where the voices of Konrad Adenauer and Willy Brandt were to be heard.

Philip Cranmer, later the Professor of Music in The Queen's University of Belfast, composed a catchy title song for the show. John Hawkesworth, later producer of *Upstairs Downstairs*, was the designer. I contributed the words and music of a number in which three guardsmen, playing caricatures of English officers in the Scots, Welsh and Irish Guards respectively, sang:

> *We're terribly, terribly patriotic,*
> *Madly, madly keen*
> *On Scotland Wales and Ireland,*
> *And although we've never seen*
> *The countries we've adopted*
> *During this too boring war,*

We like to think that they're the countries
We've been fighting for...

Easy On The Eyes was presented in what was the Divisional College, and would later house the parliament of Willy Brandt. We toured the show round the various Divisional units in the area, and I got to know well that part of West Germany bordering on Holland.

At the end of March 1946 the 2nd Battalion Irish Guards was posted to Hamburg. Division moved north to Plön in Schleswig–Holstein in 'Mons' Barracks which had been Admiral Dönitz's final headquarters. 'WELFARE' to which I was now attached, was in the Schloss Ascheberg, where we sailed in dinghies and enjoyed water skiing. We put on a cabaret called *Frivolous Forties* in the ballroom. John Hawkesworth designed a charming stage and proscenium; the audiences were seated at small tables where they were served drinks by guardsmen in uniform; well, we were all in uniform.

We were told that in a warehouse in Hannover free supplies of gramophone records (78s) were available for the troops. Tony de Lotbiniere and I went to investigate. After ordering a bulk supply, I asked for a record for myself, "I'm sorry, sir, we are not permitted to supply you with that recording of *Der Barbier von Seville*; it is conducted by Wilhelm Furtwängler. He has not yet been screened by the Allied De–Nazification Court." We could have had any number of recordings

Easy on the Eyes

Sandy and Philip Cranmer
Ascheberg 1946

of Mendelssohn and other Jewish composers and performers previously banned by Hitler, but Furtwängler was out. We were the censors now.

In the Schloss there was a charming rococo ballroom with a minstrels' gallery. John Hawkesworth designed an elegant stage, and we ran a cabaret. Our talent was supplemented by guest artists.

From this there comes to me, sixty years on, the last musical memory of my wartime years.

I accompanied at the piano a slim, blonde, leather–tanned Danish woman who had become a legend in the German and British armies alike. Her star quality illumined the Oval Room that night. Lale Andersen, whose rendering of *Lili Marlen'* had made her the darling of Rommel's North Africa Corps, as was Vera Lynn for the British. *Lili Marlen'* became equally popular with the British, and it was a thrill for me to accompany the Danish singer.

Lili Marlen' and *We'll Meet Again* shared the same theme, a soldier dreaming of reunion with his lover:

'Da wollen wir uns wieder sehen…'

'We'll meet again, don't know where, don't know when…'

When Lale Andersen came to 'Wie Einst…', ('*Like long ago…*'), I was seized by nostalgia. The war was over, I was part of history, historic song, historic singer.

We're terribly, terribly patriotic

We were in easy reach of Hamburg, and I was able to meet friends in my old battalion and to attend performances at the Hamburg State Opera.

In 1962 I was to conduct the Sadler's Wells production of *Iolanthe* in that opera house.

Tony and Sandy at the Lido

Demob

*I*n January 1947 I was given an early "Class B" release from the army. I got out ahead from my friends by dint of passing the entrance examination to the Royal College of Music, an easy exam after my musical education at school and Oxford. Thanks to four years in the army I was by now much fitter, physically and mentally, than had been the disturbed student at Oxford. God bless the army, notably assault courses.

I took up residence in a room procured by my aunt, the well–known sculptor Anne Acheson CBE, FRBS (Auntie Nan). Situated in Beaufort Street, off the Fulham Road, it was a bleak and damp top–floor room with a leaking roof necessitating buckets to catch the drips and a gas fire with a small blue flame giving out almost no heat; I used to wear a warm dressing–gown while I practised the piano.

This was the drab post–war London; no house had been painted in wartime.

Across the Fulham Road lay St. Stephen's Hospital. There, later, one of the patients was Stephen Ward, a participant in the Profumo scandal, (sexual shenanigans in fashionable Marylebone), together with Christine Keeler and Mandy Rice–Davies. The latter came out in court with the memorable utterance, 'Well he would, wouldn't he?', referring to a defendant who had denied committing a certain offence. A strangely potent comment; it was taken up by the national press, and made Mandy famous. A friend of mine often in the know was convinced that Stephen Ward had been murdered by the British Secret Service to conceal the suspected involvement of the high and mighty, including a royalty.

If you travel on top of a bus going westward along Kensington Gore, you may observe, in the forecourt of one of the buildings, the bronze bust of Gertrude Bell, the explorer. The sculptor was Anne Acheson, the first woman to be appointed a Fellow of the Royal Society of Sculptors. The bust stands in front of the Royal Geographical Society, who commissioned it. Adjacent to the R.G.S rises the bulk of the Albert Hall. Behind the Albert Hall, go down the wide steps, and you are in Prince Consort Road, facing the Royal College of Music, founded in 1882 under the direction of Sir George Grove (of the dictionary) as a modern and more lively

Anne Acheson CBE
The First Woman FRBS

rival to the ancient Royal Academy of Music. (The two institutions eventually went on to work in friendly fellowship as the Associated Board of the Royal Schools of Music).

I enrolled in the College. I was happy at last. Different from the churchiness of Oxford, The Royal College acknowledged the existence of theatres and concerts, and encompassed training for conductors. Mind you, I now think that a bloke can either conduct or he can't, and there is not much to teach him, but I was grateful to my tutor, Richard Austin, who gave me some wrinkles which have since often stood me in good stead. I won the conducting prize of the year. I also won the year's prize for musical criticism by writing a long essay as I huddled in a dressing–gown in my cold post–war digs in Earl's Court. Frank Howes, the famous music critic of *The Times*, invited me to contribute some reviews of the 'Winter Proms'. The money I won from these prizes paid for much of my existing music library.

The student population consisted of two tiers. One: the youngsters straight from school; two: the war veterans such as myself, who were granted a year to complete their music courses. Among the older group were many singers who became the opera stars of Sadler's Wells and Covent Garden in the 60s, as well as a future conductor or two such as Leonard Hancock and myself. The singers included future luminaries Elsie Morison, (later to marry Rafael Kubelik), Monica Sinclair, Marion Studholm, Denis Dowling, Andrew Downie and Eric Shilling.

Among the instrumentalists was Arthur Wilson, future principal trombonist in the Philharmonia Orchestra. Being a recently demobbed Irish Guardsman I noticed Arthur because he turned up to rehearsal in the uniform of the Coldstream Guards. He was then serving in the Coldstream band, while having tuition at the College. We never met there, but in 1959, when Arthur was already earmarked for stardom in the profession, our orchestra "fixer", (manager), for *Candide* engaged him, to my grateful surprise, as first trombone. That band, the one Leonard Bernstein had described as "neat", (an American compliment), also included the young Colin Bradbury, later principal clarinet in the BBC Symphony Orchestra. Not a bad line–up! Both Arthur and Colin became professors at the College. Both have been life–long friends.

One trouble still upset me. I had been enrolled as a student of conducting, piano and composition. Even under that excellent composer Herbert Howells, composing was still something of an agony, I thought, a waste of time for my teacher. I decided to tackle the problem head–on. Adopting a somewhat military attitude, (without much conviction – I was now a devoted civilian), I marched myself in to see the Director, Sir George Dyson, and told him of the problem. The wind was taken out of my sails when he proved most understanding; he allowed me freedom from composition studies – a final ghost exorcised.

Arthur Wilson

It was ironic that in later years composition was my forte, but in the realm of light music, the subject of later chapters. Let those who despise it scoff, but let us tolerate each other's tastes. I, for example, am not over—enamoured of Association Football, but I admire the skills of its exponents.

In December 1947, two weeks before the end of term and of my allocated course, the College was approached by the Carl Rosa Opera Company in search of a chorus master for the new season. My name was put forward. I was told to see the director again.

Although a delightful man, he was a product of the 'cathedral' school. "You don't want to go into theatre," he said, "these people do everything by telephone. No, what you should do is become music master at a public school, then organist at a cathedral." He continued to advise against it; but I believe to this day that the wily old boy was playing devil's advocate. He knew perfectly well what I wanted, and that I would not follow his advice.

I thanked him, left the room, and accepted the job. A Christmas present.

In 1947 I shared a flat close by the (then) West London Air Terminal with Tony

Colin Bradbury

de Lotbiniere and Peter Ward, two comrades from our wartime days. Indeed, I was to be best man at both their weddings. I remember with some amusement Tony's dismay at the size of my piano. Later we watched, on a miniscule television screen, the Coronation of Queen Elizabeth II. At the time I was occasionally touring with the Carl Rosa Opera Company.

Tony worked on documentaries for the BBC, while Peter was an accountant, first for a company in Plaistow and later in the West End. Years later Tony died leaving a widow and three sons. On the occasion of my eightieth birthday I invited his wife Claudia and Justin, my favourite of the boys, to my celebratory party.

While I was attending the Royal College of Music I was a frequent visitor chez my cousin Janey Ironside at 15 Neville Street, South Kensington. Janey, the new Professor of Fashion Design at the Royal College of Art, was once headlined as "The Woman Who Changed Fashion". Her husband Christopher was also a Professor at the RCA. Their daughter Virginia, then in her schooldays, was sometimes the reluctant model for Janey's latest children's wear, in which she

Main:Virginia Ironside
Inset:Virginia with Janey

would have to appear in public. She later became the well–known author and columnist.

A regular visitor to Neville Street was Osbert Lancaster. He was clearly enamoured of Janey, but I doubt if his ardour was reciprocated. I met him again in 1959 when he designed the sets for Leonard Bernstein's *Candide*, and like many members of a large public, I was an avid peruser of his witty cartoons in the *Daily Express*, and delighted in his amusing erudite comments on period architecture in *Pillar To Post* and *Homes, Sweet Homes*.

Janey was to be a partner in many extra–marital affairs, and formed a long–lasting relationship with John Wright, a student at the Royal College of Art and an up–and–coming interior designer. Christopher met Jean Marsden, whom he eventually married, Janey having long since divorced him.

Janey and Christopher frequently entertained me in Neville Street. I kept up with them both, especially Janey, to whom I owe a lot. Virginia, too, has remained a valued friend of my sister Harriet's and mine.

Harriet

Incidental

Pitch and Tempo

Ever Higher and Faster

We are at the Proms.

The concert has not yet begun, but the BBC Symphony Orchestra is on the platform, tuning up — the oboist is sounding an authoritative *A* at 440 cycles per second, with a small electronic gadget to prove him right for the benefit of unbelievers.

It is next morning — in the dim light only a few cleaners can be seen and heard. Then four strong men mount the platform, remove the piano and replace it with a different, foreign–looking model. A young man takes his place at the new instrument. He is the piano tuner; his task to ensure that the replacement is tuned to *A* = 444 cycles per second, the pitch used by the foreign musicians who will perform this morning. Audiences do not always realise that the music is played at different pitches on different occasions.

Pitch has varied from century to century and from country to country. When Robert Newman promoted the first promenade concert, and supplied the orchestra with instruments, it was on condition that they played at *A* = 435.

Then there is tempo. Over the years, many instruments, particularly the wind, have improved technically, enabling players to play difficult passages faster.

As a result, we are often listening to music played higher and faster than when it was written. In some cases, I imagine, no one would tolerate the lower, slower version.

Pitch describes the particular quality of a sound, (e.g. an individual musical note), that fixes its position in the scale.

I am indebted to Diana Deutsch's *Psychology Of Music* for the following passage:

Certain sounds used in music that occupy no particular scale position, such as those produced by cymbals or the bass drum, can be said to be of indefinite pitch. Pitch is determined by what the ear judges to be the most fundamental wave frequency of the sound, (even when, as for example with difference tones, this is an aural illusion, not actually present in the physical sound wave). Experimental studies, in which listeners have been tested for their perception and memory of pitch differences among sounds with wave frequencies known to the experimenter, have shown that marked differences of timbre, loudness and musical context affect pitch, albeit in relatively small degree. But long–term memory, called *absolute pitch,* enables some people to identify the pitch of sounds quite apart from their contextual relation to other sounds. Such aspects of pitch are discussed in *Psychology Of Music, §11.1.* This article addresses a question of special concern to students of the history of performing practice: "At what pitch level may compositions from various eras of Western tradition be performed with historical authenticity?" A related question of worldwide scope is: "To what extent have musicians of various times, places and social strata adhered to any specific performing–pitch standard or set of standards?"

Sidelights

*S*everal distinguished FRCOs[3] taught at the College. They subscribed to one fashionable feature: it was the done thing in those days for organists to cherish and define themselves by their mothers' maiden names, hence:

E. Power Biggs, FRCO
J. Dykes Bower, FRCO
C. Thornton Lofthouse, FRCO
W. Lloyd Webber, FRCO
G. Thalben Ball, FRCO
    also
William H. Harris, FRCO
Osbourne H. Peasgood, FRCO

The latter couple contenting themselves with a mere middle initial. Dr Peasgood taught me organ for a while, but I was hardly his best pupil.

Was each middle name, perhaps, the maiden name of the organist's mother; Miss Dykes, Miss Thornton etc?

Lastly, the most potent memory of all: the College boasted ninety–eight practice rooms. In a nearby mews, off South Kensington's Queen's Gate Mews, stood a pub officially called "The Queen's Arms", but to us, forever, "The 99".

Here's to it!

---

3 FRCO: Fellow of the Royal College of Organists

Opera on the Rocks

Mrs H.B. Philips, widow of a famous impresario, and now herself part–owner and proprietor of the Carl Rosa Opera Company, met me in a London Hotel. Whenever I later met her outside the theatre, she was always in a hotel, understandably when we were touring the provinces, but hardly so in London. I doubt if she had a house, flat or home of any kind; I never received a letter from a home address.

In a brief interview she accepted me as the new chorus master and, with enormous generosity, offered me a salary of eight pounds a week, and an early chance to conduct an opera; a promise on which she subsequently reneged about once a fortnight, until Vilem Tausky, the company's ebullient Czech Musical Director, bullied her into letting me have a go.

She came from Co. Derry and had a broad Ulster accent, so we could talk like a couple of natives. Immensely protective of the company's independence, she was always turning down offers of a subsidy from the newly-formed Arts Council – her downfall in the end; I couldn't help admiring her spirit. Altogether she was not a bad old so–and–so.

In January 1948 I joined the Carl Rosa at the Hippodrome, Brighton, where I was greeted by Vilem Tausky, who was to become my patron, defender and friend. I was now a member of England's fraternity of touring players; one of the Good Companions. Up to now I was more familiar with German cities than with English ones. I began to learn about England, not just Oxford and London. Being a "No. 1 company", the Rosa played the cities sufficiently big to house large productions.

We usually spent at least two weeks on each date. I acquired a fortnight's knowledge of Brighton, Southsea and Bristol in the south; in the Midlands we visited Birmingham, Coventry, Nottingham and Wolverhampton. Further north it was Liverpool, Manchester, Leeds, Hull and Newcastle; then to Scotland, usually with four weeks in Glasgow; then Edinburgh and Aberdeen.

Many of these cities had beautiful Victorian theatres. From the 1950s onwards we began to witness many changes, occasionally renovations for the better, notably in Nottingham, where the Theatre Royal is a joyously "wedding–cake" revival.

Elsewhere there was vandalism; the lovely Theatre Royal in Birmingham's New Street was demolished by commercially–minded yobs, a disaster bringing tears to the eyes of many older performers and audiences.

On tour we lived in theatrical digs, well known to every company. Except for the stars, who could afford hotels, the hoi polloi such as myself were familiar with Mrs Breckenridge in Nottingham, Mrs Somebody–or–other–else in Manchester's notorious Ackers Street, and, also in Manchester, Alma McKay's slightly more up–market establishment in Daisy Avenue. Full board, including supper after the show, normally cost 3½ guineas. Alma's place, which she called Astra House, in deference to the stars whom she entertained there, was £5 a week. A few years later, after my Carl Rosa days, I once stayed there.

So did Gypsy Rose Lee, her four strippers and her six year–old son, Erik, poor child. I was conducting the musical *Summer Song* at the Opera House. Miss Lee was performing at The Palace, prior to her coming season at the London Palladium. Our group used to meet at Alma's after our separate shows at night. She was a civilised and intelligent woman, even a touch intellectual, (she was parodied for that in the musical *Pal Joey*). She liked to discuss her show with us, for its reception in Manchester was lukewarm. Should she make changes? No, we insisted, don't change a thing; the London audience will love it as it is.

A word about little Erik. He passed his days playing in the park with a new–found local friend of his own age. His evenings were spent back–stage in the company of Gypsy and her strippers. Some boys might have enjoyed that. Erik, I thought, found his life lonely. He had not yet reached puberty. One evening, we were in the digs discussing Gypsy Rose's problems. Erik had refused supper. Suddenly he emerged into the room with a plateful of goodies which he had conned out of kind Alma. His mother was none too pleased: 'Now Erik,' she said, becoming the stern mother, 'that is *caprice, and I do not like CAPRICE!* Poor boy.

The opera had its hilarious moments. We had acquired a new stage manager, Vernon Metcalfe, a personable but inexperienced young man. On one never–to–be–forgotten evening, we were performing *La Bohème* at the Theatre Royal in Glasgow's Hope Street. Act III opens on a wintry scene in the suburbs of Paris. In our production there was snow on the ground at the start of the act, but no snow would fall until a prescribed cue. Vernon, stationed in the prompt corner, was responsible for operating the sound board, which involved giving the flies man his cues. At the vital moment he turned the wrong switch – the one that would relay his voice to the auditorium. Then, from every loudspeaker in the front of house, came what was intended as a confidential whisper: 'YOU CAN START THE SNOW NOW, HUGHIE!' A shower of fragments of white paper descended from the flies. The audience applauded, roaring with laughter. The neurotic conductor, manic with rage, ordered the curtain down, and a fresh start to the act. But the harm was done. The shivering of the four lovers was irreversibly unconvincing.

My job as chorus master, as well as having to rehearse the chorus and teach the new choristers their music, was to conduct the backstage music. In nearly every opera, a dramatic effect is achieved at some point by a soloist or the chorus singing offstage before they appear in front of the audience, as for example in Cho–Cho–San's moving entrance in *Madam Butterfly*, I had to conduct these bits, synchronizing them with the orchestra in the pit. In spite of my success in this, Mrs Philips continued to postpone my opportunity to conduct a whole opera.

I made the decision to give myself a year of this frustration, and then, if still unsatisfied, to revert to an alternative career of which I had envisaged the possibility, that of a music critic. I had, after all, already written for *The Times*!

I doubt if I would really have put the plan into action, had it not been for the fact that, exactly a year from the day I joined the company, Mrs Philips did something to make me angry – she dismissed one of my colleagues, repétiteur Emanuel Yourovsky, most unjustly as I thought. I sent in my resignation, stating my disappointment at my lack of promotion, and my alternative plans.

She was furious, and summoned me for an interview. We sat in the daytime darkness of the Dress Circle of The King's Theatre, Southsea, confronting each other, roughly as follows:

'Mr Faris, you know I have faith in you, and will give you a chance to conduct at the earliest opportunity.'

'Mrs Philips, you have said that a dozen times in the past year, and nothing has come of it. Why should it be true now?'

And so on.

We parted inconclusively, and I went to complain to Mr Tausky. He took my side valiantly, exacting from the old lady a date for me to conduct our orchestral rehearsal of *Madam Butterfly*. This took place as promised, with a bad grace, by Mrs P. My performance was greeted with approval by cast and orchestra. Before long I conducted my first professional opera performance in the Lewisham Hippodrome. On that day there was a true London smog – we still had them in 1948. I travelled by train to Lewisham, trembling with nerves, standing in a crowded compartment. All went well; I had begun my conducting career.

Before long Emanuel Yourovsky was conducting the Royal Ballet at Covent Garden, having changed his surname to Young.

My salary had risen to £10 and then £12. I could afford half a lager on pay nights. In spite of these personal betterments, it was clear that things were not going well financially for the Rosa. They were beginning to run into money trouble yet again; hence the sacking of "Monia" Yourovsky. (No pun re "Monia" and "money" – it was his friendly form of address, as "Sandy" was for "Alexander".) For me and a fellow repétiteur the axe fell at the end of my second tour. David Andrews and I, the two youngest members of the music staff, were sacked.

I went on the dole, but that period was, happily, short–lived. I became musical director for the second London season of the successful musical *Song of Norway*, opening at the Palace Theatre in Cambridge Circus, the theatre which had opened under D'Oyly Carte, as the Royal English Opera House in 1891 with Sullivan's opera *Ivanhoe*.

Proud of such a heritage, I was now a West End man, and became impresario Emile Littler's favourite conductor. *Song of Norway* was succeeded by *Lilac Time*, a switch, I used impudently to remark, *sotto voce*, from decomposed Grieg to decomposed Schubert. Later, in *Summer Song* and *Kismet*, it was the turn of decomposed Dvořák and Borodin. The appeal of these pieces depended largely on a surfeit of adroit plundering of the world's most melodious classics.

Tours of musical shows differed from opera tours in one vital respect. Whereas the opera company played a different opera every night, providing us with some musical variety in our lives, the same musical was performed eight times a week – six evening shows and two matinees. After the interest of rehearsals and a few initial weeks, this gave rise to a gruelling sense of boredom, and the problem was to keep up the standard professionally, giving, as a matter of experienced technique, the same quality of performance as had originally been spontaneous and fresh.

One small social occasion was peculiar to the world of theatrical touring. All over the country, theatre companies performed from Monday to Saturday, and travelled on Sundays – by train. With so many cross–country journeys, changes of train en route were inevitable. It frequently happened that two theatrical companies would run into each other on a platform at Crewe station, England's principal mid–country railway junction. Some of the actors from one show were more than likely to know some of the actors from another; hence Joe and Jenny from the Carl Rosa would greet Ruby and Clarence from *The Dancing Years*. Sunday licensing hours did not permit an open bar in the mornings, but the station's tea–room would do good business. Cups of tea and coffee and the Sunday papers were welcomed.

In 1951, the Carl Rosa having acquired an injection of funds, I was invited back to the company at twice my previous salary. This restored my self–esteem temporarily, but the new musical director, Arthur Hammond, a distinguished but neurotic musician and an admirable person, who was responsible for my return, did not make life easy for me, (nor I for him, perhaps), and we parted company after one tour.

I lurched back into the orbit of the Littler brothers, Prince and Emile, conducting first of all *The Merry Widow* at the Stoll Theatre, a Kingsway landmark, now sadly no longer existing.

There I met a remarkable woman who was to have a major influence on my career. Fiona Bentley had been a protégé, (if not more), of Jack Hylton, and was now working for the Littlers as a stage director. She was in her twenties, attractive, intelligent, competent, ambitious, and, it must be said, the wielder of a winning, manipulative charm. Good, indeed, to have on one's side, as she was later to prove, but not before she had effected a mischievous rivalry between myself and Cyril Ornadel, then the West End's most successful young musical director. Cyril Ornadel – the professional name "Ornadel" being an anagram of "Leonard", the name of his family's clothing firm – was Fiona's boyfriend. I began to tire of Fiona telling me, 'Cyril is brilliant at this, and Cyril is good at that', until I discovered that Fiona was telling dear Cyril exactly the same sorts of things about me. Eventually Cyril and I got wise to Fiona's wicked little game, and became good friends. It was a sad day, years later, when the two of us shared a car to East Anglia to attend Fiona's funeral after her early death.

Cyril and I were different kinds of musician; Cyril, non–intellectual, intuitively talented, a disciplinarian popular with cast and orchestra; myself the person I have already described. Each of us could probably well have done with an admixture of the other's talents.

Before "the Widow" closed, Emile Littler offered me the post of musical director and orchestrator of his forthcoming production of the P.G. Wodehouse / Jerome Kern musical, *Sally*. I wanted – needed – the job as conductor, but said to Fiona that I was not competent to do the arrangements. Fiona said, 'Sandy, don't be silly, take both jobs. I have a good friend who will help you out anonymously with any orchestration you feel you can't manage.' I took the job, after she had introduced me to Dick Barrell, an established Tin Pan Alley, (Denmark Street to the uninitiated), arranger. He was as good as his, or Fiona's, word, and ended up writing two–thirds of the orchestration to my one–third. My arrangements were poor by comparison with Dick's, but not so bad that Emile would notice.

We began by holding chorus auditions. After three days we were still short of one baritone. Fiona had an idea. She rang the Savoy Hotel. 'I would like to speak to Mr Michael Jackson please.' She was not speaking of the American performer who was as yet unborn. 'I'm sorry, madam, we have no resident of that name.' 'No, he works in the kitchen.'

Michael Jackson was, at that time, an out–of–work actor. He had previously run his own repertory company in the West Country, it had fallen on bad times and he was now earning a living washing dishes at the Savoy. He auditioned for us, turning out to have a pleasant baritone voice. We took him on. Later, after our seven month tour, he joined the advertising business, where he had a long and starry career as a director of television commercials. Another talented recruit was Peter Gilmore, who subsequently rose to fame as Captain Onedin in *The Onedin Line*.

After we set out on tour, I tackled the most significant hard work of my life. Week by week I replaced my orchestrations with new ones, learning all the time from Dick Barrell's technique, which for this purpose at least was better than that of any college professor. I awoke, too, to the fact that much of what I had not hitherto admitted to learning at Oxford and the Royal College of Music, had been simmering all the time in my subconscious, and had now surfaced to complement Dick's unwitting tuition. A moment of excitement was to come. It was preceded by the departure from the cast through illness of the lead comedian, Eddie Childs, who was succeeded by the well–known character actor Clifford Mollison. After a few nights Clifford asked Fiona, 'who did that *beautiful* orchestration of "Look for the Silver Lining?" Said Fiona, 'Oh, Sandy did that, he arranged several of the numbers,' Fiona told me. It was as if the inhibitions of childhood and studentship had left me. I was a professional arranger, acknowledged by the public listener.

In twenty years' time I was arranging for Domingo and Pavarotti.

Michael Jackson

Wedding in Paris

edding in Paris was notable for the implacable hostility between Anton Walbrook and Evelyn Laye. The cast were aware of this; the audience thought all was wine and roses.

Anton Walbrook, an Austrian, had become a star in Berlin and subsequently internationally known both on stage and screen. He will be particularly remembered for *Dangerous Moonlight, 49th Parallel, The Red Shoes* and *La Ronde.* When I met him first at his home in Frognal, Hampstead, I found a quiet, sensitive, polite homosexual, and warmed to him from the start. Anton made his first venture into musicals in *Call Me Madam* at the London Coliseum. As a result of his success, *Wedding in Paris* was written as a starring vehicle for him. But Evelyn Laye, ("Boo" to her friends), stole a march on him. Boo had been in the doldrums for many years after her initial considerable fame. She had been playing on tour after tour, and was popular in the provinces, without making it back to the West End. George and Alfred Black, the producers, and Charles Hickman, director, seized the opportunity of casting her in the co–starring role of an attractive middle–aged widow. Laye still had her looks; blonde and blue–eyed, and she took care of her weight. She also took care of the press, whom she had cultivated assiduously during her temporary exile from the London stage.

The show opened on a Saturday. *The Sunday Express* Beverley Baxter raved. A front page headline read: 'It Was The Greatest Night Of Evelyn Laye's Life.' Anton never forgave her. Some weeks after the opening, as he gave me a lift on the way back from our recording at Abbey Road, he told me a story:

'Sandy,' he began, 'do you believe in astrology?' I looked at him enquiringly. 'We can do nothing; *everything is decided!* I tell you something. When I was a young actor in Vienna, I was called to Berlin to star in a new play. A middle–aged German woman was to play opposite me. Sandy, she stole my thunder, she became the star, I was now just a secondary actor – exactly what has happened with Boo.' He went on, 'Today I discover that that German woman was born the same day as Boo. *To the day!* Sandy, we can do nothing. Everything is decided!' These last words were delivered in a dramatic Teutonic whisper.

At a loss for an adequate response, I kept silent.

The Laye–Walbrook war apart, Anton was constantly ill–at–ease. He habitually criticised actors, stage management and the music. About once a month I would be sent for:

'Sandy, the orchestra was *horrible* tonight.'

(*I put on a calm imperturbability.*)

'Oh really, Anton, which number?'

'Every number, but *Strike Another Match?*'

'What was wrong with it?'

'This drummer, I think he is mad.'

He spoke of Tristan Fry, a budding genius.

'Well, Anton,' I said, 'normally you sing that number standing downstage on the O.P. side; tonight, for reasons best known to yourself, you stood downstage on the prompt side, right on top of the drums; they must have sounded much louder.'

'I think he is mad.'

I said nothing to Tristan about this. The next evening I met Anton on the stairs:

'Sandy, tonight the orchestra was different, *like night from day!*'

'Thank you Anton, glad it was OK.'

Evelyn Laye was, in fact, an amusing and, (Anton apart), friendly person. I used

Anton Walbrook and Evelyn Laye

to drop into her dressing room at the half–hour call to say good evening. She would perhaps be fiddling with a false eyelash, 'Hello, darling, I'm just putting on the scaffolding.' She had a horrible song, "In the Pink", to sing in Act II. She stood swathed in pink chiffon:

[Tango rhythm]
My heart is light as wine tonight,
And everything is fine tonight,
For all the world is mine tonight,
For I — [te–tum–tum–tum] — am **in the pink!**

There seemed to be about 117 verses of this awful song. Boo would frequently forget the words. Never put out, she would fix her smile on some elderly lady in the third row and, moving her lips with a semblance of perfect diction, would invent complete gibberish. I imagined the old lady in the audience saying to her friend, 'I didn't quite catch that, my dear.'

The show was playing at the Hippodrome. On my way of an evening I used to walk along Lisle Street, notorious for its prostitutes, on my way to the stage door. One rather attractive French girl used to loiter in her doorway, waiting for custom. She obviously got to know my face:

'Bonsoir, chéri, tu viens?' 'Er, not tonight, thank you, I've got to get to the theatre.' Off the hook.

Opposite the Hippodrome was Wyndham's Theatre, then showing *The Boy Friend*. After our performance I would often pick up Stella Quilley there, and we would go together to join her husband Denis, playing in *Airs on a Shoestring* at the Royal Court Theatre. There we would eat on the top floor at Clement Freud's popular club.

Happy days.

Twice Nightly

*B*lackpool is a holiday resort fronting one of the dreariest stretches of the Irish Sea. In the winter, off–season, it presents an aspect of almost unparalleled dullness, but in the summer it boasts many amenities for holidaymakers who turn up in large numbers from the nearby northern towns, Preston, Blackburn, Burnley etc., and further afield, from beyond the Pennines and Scotland.

The attractions are the Tower, where may be seen boxing and wrestling matches among other entertainments; the Winter Gardens with its two theatres and large ballroom, the Grand Theatre and many hotels, lodging and boarding houses of every description. But the year's great attraction is THE LIGHTS, a spectacular display stretching the length of the front, which draws crowds from far and wide during the late summer when the evening dusk shows the display to its best advantage. Early each autumn Blackpool was to become the venue for a party conference, Labour, Conservative or Liberal Democrat.

The summer of 1953 was one of the hottest on record, and we used to spend our days sunning ourselves and swimming at the south shore pool; "we" being the members of the cast of *The Show of Shows*, playing at the spacious Opera House nightly at 6.15 and 8.50. Because, once the show had opened, there were no daytime rehearsals, we could lie by the pool all day long, before mounting our bicycles to go to the theatre.

The Show of Shows was not a "book" show, rather a cross between a variety show and a revue. George and Alfred Black, the brothers who had inherited the mantle of their father, the great impresario George Black, had assembled an impressive array of star acts, led by Harry Secombe, the South African Eve Boswell, and *Les Compagnons de la Chanson*. The last, a group of personable nineteen and twenty–year olds, with pleasant individual voices and an impeccable ensemble, were to me by miles, or should I say kilometres, the highlight of the evening.

Harry was Harry, the post–war Goon loved by all. His dressing–room was on the same floor as mine, and I used to visit him between the shows for half a lager, (I was not for many years to come the over–imbiber of whisky). There was always a pile of the latest hardback books on the table — Harry was a voracious and serious reader. Our conversation took one serious trend. Harry had a strong tenor voice, sometimes, I thought, a little strained by a slight tightening of the throat. He used to discuss with me the possibility of giving up his comedy career in favour of becoming an opera singer. I have often regretted that he never took this courageous step, which was well within his powers. By the time he became famous in TV's *Songs of Praise*, the voice had mellowed and matured. He was agreeable and easy to work with.

Eve Boswell had made a hit with *Sugar Bush*, and was billed as *The Sugar Bush Girl*. George and Alfred felt she should feature the very latest song hit, which turned out to be a setting with words of the theme from the new Charlie Chaplin film *Limelight*. Ronald Hanmer, the quickest orchestrator I have ever known, turned out one of his lightning arrangements, and we rehearsed it at the piano with Eve. Unfortunately, by the time we came to go through it with the orchestra, Eve had remembered it wrong! She added an extra beat to the end of each phrase, so that this three–four melody now went "three–four, three–four, *four*–four" on each repeated phrase. Nothing would induce Eve to change, so all the orchestral parts had to be altered. I am afraid dear Eve was a bit of a nuisance.

In between the solo acts, there were comic sketches or production numbers, some including the Tiller Girls.

The finale of the first half was a sequence entitled *Our Heritage the Sea*. This began with Queen Elizabeth I delivering her famous speech at Tilbury. The Queen was surrounded by showgirls, each clad in Elizabethan corsage and a ruff. The stage was then transformed into a sea scene for *The Defeat of the Armada*. There were several battleships and much gunfire with profuse bursts of smoke, the climax coming when one of the ships sank, (through a trap door), with a final almighty burst of smoke that sent the audience coughing and spluttering into the bars, which naturally did splendid business.

The showgirls added a splendid *je ne sais quoi* to the proceedings; actually I knew exactly *quoi*, but let us continue. Each lady was about six feet tall, female height being an essential of showgirldom. Two flights of stairs had been erected from either side of the dress circle down to the stage, and on these steps the lovelies would be displayed in spectacular costumes.

Adjacent to the Opera House auditorium, under the same roof, was the Empress Ballroom. Here on Saturday nights, Geraldo would preside with his famous orchestra. The public would throng in couples to dance the quickstep, the tango, the foxtrot, the "Hokey–Cokey", ('You put your right foot in, you put your right foot out, you put your left foot in and you shake it all about, etc., etc.), the samba, the rumba and other dance favourites of the age. Geraldo, (Gerald Bright), silvery–

Peter Gilmore and Anne Stallybrass

haired, in a tuxedo with a red buttonhole, would stand smiling graciously at the crowd of dancers, elegantly waving his conductor's baton in a manner bearing no relation to the tempo of the music, while his faithful musicians, ignoring his "beat", would keep the strict time essential for the ballroom couples.

We did not perform on Sundays, but this was better than just a night off. Every Sunday evening there was a concert in the Opera House featuring one of the biggest singing stars of the time. It was there that I saw live for the first time Frank Sinatra, Billy Daniels, Tony Bennett, Billy Eckstine and others, artists with whom I was familiar on disc, but to hear and see whom I could not afford to travel to Wembley or wherever; perhaps I could never be bothered to make that necessary trek. Although these personalities performed in a musical medium somewhat different from my own, their stunning artistry added to my education.

I shared digs in Blackpool with a young Peter Gilmore, still a long way from his stardom as Captain Onedin in *The Onedin Line*. We became and have remained close friends, not before a certain unexpected clash. I use the word "clash" literally; one sunny Sunday morning we took our bicycles for a leisurely ride around the wooded back avenues of the town — by far the pleasantest part of Blackpool. Riding idly in the sunshine, we were not paying much attention to each other, when suddenly I swerved right and Peter swerved left simultaneously. Crash, bang, fall! And there looking down at us was a policeman, delighted to have his boring Sunday beat enlivened by two careless idiots, plus gaining a chance to make a fair cop. It took a lot of hard talking to dissuade him from arresting us, but with a bit of name—dropping and, I seem to remember, the offer of free tickets to the show, we remained free men.

Blackpool was not so dull after all.

Glebe House

When, in 1951, my mother retired from the headmistresship of Victoria College, she remained not only a governor of the college but a senator of Queen's University. She retired to an old country rectory in County Antrim, known as Glebe House, which she shared with two sisters, my Auntie Hazel who had retired with an OBE from her position as head of a hospital in Lahore, and its chief gynaecologist, when the British Empire dissolved; and Auntie Nan, (Anne Acheson), a sculptress who had become the first woman to be made a fellow of the Royal Society of Sculptors. Her greatest distinction, however, was the invention of the plaster cast, which she conceived while helping the casualties of the First World War. She became a CBE in 1919.

Glebe House was Georgian; a gracious, albeit now shabby u–shaped mansion with a central courtyard, set among trees beyond which was a view of Lough Neagh. It housed a flock of Chinese geese. Why we had Chinese Geese, I will never know. Noisy, angry birds.

During this time, preceding my aunt Hazel's sad early death from cancer, I had the unhappy duty of conveying the news to my mother in the Royal Victoria Hospital that my aunt had an incurable cancer.

Happier news was the birth of three more of my brother's sons. Eventually, after Uncle Sam's death, aunt Molly came to share Glebe house with her sisters. When, one by one, they died, my mother moved into a small flat in Belfast where my elder sister Katharine kept her company until mother had to move into a nursing home upon the onset of her prolonged final illness.

Harriet and I heard the news of her death on 31st December 1972 while on a Christmas holiday in Tunisia. On a rushed series of flights between Djerba and Belfast, we made it in time for the sad funeral.

My mother was buried beside my father in the churchyard at Coagh.

Harvard in Salzburg

*F*or the sensitive painter that he was, John Hawkesworth had a deceptively military manner, perhaps because he was the son of a general. We met in Germany in 1946. Both of us were officers in the Brigade of Guards, John a Grenadier, I an Irish Guardsman. I had produced a revue for my battalion, and was sent to do another at Guards Division HQ in Bad Godesberg. John designed the sets for the new revue, *Easy on the Eyes*, a pun deriving from the divisional emblem, an open eye.

John was greatly attracted to my music for the show. 'After the war,' he said to me, 'I shall produce a documentary film about the Rowlandson cartoons, and you must write the music.' My secret reaction was, 'Don't worry, Sandy, it will never happen.' But happen it did. In 1955 *Rowlandson's England* was shown as the short film accompanying the main feature *To Catch a Thief* at the Royal Film Performance. My music adorned the screen with Cary Grant and Grace Kelly. On the strength of this little success I received an invitation from America to attend *The Salzburg Seminar in American Studies*, an event sponsored by The Commonwealth Fund of New York, now the Harkness Fund, and organised under the aegis of Harvard University.

I had a birthday on 11th June 1955. The party went on till 2 am, and I stayed up all night to catch an early train to Paris. I spent a day in Paris, of which I have no memory, probably because I was hungover, save that of catching a night train to Salzburg. Where was my luggage all that day, I now wonder. I must have travelled first class, for I had a sleeping compartment to myself where I slept like a log. On waking I raised the blind, and remember the joy of seeing Lake Constance in the sunshine. Who would want to travel by air, I asked myself. We travelled through the Alps, arriving in Salzburg on a sunny afternoon.

Waiting to disembark from the train, I met a fellow passenger bound for the same destination, Leopoldskron, once the palace of the Prime Archbishop of Salzburg. The young man introduced himself as Troy Kennedy–Martin. This meeting established a long–standing friendship during which, years later, Troy was to create, among other TV and cinema hits, *Z–Cars* and *The Italian Job*.

Mozart's father was Vice–Kapellmeister to the Archbishop of Salzburg, and the composer spent much of his childhood there. In the twentieth century it was remembered as the setting for Max Reinhardt's famous 1935 production of *A Midsummer Night's Dream*.

The Salzburg Seminar was a holiday–like month–long course in a variety of subjects, including music, architecture, philosophy and the arts in general. The teaching staff consisted of professors and lecturers from Harvard. The students, an eighty–strong group of young post–graduate intellectuals from all over Western Europe, sat at the feet of the good and the great of the Ivy League. Apart from illustrated lectures, we had diversions such as a witty talk from the visiting Al Capp, creator of the cartoon *Li'l Abner*, and an afternoon's trip to Hitler's eyrie in Berchtesgaden. Not much of it left.

The Salzburg episode began with my birthday party in South Kensington, and ended with a party in Leopoldskron, for which I wrote a song, "*What Would the Archbishop have said?*", enumerating a few of the students' shenanigans of the past month.

A sequel to my Salzburg visit was my appointment as a Fellow of the Commonwealth Fund of New York. The New World awaited me!

New York, New York

It's a Wonderful Town, The Bronx is Up and the Battery's Down

*I*n September 1956 I set sail from Southampton, bound for New York, on the French liner *Liberté*, one of the grand old transatlantic ships, before our own *Queen Mary*.

I do not altogether recommend transatlantic ocean travel. Whereas, on a cruise, one calls in at pretty towns and islands, unending sea becomes pretty boring, as does the unchanging company of one's dinner companions. In my case, however, there came a wondrous reward when, at dawn on the last day of the journey, we rose to see the spectacular silhouette of Lower Manhattan.

You don't get that sight from an aeroplane.

I had been appointed a Fellow of the Commonwealth Fund of New York, an institution which awarded to young Britishers, and others, a generous year's funding for tuition and travel in the States; the theory being that we would return home as little American ambassadors. A condition was that we would undertake no paid work in the United States for a further two years. Alistair Cooke, a former Fellow, was excused this proviso, probably because he already worked in America for the Manchester Guardian.

On arrival I was escorted to a comfortable hotel on 42nd Street. That evening, being on my own, I decided to go to a theatre. A popular play of the moment was *Will Success Spoil Rock Hunter?* The play being an ordinary straight comedy, I was surprised to see a queue of American sailors outside. This little mystery was explained when the curtain rose to reveal, on a masseur's table, Miss Jayne Mansfield, for the most part naked, her monumental endowments rivalling the towers of Manhattan. The play was good too.

My host from the Fund was Lansing V. Hammond, a charming, kind and good man, who introduced me, that half–century ago, to the Americans who enlarged my musical experience and my limited worldliness.

Bernard Wagenaar, a professor at the Juilliard School, became my teacher of composition. Perhaps his greatest value to me was his attitude; he treated me as a composer rather than a pupil, and took pleasure in my efforts (or appeared to do so). He and his wife became my friends, on one occasion inviting me to stay in Martha's Vineyard, at Edgartown (of Moby Dick fame). Mrs W. was a rich New England hostess; very rich – she allegedly owned Chappaquidick Beach, which had not yet acquired the notoriety associated with Teddy Kennedy.

The orchestrations for *Oklahoma*, *South Pacific*, *My Fair Lady* and other Broadway musicals were the creations of Robert Russell Bennett. I had the good fortune to meet this – by now silver–haired – sixty–year–old, whose slight limp did not prevent him being an enthusiastic tennis player. He was, at the time, engaged on the orchestration of *Bells Are Ringing*, a show destined for Broadway, but at present performing in Boston while struggling with the customary misery of re–writes.

On arrival at the theatre, the company was rehearsing, under Jerome Robbins, the director, an elaborate re–arrangement of a major production number, which would involve Russell in a long night's chore of re–writing the orchestration. I knocked at his bedroom door to bid him a quick goodnight, but he called me in.

'Come in, come in!' He sat me down and entertained me with a long and fascinating rigmarole about his past, including such adventures as a taxi journey to Wimbledon in the company of Ivor Novello; a bizarre couple, I would have thought. Russell sat in an upright armchair, a music pad on his knee, writing in pen and ink. During the evening I only saw him make one alteration, scratching an offending note out with a razor blade. As he completed each page, he would give it to a music copyist, called from the neighbouring room. He had no apparent need to refer to the previous page, having, it seemed an exact memory of what he had written for each instrument in the preceding measures. In the course of the night he wrote sixty pages of score, eight bars to the page. I was told that he earned $25 a bar.

That evening we watched the show, then went backstage, where I had the thrill of meeting the exquisite Judy Holliday, a comedienne who could make you laugh and touch your heart at the same time. She had made her name in the film *Born Yesterday*; I saw her, too, in a lesser known movie called *Full of Life*, a funny and moving story about a pregnancy. Judy died young, leaving us the poorer for the loss of an entrancing artist.

There was a further happy diversion. A former Oxford friend of my brother's took me with his children to see a baseball match at Ebbett's Field, at that time the home of the Brooklyn Dodgers. There, under the guidance of a 12–year old boy, I learnt the meaning of a "bunt", (since forgotten), and had the unique experience of seeing the immortal Micky Mantle score a home run, (never forgotten).

Aaron Copland gave me lunch at the Harvard club. We discussed the forthcoming Bernstein productions of *West Side Story* and *Candide*, the latter of which I was later to conduct in London's West End. Copland was doubtful whether the varied pastiche in Candide would hold together as a convincing whole. In the event the score worked brilliantly. It was, rather, Lilian Hellman's libretto that caused critical comment, in that it involved a self–indulgent pseudo–philosophical expansion of Voltaire's snappy, cynical and, above all, concise novel.

A year or two later I had a singular delight. Aaron Copland was a world famous composer, but it was I who had the honour of introducing him to a London audience as a conductor. He stayed in the Cavendish Hotel in Jermyn Street, later used as the model for *The Duchess of Duke Street*. I knew the hotel slightly from having been at a party there as a young officer in the Irish Guards. (I actually met the great Rosa Lewis, owner of the hotel and a long-time friend of King Edward VII). The big occasion now was to be a concert in the Festival Hall, sponsored by the World Record Club with the Sinfonia of London orchestra. The programme would consist of Copland's own music, conducted by the composer. The Sinfonia of London was a breakaway group from the old London Symphony Orchestra, many of whose most distinguished luminaries, including such stars as Leon Goossens and the bassoonist Archie Camden, had joined the new group.

Meantime, *Candide* had made a success in Boston and on Broadway, and eventually started rehearsing in London in April 1959. When it came to finding an actor / singer to play the part of *Candide*, I recommended Denis Quilley. Leonard Bernstein insisted on hearing his voice, so Denis and I made a tape and sent it to him. Back came a telegram: ''squisito! You have the job!' Denis subsequently lost this precious memento.

Back in New York, March 1957, I gave up the chance of attending that year's final performance of *Götterdämmerung* to join an American girl (Ann Davidson) and a German youth whose name I forget, in a car trip round the United States. I passed a driving test in uptown Manhattan. We acquired a 1953 Chevrolet coupé, and set off south, hitting Washington briefly, and reaching New Orleans in time for the Mardi Gras. We parked by chance in Basin Street, where we made obeisance to the Jazz Greats.

Leaving New Orleans along the Louisiana Gulf Coast road, we turned left somewhere to visit a salt mine. I suspect that Ann Davidson's family had a commercial interest here. Ann never boasted about any family wealth, but one could tell she was not short of a dollar. Picture Gloucester Cathedral underground and you have this salt mine. Huge pillars of salt, (shades of Lot's wife), support the roof. The temperature remains constant at 72 Fahrenheit all year; a healthy infection–free ambience for the workers.

I parted from my companions to escort a nonagenarian widow into Mexico. The lady, Mrs Florence Marmon, was the relict of the rival of Henry Ford who invented the once popular Marmon car. I spent a few amusing days with her in San Miguel de Allende, an artists' colony graced by much beautiful Spanish architecture.

I left the lady to spend a few days in Mexico City and Acapulco, then flew to join my friends and the Chevrolet in San Francisco.

Travelling coast to coast across America, one finds, firstly, that almost every town is like a familiar film set; Sacramento, Salt Lake City, Laramie, Reno ('The Biggest Little City In The World'), and so on; secondly comes the observation that all state capitols are the same, being modelled on the great Daddy Capitol in Washington D.C.

While high up in the Rockies, in deep snow and with chains on the wheels, we made a diversion to visit a molybdenum mine; I was becoming a mining expert by now.

My two friends had a penchant for attending assemblies in capitols, which I found rather monotonous, until, that is, we came to Madison, Wisconsin. Here we fell in with a party of schoolchildren, their guide being an over–eager young man, who spotted us and shouted, 'Hi, Folks! Where you from?' We told him, London, England; Wiesbaden, Germany, and New York, New York.

'How about that, children! London England; Wiesbaden, Germany and New York, New York! Welcome to Madison, Wisconsin, folks! Join the party! Give them a hand!' Friendly American welcome.

The party was then led into the State courtroom, a square chamber with a large mural covering each wall. When we reached the fourth wall our cicerone was in his top form:

'This painting, folks and kids, depicts King John the Thirteenth of England signing the document known as 'Magna Carta' which gave to the people of England almost the same form of democracy as we now enjoy in the United States of America.' He nodded to me for agreement. I was not going to argue, although it was a bit rich, considering we were in the constituency of Senator McCarthy, Chairman of the Committee of un–American Activities and scourge of democracies.

Bouts of travelling apart, I had lived in New York for a year. Two days before I left for home, I saw, thrilled, *My Fair Lady*, with the original cast, the stars of which, with the exception of Cathleen Nesbitt, who had been a school friend of my mother's, were about to leave for London to perform the show at Drury Lane. I sailed from Hoboken the following Monday on the world's newest luxury liner, the Holland–Amerika ship Statendam, a one–class ship with plate glass windows where the Liberté had had portholes, and which had en suite toilet facilities in every cabin. My agreeable cabin mate was a fellow of the Commonwealth Fund, a budding young German diplomat called Otto von der Gablenz. I congratulated myself on the fact that I would not have to join the fight for seats for *My Fair Lady* in London, but could swank about having seen the show in New York.

When I got home, a friend telephoned to say that he was to be in *My Fair Lady*;

would I like to escort his wife to the opening night? So I saw the show again, the sets looking even better on the deeper Drury Lane stage. For personal reasons, however, I regretted the absence of Cathleen Nesbitt. Though I had never met her, we had spoken on the telephone in New York.

Leaving the theatre after the performance was like walking into the set again; into Covent Garden, where the story of Professor Higgins and Eliza had unfolded.

I do not want to see *My Fair Lady* for a third time; two such potent memories are not for repetition.

The West End

Irma La Douce

I was in a meeting with Donald Albery, Peter Brook and others, discussing Peter's forthcoming production of *Irma la Douce*; I had been summoned as a musical consultant.

'Shall we need a conductor?' someone asked. I thought: 'they mean, will they need *me?*' I don't know what answer they expected, but the one they got was 'yes!' *Irma la Douce*[4], had been a great hit in Paris, where it was still running in a tiny theatre. The music was supplied by a quartet stationed in a box adjacent to the stage, providing easy contact between singers and band. The London production, with a short tour in advance, was planned with a larger band situated in the orchestra pit. I pointed out that this was a hazard in terms of any decent ensemble. They rejected my advice, and engaged a pianist/conductor, who, as I had foretold, found it impossible to liaise with the singers; he could not see the singers, nor even hear them clearly. Nor could the musicians in the orchestra. When the brass, for instance, are playing, they cannot hear the singers at all, and are dependent on a conductor's beat. This is normal in every musical theatre. After a few weeks of the tour, I was summoned to the Theatre Royal, Brighton, to rescue the situation. The music had become chaotic; one or two musicians were misbehaving and I had to fire them. I hated doing this, and vowed that I would never sack any musicians whom I myself had engaged. I took over conducting, and things went well. In the event, after a plea from Lionel Monte, the fixer, I re–engaged one of the fired musicians, a good trombone player, who proved to be also a congenial drinking companion after the show.

Elizabeth Seal came fresh from her triumph in *The Pajama Game*. She and Keith Michel led an otherwise all–male cast, which was awash with current and future stars, including Clive Revill, Ronnie Barker, Gary Raymond, Julian Orchard and others.

---

4 Music by Marguerite Monnot; French book and lyrics by Alexander Breffont; English version by Julian More, David Heneker and Monty Norman. I accepted a six–month contract, having already signed up to conduct Leonard Bernstein's Candide in April 1959.

The show settled down to a four–year run, during which, from time–to–time, other famous actors such as John Neville and Denis Quilley took over leading rôles.

On Saturdays we performed at 5.00 and 8.00 p.m., finishing after eleven. One Saturday, shortly before I left, I dropped into Liz Seal's dressing–room for a goodnight/weekend whisky. The telephone rang; it was the stage doorman. There was a 'Mr Mac' to see Miss Seal. Liz sighed and said, 'send him down'. 'Mr Mac' turned out to be Groucho and Harpo Marx. They had been out front and were considering taking the show to Broadway. (In the end, David Meyrick acquired it). We had a delightful quiet chat, without, I'm glad to say, any attempt on the Brothers' part to be funny — with one exception: after twenty minutes or so, Groucho said politely to Liz, 'Well, we mustn't keep you — although I wouldn't mind!'

Candide

Rehearsals for *Candide*[5] used to begin at 10am in the stalls bar of the Saville Theatre, where we would sit for a comfortable hour listening to Robert Lewis, the director, discoursing about Lee Strasberg's Method School acting, and encouraging the cast to follow this theatrical religion — a cult which spawned Marlon Brando, Shelley Winters, Rita Moreno, Dustin Hoffman and many others. The general opinion in our English group was that the good actors would be good actors anyway, and the others paid little attention. Bobby Lewis had forbidden Lillian Hellman to attend the theatre until the final day of rehearsals.

Denis Quilley describes in his autobiography how, when Hellman finally appeared, she tried to persuade him to alter his entire conception of the part of Candide; this on the day before the opening night. Denis quietly ignored her advice.

The choreographer of *Candide* was Jack Cole, a figure of unchallenged supremacy on Broadway and in Hollywood. He was welcomed by our English dancers with a respect amounting to adulation. Because I came to know him outside the theatre, and learned a lot from and about him, I make no apology for indulging in a digression about this remarkable man.

Jack came to my flat one day when we both had a respite from rehearsals. I played him a recording of two Haydn symphonies which I had recently conducted with the Sinfonia of London Orchestra. Taken somewhat by surprise at his obvious

---

5 CANDIDE, comedy in 2 acts; book by Lillian Hellman, (assisted by Michael Stewart), based on Voltaire's satire; music by Leonard Bernstein; lyrics by Richard Wilbur; additional lyrics by John Latouche and Dorothy Parker. With Denis Quilley, Mary Costa, Laurence Naismith, Edith Coates and Ron Moody. Sets by Osbert Lancaster.

Denis Quilley

liking for classical music, I asked him who was his favourite composer. Purcell, he said, an unlikely answer from a Hollywood choreographer; though I was reminded of another such jolt when I heard Nelson Riddle say on the radio, 'When I sit at in my studio in Malibu, gazing at the ocean, I love to put on the music of your great English composer Ralph Vaughan Williams.'

Jack and I chatted. He told me of the occasion when he was telephoned by the great Howard Hughes, telling him that Mitzi Gaynor was unhappy with the choreography of her new show, which was on tour in San Francisco prior to its Broadway opening. Jack did not like taking over from a dismissed colleague. He visited Hughes to discuss the problem, and named an enormous fee, hoping that Hughes would refuse, thus ending the matter. Hughes said 'That's far too much.' Jack replied, 'Mr Hughes, that is the sum that would overcome my distaste for doing a job of this kind.' 'OK then', said Hughes, and took him to his private airport where a large jet was parked. Hughes summoned a wandering crewman of some kind. 'Do you know your way around these things?' A nod, 'Yes.' 'Move the blocks, then.' Jack was led on board. Hughes took the pilot's seat. He looked at the controls for a moment, then said, 'I never flew one of these things.' Jack, who was terrified of flying at the best of times, began to tremble. However, they arrived safely at San Francisco, where Jack was installed in a luxury hotel suite that was permanently at Hughes' disposal. Subsequently, he completed his distasteful task with success, and came away considerably richer, leaving Mitzi happy.

Candide was presented by Linnit and Dunfee, the firm then headed by the Hon. Geoffrey Russell, later, after a legal boxing match, to become Lord Ampthill. After four weeks tour, in Oxford and Bristol, the show opened at the Saville in Shaftesbury Avenue. The reception comprised acclaim for Bernstein's score, but no more than faint praise for Lillian Hellman's book, which lengthened and weakened Voltaire's terse, witty and concise novel into something of a wordy philosophical sermon. This, however, had nothing to do with an unseemly outbreak of booing from the upper reaches of the house, a demonstration initiated by the bitter playwright and composer Sandy Wilson, whose show, *Valmouth*, had been compelled to end its run by vacating the Saville in favour of *Candide*. Wilson wrote an unbelievably vicious letter to *The Observer*, complaining of what he saw as an injustice. The fact, as Geoffrey Russell pointed out in a reasoned reply, was that the theatre had long since been booked for *Candide*, and that *Valmouth* had generously been allowed to occupy the house while *Candide* was in preparation.

Leonard Bernstein attended the show a few days after the opening. We met him the following day in Claridge's. He emerged from his bedroom in a Noël Cowardish sort of dressing–gown and a pair of green slippers embroidered with a large "L.B." With one criticism re one over–fast tempo — L.B. was on my side against that of Bobby Lewis — he praised the performance.

The show ran for sixty days, during which it acquired a coterie of admirers. An excerpt was shown on BBC Television's semi–intellectual programme *Monitor*, in which Leonard Bernstein was interviewed and, to my gratification, complimented the 'neat' orchestra.

Many years later, "Lenny", as he now was to us, was being shown around the unfinished National Theatre, and ran into Denis Quilley, who was rehearsing *Tamburlaine*. After a brief conversation he asked Denis, 'How is Sandy?' Denis said, 'Well you know the TV series *Upstairs, Downstairs*?' Lenny immediately burst into loud song with my theme melody for that series. Fame.

A few days before the opening night of *Candide*, a sadness had happened. Jack Cole suddenly disappeared, having apparently left the country. His dancers, revelling in his work, and standing by with a first night present, were devastated. No one knew what had upset him, or, if anyone did, they weren't saying. I reflected on a remark Jack had made to me quietly, privately, 'Sandy, we all have our problems.'

Paul Collins, the leader of the *Candide* orchestra, used to deputise for a violinist friend in the Philharmonia. One night he was seated within earshot of the conductor, the aged, ailing Otto Klemperer. The Festival Hall was packed with an audience aware that this might be the venerable artist's final public appearance.

Klemperer limped onto the platform, bowed to audience and orchestra, raised his baton to inspire a performance of Beethoven VII. Silence in the hall. The maestro raised his baton, paused, then slowly dropped his arm. Hugh Bean, the leader, leapt up to the podium, 'Are you alright, Dr Klemperer?'

The old man looked at him, despondent, 'What a life!' he muttered, and began the Beethoven symphony.

The Sixties

*I*n 1960 Sadler's Wells decided to institute a policy of producing light operettas in parallel with their usual serious opera programme. I was the new operetta conductor, Wendy Toye the new director. We both had experience in opera as well as West End musicals, and had once worked together.

The world's sixties were my forties, which proved to be one of the most fruitful periods of my conducting career. I am now ashamed to say that I took no notice of the Beatles, but at least I did not grow my hair long or indulge in drugs other than whisky (and wine with meals).

I began my first orchestral rehearsal under the scrutiny of the bosses (Norman Tucker, the Artistic Director, and his second–in–command Edward Renton). The members of the orchestra, none of whom knew me, were friendly and cooperative; until, that is, a would–be clever–clever pedantic know–all tried to disconcert me.

We were playing a recitative passage, where the orchestra interjects single chords (maybe two or three in succession) between the vocal passages. They were playing these chords beautifully but rather too smoothly in the context. I explained that this was a brittle comedy, (it was *Orpheus in the Underworld*). I asked them to make the chords shorter and crisper. Everyone knew what I meant. Except that is, Mr Know–all:

"Mr Faris, exactly how long would you like these chords?"

Me:

"Just a little bit shorter than you played them last time."

We made to start again. Not a hope.

"Mr Faris, if you will tell us exactly how long you want the chords, we will play them that way."

The orchestra was now shuffling their feet; they knew this old guy. He made one more attempt at sabotage. My patience snapped.

"Very well," I said calmly, "I will tell you exactly how long the chords should be. Play each written crotchet as if it were a quaver tied to a double–dotted semiquaver, with a pause over the second dot." The other players practically cheered. The man never spoke to me again (a bonus). In the pub after the rehearsal musicians were buying me drinks. They had been waiting for someone to nail this guy. The quotation about the double dots became famous. I became a popular conductor for the next six years.

Sadler's Wells Theatre had three special features:

One: It stood adjacent to three good pubs – The Shakespeare's Head, The Harlequin and The Empress of Russia. Each of these boasted an extension on the theatre's telephone exchange. Interval endings could be sounded, delinquent drinkers could be summoned back to rehearsal; and, since there was also an extension on the conductor's podium, he could, during a dialogue passage towards the end of an operetta, order his chosen drink for after the show. I sometimes claimed to have done this, but I was merely jesting. I never used this particular facility, however much the temptation.

Two: Mr Sedziak, a Canadian expatriate of Czech origin became a rabid fan of *Orpheus*, of myself and the cast. He attended every performance, usually sitting in the second or third row of the stalls, near the centre. When I entered the pit he would shout out "Bravo, Alexander and his ragtime band!" After the first occasion,

Norman Tucker
Director, Sadler's Wells Opera 1948 – 1966

the orchestra learned to expect this outburst, but it left each new audience somewhat bemused.

And *three*: I could always park my 2½ litre Riley.

After our success with *Orpheus* came *La Vie parisienne*, again starring the exquisite June Bronhill.

Although in my mind the Sixties have always belonged to the Wells, I made various diversions. My first departure was only a few steps away from the Wells; down the road to Covent Garden and the Royal Opera House. I was to conduct *Façade* and *Coppélia* in a double bill. All went well except for one *glitsch* when I had a trivial run–in with the odious orchestral manager. Dame Ninette de Valois took my side in a matter too boring to relate, which ended with me being offered the job of principal conductor of the Royal Ballet's second company. I turned this down on the grounds that there was no chance of being promoted to the first company, where John Lanchbery was firmly and deservedly entrenched for the foreseeable future. Meanwhile I was working with England's youngest up and coming star dancers. I remember with joy the premiere of Lynn Seymour and Christopher Gable, together in their first *Swan Lake*, and — a different kind of honour — conducting for the venerable, but still magical, Alicia Markova as *The Dying Swan*.

Then came the momentous occasion when the Wells presented the first non–copyright production of a Gilbert and Sullivan opera. So prestigious was the

Theater an der Wien
A historic venue on our European Tour, 1962

proposed event that Sir Malcolm Sargent proffered himself as the conductor. 'No thank you,' replied Norman Tucker, 'we have a perfectly good conductor of our own'. Yours truly.

The right to perform the Gilbert and Sullivan operas was originally vested in the D'Oyly Carte Opera Company. Sir Arthur Sullivan died in 1900. His music remained in copyright until the end of 1960, after which anyone was at liberty to perform it as happened promptly in the Cranko/Mackerras ballet *Pineapple Poll* — but not in conjunction with Gilbert's words, which were still protected from general use. Sir William Gilbert died in 1911. The copyright in the words expired at midnight on 31 December 1961. On the following day we performed Frank Hauser's superbly directed *Iolanthe* at the Royal Shakespeare Theatre in Stratford–upon–Avon.

The town was deep in snow. I had to get permission from the Regimental Adjutant of the Irish Guards to allow their band, who took part in the performance, to stay in Stratford overnight. This pleased them hugely, as it got them off the next morning's drill parade.

Sadler's Wells now had a high European reputation. Before many years passed the Company would move to the London Coliseum, and eventually become The English National Opera.

The latest project was a European tour, largely in Germany. The touring repertoire was to consist of *Peter Grimes*, *The Rake's Progress*, both conducted by Colin Davis, and — yes or no? — *Iolanthe*, my own assignment. The majority verdict was against including the latter, on the grounds that its Englishness would not appeal to German audiences. Then, like a deus ex machina, the West German Ambassador attended a performance of *Iolanthe*, laughed all the way through, and insisted that it should be included in the repertoire.

We soon set out for Stuttgart.

The Stuttgart Opera House fronts a small park criss–crossed with paths not unlike those on Primrose Hill, save that they are on the flat. On the evening of our German premiere the theatre was alight, and a strolling audience was gathering, peopled, apart from the locals, by groups of German, English and American diplomats. Backstage an apprehensive cast was awaiting the evening's adventure.

The conductor is first on.

I stood in the dark beside the uniformed German flunkey who had escorted me through the labyrinth that lies under the stage of the Stuttgart Opera House, waiting for a green light, the signal for me to enter the orchestra pit to conduct the overture to *Iolanthe*.

A bizarre choice, perhaps, *Iolanthe* for Sadler's Wells to present to a German audience as part of the repertoire of its first tour of European cities; but the West

German Ambassador had insisted on its inclusion in the programme. Moreover, this production had already made its mark in the history of British musical theatre.

I was apprehensive about the evening to come, fearing a frosty reaction from the audience. The Germans, I thought, will hate Sullivan's music. They will either not understand the jokes, or not think them funny, in their bewilderment at watching the English make fun of their own House of Lords.

A green light. As one walking the plank I entered the pit, bowed to the audience, and to the orchestra. (We had brought our own orchestra with us, thank goodness). In retrospect I think the Germans expected a rumpty– tumpty jingle of an overture. After about twenty seconds I was aware of their silent surprise at hearing an enchanting pianissimo misterioso – Sullivan imitating Mendelssohn. This was one of the three overtures that Sullivan himself composed. The others were, in the main, cobbled together by musical directors. The overture ended brightly, to enthusiastic applause.

Although there was a smattering of English and Americans in the audience, there must have been a majority of Germans who understood English. They laughed at all the jokes save those involving a political reference which they could not be expected to comprehend, e.g. Captain Shaw.

At the end of the performance we were given the greatest ovation I had ever experienced. I asked the late John Cranko (then Ballet Director at Stuttgart) why they had liked it so much.

"Because the Germans love operetta, but the standard here is so bad that they didn't know what had hit them."

The remainder of the tour, and a subsequent one, took us to Munich, Cassel, Hamburg, Vienna, Prague and Brussels. We had happy experiences everywhere, but none to compare with that ecstatic evening in Stuttgart.

My next departure from the Wells was as one of a trio, the others being June Bronhill and Wendy Toye; Wendy to direct and June to star in *Robert and Elizabeth*, a musical based on Rudolf Besier's play *The Barretts of Wimpole Street*. The London producer, Martin Landau, had acquired the West End rights from an American judge. Unfortunately, the libretto was sadly in need of re–writing. There ensued a rumpus of litigation between Landau and this irascible judge. The outcome was that Ronald Millar, (later to become knighted for writing Mrs Thatcher's speeches), was permitted, (thank goodness), to write a new book for the London version, while Australian Ron Grainer, (known for TV's *Steptoe and Son*), composed a remarkable score in what I think of as "20th Century Classical".

Sadly, two years later, an American legal judgement stopped a possible Broadway production, despite the hopes of US producers.

A long rehearsal period turned out to my personal advantage. I was chatting with Ron Grainer in his flat in Queen Anne Street. Ron was working hard at the orchestration of his own music. I was, at that stage, solely and contentedly the musical director. Suddenly, Ron said, 'Sandy, with all these alterations, I'm very pushed for time; would you like to arrange some of the music?' I was thrilled at such an offer. I expected no credit; Ron would pay me out of his own fee, although I would have happily done it for nothing; I was well paid as the conductor. I arranged about five numbers. When the publicity came out it read: "Orchestrations by Ron Grainer and Alexander Faris". This unsolicited credit was typical of Ron's generous nature, and was to my benefit over the years, long after dear Ron had met an early death from cancer.

The long rehearsals proceeded and we went on our prior–to–London tour. I was enabled on my present salary to reside at the Queen's Hotel in Leeds, theatrical digs being now mercifully a thing of the past; but I more than once had to sit up most of the night scoring yet another new number for the show. Eventually we opened at the Lyric in Shaftesbury Avenue to a resounding success. I remember a touching moment at the first night party when John Clements made a dramatic entrance with his stricken wife Kay Hammond, who died of a debilitating illness. How I recalled her brilliant comedy performance in Coward's *Blithe Spirit*!

A happier moment was the night when two Australian lady friends of June Bronhill came to the show.

In the second act, June, as the bedridden Elizabeth Barrett, had to sing a dramatic soliloquy as she rose from her sickbed, enlivened by her love for Browning. The Australian ladies were rightly impressed by June's ability to repeat such a dramatic performance night after night, (we were now at about night two hundred). Next evening June told me that on the night in question, she was expecting guests for supper after the show. 'I didn't tell my friends, Sandy,' she said, 'but as I rose from my stage sickbed, singing with passion, I was thinking about the supper party. "Now", I thought, "if I put the potatoes on while they're having their gin, the timing should work out about right"; I didn't tell my friends.'

The digs days were over, the hotel nights past and gone; it was night sleeper time. While I was still conducting the *Barretts* eight times a week, (six evenings and two matinees), the call came from Rosebery Avenue: would I now conduct intermittent performances on tour of *Orpheus* and *Iolanthe*? A new routine commenced. I would do the evening performance of *Robert and Elizabeth*, then take a taxi to Euston to mount the night sleeper, first class of course, to Edinburgh, Glasgow or Aberdeen; conduct the next day's performance of whichever operetta, and return by the following morning's day train to join the Barrett family again.

These night and day journeys were a joy. In those days the night trains had bars still open after midnight. Regular passengers got to know each other. By day, I came to know the Forth Bridge, the Tay Bridge and the eastern coastline of England and Scotland. It was a hard but supremely rewarding life.

The continuously successful West End run of *Robert and Elizabeth* came to a rude end when the theatres of Shaftesbury Avenue suffered a sudden increase in their rates. Even full houses could not support the burden. The show then went on tour and was later to be revived on two occasions; one at the Chichester Festival. By that time, Ron Grainer was dead. Ronald Millar regarded me as the guardian of the musical legacy. Some years later, after my expedition to the Antipodes, Ronald invited me to dinner at Brooks's Club in St James's. He had a project in hand: to make a musical out of his successful play *Peter Abelard*. I offered my services, but before long was aware that Ron's invitation was by nature of an unmentioned farewell — he was, I was convinced, conscious of his impending death.

I had worked off–and–on for some years with Ron Grainer and Ronald Millar. I now said goodbye to the second of two well valued colleagues.

Down under

Australia

*I*n July 1962 an eight–strong group from Sadler's Wells set out for Sydney to head an Australian production of *Orpheus in the Underworld*.

Robert Blake was to re–direct Wendy Toye's scintillating production; Iris Kells to take over as Eurydice from June Bronhill. (As I write over forty years later, the unsurpassable June, who has suffered a brain tumour, is stone deaf and can only lip read; that once infallible voice can no longer sing in tune).

After a short flight to Rome, we boarded an Alitalia DC8 bound for Sydney. On its return journey this aircraft crashed near Bombay with no survivors; an inanimate exception being one postcard which I had addressed to a 12–year old nephew in Belfast, and which turned up two years later as an enclosure in a letter from an Australian lady who found it among her papers. She and her husband had boarded the same plane in Sydney, but survived, having disembarked at Karachi. I still have the postcard.

We recruited our Australian singers from the Elizabethan Trust, an organisation which ran, among other things, the Australian National Opera Company.

The Company was at present on tour in Brisbane, which gave Bob Blake and me a welcome visit to that city in order to take auditions in the mornings and witness the evening performances. Brisbane reminded me of a western town in an American movie. It had bars with slatted double swing doors, which one expected to burst open admitting a gun–toting John Wayne, shouting 'Don't nobody move, this is a stickup!'

The Australian singers were of the high standard one learns to expect in that country. I attribute this to the sunshine and the healthy life the youngsters lead, although it may be that some of them inherit romantic Irish voices from their chain–rattling ancestors.

We assembled a fine cast and returned to Sydney where Bob and I were allotted a comfortable furnished flat, high up in a modern block in swanky Pott's Point, with a balcony view of Sydney Harbour, enhanced by the presence of a nearby dry dock, which was occupied for the duration of our visit by the P&O liner *Caronia*, undergoing repairs after damage on its recent ocean journey. At night the great ship was dressed over–all with lights, whose reflection on the harbour waters created a kind of fairyland. Round one corner from our block was the equally swanky, if faintly notorious King's Cross. In the other direction was Woolloomooloo — dockland. The name was a shibboleth; to prove one's right to true Australianship one had to be able to spell and pronounce it. Internally the apartment was comfortably appointed, with one exception: there were no egg cups, an omission giving rise to the curiosity about Antipodean diet.

The orchestra that shortly joined our vocal rehearsals was of a less high standard musically than the singers. The cream of musicians in New South Wales was absorbed by the Sydney Symphony Orchestra. However, we soon mounted an acceptably musical performance in the Tivoli Theatre, (no longer there, alas), and the show was well received by press and public.

I had an affection for the old Tivoli Theatre, even though my under–the–stage dressing room smelt permanently of coke fumes and urine. The auditorium had an old–time Victorian grandeur reminiscent of such as the Hackney Empire, providing a shabby–ornate but welcoming theatrical venue for audience and performers alike.

Not so, alas, the embryonic Sydney Opera House, still in its concrete and scaffolding state, which was the cause of a burgeoning scandal.

A stage manager on holiday from the Royal Opera House at Covent Garden had written to the press pointing out that the shell–like roofs, reaching down to the floor, would prevent the flying of stage cloths from more that a few feet up–stage.

As visiting firemen, the Sadler's Wells contingent was invited on a tour of inspection of the rising building. I found myself beside an Australian conductor contemplating the orchestra pit intended for the smaller of the new opera house's two auditoriums, supposedly big enough to accommodate the orchestra for a Mozart opera. My colleague and I turned to each other in disbelief. The structure, cast in concrete and therefore unalterable, was in the shape of half a slice of lemon, tapering to nothing at either end, where there would not have been enough space for one cello to handle his bow. We were supposed to make conciliatory remarks about the building, but I chickened out of this requirement, avoiding contact with any local authorities.

Though externally destined to become one of the world's most beautiful buildings, the Sydney Opera House was drastically unsuited for its prime purpose of presenting opera.

The whole scandal caused some malicious delight to the citizens of Melbourne. The latter city and Sydney thrived on a rivalry akin to that of Glasgow and Edinburgh. But Sydney had its revenge after a few months when a lorry fell through the roadway of Melbourne's vaunted new bridge over the river Yarra.

After a three–month run in Sydney we moved to Melbourne, headquarters of Garnett Carroll, the dictatorial impresario of the Australian Commercial Theatre. Garnett was not an unpleasant man, but he was a bit of a stingy old so–and–so, (I once referred to him in an end–of–term party lyric as 'Garnett, that semi–precious stone'), in that, throughout our whole Australian run, he never gave us a day off other than a Sunday. This meant that those of us on a once–in–a–lifetime visit to Australia had no chance to see any of its beautiful countryside other than on a day's trip to the Blue Mountains. It was on such a visit that I bought a full–size boomerang, which I sent to my godson in London with a strict warning that it was not just a toy, but could also be a lethal weapon.

Melbourne is a handsome Victorian city, but not as much fun as Sydney. However, we were equally successful in its Princess Theatre.

Let me here introduce Ron Austron, a tenor of excellence, not exactly fat, who played the King of the Boeotians. Ron was a genius in another respect; he had an infallible gift for nosing out the time and location of parties. The dwellers in Melbourne, being hospitable folk, gave parties every night. All were welcome, if you wanted to know where the party was on any given night; all you had to do was to ask Ron and bring a bottle. Thus it was that on one occasion I found myself at a party having a long talk with Fred Trueman and Ted Dexter. I later became friendly with Ted in a different context, of which more anon.

I finish this chapter with a digression: I am a European. It came to me once in New York, which I love, that I was a foreigner, in alien corn. I am by blood Irish; English by adoption, a Londoner by profession, affection and the passage of time, but recently when I called a cab in Sydney, realising that the driver was German. I exclaimed: "Oh good! Somebody from home!"

I am a European. Australia, I still love you.

New Zealand, here I come!

New Zealand
Auckland, Christmas Day, 1962

After one night in an Auckland hotel I rented a flat in the suburbs. Following our first night's performance of *Orpheus* I returned to my new residence to hear the telephone ringing. I answered, mystified as to who could have found me there.

It was June Lewis. Australia had caught up with me.

I had had a month–long affair with this June Lewis, who lived in the same Melbourne block and whom I met at a party. She was a thirty–year old divorcee with a son of eight called Mark. June and I carried on an active nightly sexual affair, which broke up acrimoniously when June suspected me of bisexual leanings. I hadn't expected to hear from her again. But here she was on the phone; she must have gone to considerable trouble to track me down at my day–old address. We had a friendly reconciliation, my last contact with her. But years later a young Australian called Mark, of an appropriate age, turned up as a barman in my local Primrose Hill pub. I didn't have the nerve to ask him if I might have had a fling with his mother.

'I recognise that horrible Hammond organ', I said as a foursome from our *Orpheus* company, (John Fryatt, *Orpheus*; Cynthia Morey, *Calliope*; Patricia Bancroft, our company manager, and myself, the conductor), were enjoying a picnic lunch on Mount Eden, while over the air came a recording of Christmas pieces which I had conducted two years earlier, with memories of that hated instrument now long since outdated.

Since coming to New Zealand we began to alternate performances of *Orpheus in the Underworld* and *The Merry Widow*, both of which went down well with the Kiwis. The orchestra in New Zealand was not up to the standard of the Australian one, but we were lucky to have a superb lead violin. He came to us for an ironic reason: he had been sacked from the New Zealand National Orchestra when it was discovered that he was a kleptomaniac. He played the solos in the two operettas beautifully.

After our visit to Auckland, we made a brief excursion to Rotorua, with its magnificent geysers and the constant smell of sulphur, and then spent a few days in Palmerston North before proceeding to Wellington.

Palmerston North is a dump, and its theatre has the worst orchestra pit in which I had the misfortune to conduct. Not only that, but a few of us were accommodated in the Station Hotel, where we were kept awake late at night by the shunting of trains. We alleviated this problem by having sessions of warm gin and Fanta; fortunately, before long we were on our way to the handsome city of Wellington where I conducted two concerts with the National Orchestra of New Zealand. These were promoted by my friend James Robertson, formerly Musical Director of Sadler's Wells. The orchestra and I were only quite good.

Next stop, Christchurch, New Zealand's most English city, lying in the lowlands, albeit near the heights of Mount Cook, whither a party of us flew on a Sunday, lunching in the hotel at the summit, then slithering about on the Tasman Glacier.

Christchurch does not possess Cambridge's multiplicity of colleges, (it has one university of excellence), but it resembles England's Cambridge in that a gentle stream flows through the meadows, reminding one of the 'Backs' in the English city.

At the end of a happy Christchurch season, the company split up to depart for their various homes. Cynthia Morey, John Fryatt and I travelled together, stopping

Cynthia Morey and John Fryatt

for a night in Fiji – I still have the hotel room key, not much good to them now. We proceeded to Hawaii where we stayed in the Halekulani Hotel. The Halekulani consists of a central building surrounded by a series of bungalows, and is extremely fashionable. We spent time sunbathing, but I was brave enough to have some water–skiing lessons on Waikiki Beach. I was strictly instructed not to let my feet fall to the ground, but rather to do 'belly–flop' dives, but I dropped my foot once and got from the coral a nasty cut which remained poisonous for several weeks.

A great pleasure was a day tour of Oahu. Leaving behind Waikiki and Diamond Head, (later familiar to TV viewers from the series *Hawaii Five–0*), we circumnavigated the island in a hired jeep decorated with a candy–striped canopy; travelling partly on the coast road, but later through fields of sugar cane. Not the most picturesque crop I've ever seen.

Before arriving back in Honolulu my mind was rudely wrenched away from the frivolity of water–skiing and candy–striped jeeps; the sudden nearby spectacle of Pearl Harbour had given rise to more serious contemplations. What effect, I wondered, did that bombing have on the progress of World War II? If the Japanese attack had not taken place, would America have joined us when she did?

With brief stopovers to visit various friends whom all of us knew in San Francisco and New York, we were more than happy, after nearly a year's touring, to return to London and beloved Rosebery Avenue.

New York Again

As I write in 2005, I am saddened to hear of the premature death of Otto Plaschkes, who engaged me in 1966 to compose the score for *Georgy Girl*. Though I failed in two attempts to write a satisfactory title song —Tom Springfield and Jim Dale later wrote the hit *Hey There, Georgy Girl!* which gave a carefree lift to the opening of a cynical, witty and at times touching film. I was never jealous of their deserved success, and had my own reward when Bosley Crowther, critic of the New York Sunday Times, writing of the extensive background score, singled out two of my musical passages for special praise:

'… and the musical score of Alexander Faris, which is brightly and cleverly composed of satiric symphonic interpolations and modern jazz passages, is a splendidly witty commentary on a basically tender, touching theme.

'… or why it's sad for just a moment to see the roommate disappear from all their lives with a totally anonymous sugar–daddy to the dying strains of Tchaikovsky's First Piano Concerto.'

So I found myself on a second visit to New York, this time with the loan of a Brooklyn Heights apartment belonging to actor Alan Arkin, a friend of a friend. I wrote earlier of seeing the skyline of lower Manhattan in the dawn from the deck of the liner *Liberté*. Now, with New York in a blizzard, I looked across the East River to the same skyline, which, lit up and bedecked in snow and ice, outdid any potential Disney fairyland. A small extra bonus in my borrowed apartment was that I could see the newly–starry Norman Mailer pass by on the stairs. We never spoke.

One wintry afternoon, after attending a matinee performance of *Man of La Mancha* in downtown Manhattan, I took the uptown subway and disembarked without realising that I was in Harlem. I went into the nearest bar and was greeted by surprised black faces but no comment. After a quick whisky, I left to make my way towards Morningside Heights where I was due at a party. The route was roundabout, and I asked the way from a middle–aged couple who pointed out, with some hesitation, that it would be quicker to walk across the narrow park.

I decided on this route because I could see, higher up, the railings of the upper perimeter. Easy, I thought. I was, alas, dreaming the impossible dream, the theme number of the show I had just attended.

I had not noticed that halfway up the hill was a clump of trees, providing cover for the unwary. When I reached it, I was seized upon at knifepoint by two black teenagers, who demanded my money, emptying my pockets, and throwing into the snow all my possessions, including my passport. The two boys soon discovered the unpalatable fact that I only had seven dollars.

'He's been drinking!' exclaimed one. It was the only occasion when whisky may have saved my life, the distraction causing the couple to lose their concentration for a moment, thus allowing me to make a break for the railings at the top of the park, only a few yards away.

The scene became irretrievably American. A matronly woman saw my predicament as I climbed the tall fence. She came to my aid and I thanked her, making to go. 'Oh, no!', she insisted, 'You must call the cops!'

So we went to a nearby station and explained the situation. All I wanted was to get to my friend's apartment, ashamed of my stupidity in laying myself open to such an unwelcome adventure. But escape from the constabulary was firmly forbidden, albeit with great charm.

To envisage the acme of pointlessness, picture two uniformed Yankee policemen escorting one English, (well, Irish), composer around Harlem on a dark winter's night, in a marked car, in search of a couple of black youngsters, who, having just mugged a stranger, had had half an hour to disappear into the depths of New York's teeming Afro–American ghetto.

I perhaps do the cops an injustice; later, in the snow by the copse, they found my passport. But no seven dollars.

Our party now proceeded to another police station, the 26th Precinct. Suddenly I was in a novel by Ed M°Bain. Every detail was correct: US flag, picture of the President, (Lyndon B Johnson), slatted rail. I was submitted to a friendly interrogation about the reasons for my visit to New York. The cops were enthusiastic, and were all going to take their wives and girl friends to see the movie. One of them then drove me back to my friend's apartment, where I was greeted with sympathy and no surprise — 'Gee, it happens all the time!' My red face gradually lost its flush. Finally, Lansing Hammond, my sponsor at the Commonwealth Fund, handed me twenty–five dollars. 'Fund money', he said, but knowing his generosity, I think it came out of his own pocket.

One evening I went for a drink in Sardi's. At the next table sat Marlon Brando. We didn't speak. Some things you lose.

No more adventures this time. I failed to land a further film music commission, and returned on a dreary plane to Heathrow. No more romantic liners.

Colline Des Primevères

I had to look up the French for primrose. Primrose Hill has been my home for forty years.

After in 1956 and 1957 I spent a year on a fellowship in New York and later another year in Australia and New Zealand conducting the Sadler's Wells Opera, I then returned to my beloved London to search for a new abode. After a visit to Victoria Park in Hackney, I found my present flat in Primrose Hill. It was the best choice I ever made. In those days Regent's Park Road was a village high street. The lighting was poor, but we had good tradesmen and shops. There were three butchers, two pubs, a baker, a cobbler and a post office. There were no cafés, with the exception of a bistro run by students who provided excellent food, but did a moonlight flit, leaving debts up and down the road.

Then property prices rose and a transformation took place. Boulevard replaced village street; people dined out on the pavement. Many of the tradesmen left, forced out by rising rents, to be replaced by young rich folk, their all–terrain vehicles, their bistros and boutiques. The once dingy Queen's Hotel, twice refurbished, disappointingly to my mind, its wonderful old mahogany woodwork covered with paint, is now a bright gastro pub run with courtesy by excellent young staff. Sadly, by the omission of the apostrophe in the pub's original title, a fragment of history has been forgotten. *The Queens* once *The Queen's Hotel*, referred to one queen, Victoria, with memories of one of the pub's visitors, her son Edward VII, en route for a rendezvous with his intimate friend, actress Lily Langtry, who lived a hundred yards away in St George's Terrace. The title has been altered to *The Queens* (unintentionally suggesting a sexual motif).

The street is already awash with teenagers; young couples with their babies and a plethora of dogs, young and old, large and small. My friend Michael Jackson, a regular *boulevardier* has watched thirty dogs passing by as he enjoyed his morning café-au-lait. I can empathize with the babies, but become tetchy when confronted on my walks by a phalanx of prams, single or double.

The good and the great have moved into Primrose Hill. My neighbours, some of them pub fellows, include Kingsley Amis, Peter Quennell, Robert Stephens, Alan

Bennett, Simon Jenkins, Joan Bakewell and others. Such celebrities nod at me or exchange an odd friendly word at the bar, but I often feel that they don't quite know who I am or what I do.

New arrivals turned up. Germans, Ulrich and his wife, Gisela, came to live in Regent's Park Road. Ulrich, being a reporter for the German newspaper *Bild*. Gisela worked in an antique shop in the West End, but she was also a brilliant interior decorator, and undertook to decorate my flat, which she did with panache and great skill. Gisela repapered the flat with Japanese grass cloth obtained at enormous expense at Sandersons and which I could now no longer afford, in addition to which she designed an elegant archway to replace a square entrance from the hall into the rest of the flat.

A second renovation was designed by my neighbour David Gloster, an architect and good friend, in conjunction with my sister Harriet who paid for a new kitchen. The original set-up, which had been cobbled together from a basement, was prone to damp and associated creepy–crawlies. Wandering ivies had found their way through the breeze-block outer wall and were attacking, like some John Wyndham creatures, through the locks and cracks, into my life.

Harriet came, saw and issued an ultimatum: things had to change. She commissioned David to do the work. He decided correctly that the entire area be tanked to avoid damp before renovation started.

This gave me a problem, Without a kitchen I couldn't carry on living at the flat. I moved out to stay with relatives, while Nigel the builder moved in. Nigel tended to be away when he was wanted. I dubbed him St Nigel the Absent. The changes were duly completed, with built–in units including washing machine, tumble dryer, fridge and an elegant gas hob. No oven; Harriet said, 'Sandy, you never do a roast.' Instead, a microwave.

Gisela and Ulrich's marriage foundered, he returning to Stuttgart, where I visited him at the scene of my happiest success, *Iolanthe*, at the Opera House, and where, on the grass forecourt of the theatre were paths like those on Primrose Hill, one of which bore the name 'John Cranko Allee' after the late Director of the Stuttgart Ballet who had died in 1973 after suffering an allergic reaction to a sleeping pill taken on a transatlantic flight. Would that our local paths and woods were named for our distinguished artistes, as in France and Germany, rather than for wealthy English landowners (Cavendish, Grosvenor etc).

Ulrich returned to London, hoping for a reconciliation with his wife, but sadly she would not take him back. One afternoon, I met him in the Princess of Wales, and was shocked to see how ill he looked. He adamantly refused my offer of an ambulance to take him to hospital; eventually I left for home. Three days later I heard that he had died of pneumonia.

Alan Spencer

Other new friendships included two brothers, Richard and Andrew Benbow, who looked after my spaniel Sacha on the evenings when I was conducting at Drury Lane.

Neighbouring Sharpleshall Street was home for many years to Terry Mitchell and Alan Spencer. Terry once played the boy cellist (and the cello) in *A Little Night Music*; Alan, the choreographer for D'Oyly Carte and later director of many Gilbert and Sullivan and other productions.

Both always helped me in looking after my flat and contributed greatly to the success of my 60th, 70th and 80th birthday parties.

I became friendly with Annie Clough, who had become my agent after the sad death of John Cadell, son of the famous actress Jean Cadell.

John's death was followed all too soon by the even sadder death of his young actor son Simon, possibly best known for his role in the television series *Hi–de–Hi*.

Another familiar rendezvous was The Lansdowne public house run by the friendly Jim McGrath. A group of happy friends used to meet in front of one of the two wood fires at either end of the bar. The Lansdowne was gutted by fire in October 1984. We all mourned the death of Jim's dog who, for no apparent reason, re–entered the inferno.

At one point along the way I composed an eccentric piece entitled 'Blanche could never touch anything fried', which Bill Drysdale brought to life on stage with sparkling choreography.

A Common Occurrence

I have been mugged — who hasn't nowadays? Once in New York, this time London style; in my own flat, due to my own naïveté, or stupidity.

I had had my afternoon nap. The doorbell rang. A seemingly pleasant youth asked if one Gerry lived in this house. I said no, went to close the door. The boy pushed the door open, knife in hand. I was at his mercy — he tied me up, hands behind my back, ankles together, left me face down on the floor, and proceeded to search the flat — thoroughly, he was an experienced operator.

Sitting room, bedroom, hi–fi in the hall with its cassette player and turntable, steel filing cabinet — he had found the key in my pocket — found my grandfather's gold watch, though not the gold chain. My nephew would never see this bequest from his uncle.

Bank card. I was too frightened to reflect that, as he didn't know my PIN number, it would be of no use to him. I saw him drop it on the floor. When, for some reason, he untied my hands, not my feet, I jumped on the card to hide it. He was now heavily laden because of the hi–fi equipment. 'Don't call the police for at least two minutes!' He must have had a van outside. I called the police.

I had twenty–three visits from the police, men and women. Interviews, finger–prints, mine and they hoped his, a fearsome but in a way therapeutic procedure in my shaken condition; I had nothing but admiration for their skill and determination to find the little shit. Two days after the event two police officers visited me.

'Is he behind bars?'

Not exactly 'yes' or 'no'.

'You won't see him again.'

So it was yes.

The Great Waltz

One Friday evening I was in my flat, enjoying a nightcap with a friend. We were both rather drunk. At midnight the telephone rang. It was Harold Fielding, the impresario. He had a very high voice. 'Oh, Sandy!' he squeaked, 'I'm so sorry to trouble you so late, but we are in a terrible fix with our conductor of *The Great Waltz*.' I knew him; it was Bernard Grun, a delightful man and a good musician, but no conductor. It appeared that the cast and orchestra were up in arms, and the show was due to have its first preview on Monday.

'Could you possibly take over in time for our Monday opening? Bob and Chet, (Robert Wright and George Forrest, the American writer and composer), would take you through the score tomorrow morning.' A tough assignment; I accepted, doing my best to conceal my drunken state. So much for a peaceful nightcap; a quick good night and an early start were indicated.

Saturday

10.00 am to 3.00 pm Intense study of score with Bob and Chet in Harold Fielding's office.

5.00 pm Vocal and piano rehearsal with cast in the dress circle bar of the Theatre Royal, Drury Lane. I was received with applause and cheers, with, if I remember rightly, tears of joy from the star, Sari Barabas, the Hungarian former prima donna of the Vienna Opera and Glyndebourne.

7.30 pm Full rehearsal with orchestra. Sighs of relief from the musicians. A moving telephone call from Bernard Grun, saying, 'If anyone had to take over, I'm glad it was you, Sandy.' I thought, there's generosity of spirit. Typical of Bernard.

Harold Fielding, aware of the shortage of time and the consequent difficulty of my task, offered to cancel the Monday preview, a major concession on his part. I refused on condition that I would not be too harshly blamed should there be an occasional *glitsch* on the night. In the event the occasion went remarkably well. The performance on the subsequent Thursday's press night was *glitsch*–free and there were happy faces all round.

My agent John Cadell, whom Harold respected as 'a rare gentleman among agents', was on holiday during all the fuss. His secretary agreed on generous provisional terms, and I acquired a contract for a seven–shows–a–week engagement. This gave me Monday nights off and a consequent two–day weekend.

All very well, one might think, except that my deputy conductor, Reg Cole, did not get on with Sari Barabas, the result being that my arrival at the theatre on Tuesday evening was always greeted with a screaming tirade from that lady: 'Sandy, Reg was terrible last night, please tell him how to do it!' etc. etc. Reg, a good chap, was a middle–aged experienced conductor of shows of the variety and music hall type, but in the case of any remotely operatic music, which this was, he was a fish out of water. He was at a loss about how to get the orchestra to accompany Sari's impassioned *rubato*, and this is something that no one can teach. Reg was a good violinist, playing in the orchestra from Tuesday to Saturday. He was, incidentally, an enthusiastic freemason, which I respected, albeit knowing little of that world; I was happy to allow him a night off to receive some honour in the field. Oddly enough, I felt some measure of pride in his distinction.

I continued with the Monday nights off and Tuesday night's rows for the eighteen months of the show's run.

Upstairs, Downstairs

*I*n the autumn of 1971, after a long gap, I heard from John Hawkesworth. It was a pleasant surprise, the more so as he was ringing me with an offer. London Weekend Television were planning a series about an Edwardian family. Would I like to submit a musical theme for the series? (Not straightforwardly, to *write* a theme, but to *submit* one; fair enough, they might not like my submission.)

I attended a meeting of the LWT team, where John was in the chair. An argument was in progress regarding the title of the series. There was a strong contingent in favour of entitling it *165, Eaton Place*. Crummy, I thought. Somebody, John probably, stuck out for *Upstairs, Downstairs*, and won the day. The theme, they said, should be very English, perhaps rather Elgarian in character. Someone muttered 'like *Land of Hope and Glory*'. Hmm, I mused, a hard model to match.

I went home and wrote a theme tune overnight. I was not entirely enamoured of it myself, nor was the production team next morning.

But lucky Sandy got a second chance: *submit* another tune. 'Perhaps,' suggested someone, 'more like Elgar, less like Eric Coates.' I tried again and again produced something overnight. It was better than my first attempt and was immediately approved by the team. I did an orchestration, in a dignified slowish $\frac{4}{4}$ march time, and my resident copyist, Giles Hewlett–Cooper, set about copying the orchestral parts. These were nearly finished, and a motor–cyclist was on his way from north London to collect the score and parts when, tinkling at the piano, I found that the theme worked rather well in waltz tempo. Giles and I produced a new version, keeping the messenger waiting. Both versions were accepted, but before long every director of an episode opted for the waltz, and it was that which became well–known.

This theme proved so catchy that I began to be worried that I had pinched it from an existing tune. Plagiarism, which nobody bothered about in the 18th century, could now prove a costly business. I became anxious about this to the point of paranoia, asking everyone I knew, every classical musician, pop musician, jazzer, show musician and every rag, tag and bobtail individual if they recognised this tune. No one did, and I breathed a sigh of relief.

The show came on air in black and white for the first six episodes. As a result of its instant popularity, the succeeding episodes were transmitted in colour. In 1975 I won the Ivor Novello Award for the Best TV theme of the year. I received a statuette, pretty, but so heavy that it would have made an excellent door–stopper or murder weapon, (I thought of this when I was mugged some years later), but I put it on prominent display, hoping for some appropriate adulation. Someone occasionally asked, 'what's that thing?' I was paid a ridiculously small fee — perhaps that's why they gave me the job — a cheap composer.

They forgot to give me a screen credit. Their red faces failed to console me. But the grey skies turned to blue. John Hawkesworth and Freddie Shaughnessy, the script writer, had planned six episodes. Emboldened by their sudden success, they embarked on a further series. To make up for the previous omission I was rewarded with a solo credit; the screen all to myself, my name in the *art nouveau* calligraphy of the period – a welcome boost to morale and my professional image, to be displayed world-wide in the coming sixty-eight episodes. Concomitant royalties; some things you win.

On the tenth anniversary of the series, there was a party in LWT's new premises on the South Bank. John Hawkesworth apologized for the meagre amount that I had been paid for the music. I said, 'You can stop apologizing right now, John, the royalties are rolling in nicely.' He said, 'More than mine are.' He later engaged me to compose theme music for *The Duchess of Duke Street*. Not so much of the "submit" this time.

Clifford Makins

Formative influences: for the piano Miss Winifred S. Bell, than whom I could imagine no better teacher; but when I showed signs of a developing musicianship I needed an introduction to harmony, counterpoint and the wider repertoire of classical orchestral music.

George Smith was the music master at Victoria College, my mother's school. He was an ebullient character, middle–aged but so far a bachelor (that was to change soon after I met him) and a profoundly learned musician who proved a valuable *guru*.

I was then a schoolboy. Later, in my sixties, I met my second great mentor, Clifford Makins, who was to influence my career — and my life — for years to come.

After my eighteen–month stint conducting the musical *Billy* at Drury Lane, I was wilting from the strain of an eight–show–a–week routine, and wondering what the future might hold.

When I first met Clifford he was living in a ground–floor room in no.8 Rothwell Street, a few doors away from my flat. He was divorced, had two sons, hefty likeable lads, with whom, after Clifford's death, I remained on Christmas card terms. He was deeply devoted to Ann Melsom, whom he would liked to have married. Sadly, Ann, a devout Catholic, felt that she could not marry a divorced man. Eventually Clifford married *Observer* political writer Nora Beloff, who looked after him during his terminal illness.

He was succeeded in no.8 Rothwell Street, first of all by my copyist Giles Hewlett–Cooper, subsequently by David Llewellyn, a promising journalist whom Clifford nurtured as he had me. As a result of Clifford's encouragement, David rose to become a sports writer in his own right, featuring prominently in *The Independent*. David was to marry my niece Hilary.

Giles was a brilliant musician. His ambition as a composer never bore fruit, but he was one of the best copyists I have ever known. He interpreted my work on paper better than anyone. Sadly he died early of leukaemia. The card he wrote to me the night before he died still stands on my shelf.

Clifford would turn up in the morning armed with his personal miniature gin–and–tonic. After brief 'good mornings' we would adjourn to the Queen's. Ensconced behind an arras on a raised area at one end of the room Clifford would keep a lookout for the arrival of any boring bête noire, whereupon he would declare, 'Stand by to repel boarders!'

In 1974 Donald Mitchell, music editor of both the *Daily Telegraph* and publishers Faber & Faber, had approached me more than once with an offer to publish a biography of Offenbach. I had then a modest réclame as an Offenbach conductor at Sadler's Wells. I twice agreed to his offer and twice did nothing about it. I needed money and Clifford urged me to write the book. I asked Donald if the offer still held good. He replied, 'Yes, but you must do it this time.' I began to save part of my salary for conducting *Billy* at Drury Lane. By the time that show closed, I had enough from those savings plus an advance from Fabers' to become an author rather than a conductor. The British Library became my second home. I used to spend every morning there with a break for elevenses in the Museum pub — the whisky drinking had already taken hold in my mid–fifties.

During this time I had a dog called Sacha; a golden Cocker Spaniel whom I had bought from a member of the cast at Drury Lane. In order to look after this animal, I enlisted the help of two neighbours — brothers Richard and Andy Benbow — I gave Sacha his morning walk and my neighbours fed him and took him out in the evening while I was conducting a musical.

Clifford Makins

Then came France. During the next four years I paid many visits to France, interspersed with salary–earning episodes conducting shows in London — *The Yeomen of the Guard* at the Tower of London, *Bar Mitzvah Boy* and others. But I spent weeks at a time in the little Hôtel Prince Albert on the right bank, near the Opera and its library, near the Bibliothèque Nationale, and near also to Offenbach's own theatre, the *Théâtre des Bouffes–Parisiens.* The hotel was run by two French brothers, both of whom spoke perfect English. I had been good at French at school, having come second in the Northern Ireland equivalent of A–levels, but in spite of some conversation with Frenchmen and Belgians during the north–west European campaign, my French conversation was somewhat halting. I made a deal with the hotel brothers that we would converse in French only. I spent every day, after a morning café–cognac in a corner bar, reading old newspapers in the music department of the Bib. Nat. Being immersed in reviews of Offenbach operettas in the newspapers of the Second Empire, I began to read French almost as easily as English. Speaking remained a bit hesitant, since I lived a lonely researcher's life, seldom finding anyone to speak to.

Antonio de Almeida, the Musical Director of the Nice Opera, was then the world's greatest expert on Offenbach, to be succeeded after his early death by myself and now by others, French and American, who have had the good fortune to discover hitherto unknown Offenbach scores that have come to light in various châteaux and elsewhere. I was up to date when my biography of the composer was published on the day of the centenary of his death — the day after, actually, as the anniversary fell on a Sunday. Good luck to my successors.

'Tony' Almeida, as he was to me, was a man elegant of dress and charming in manner. More than that, he started me off on a chain of introductions, to begin with, M. Pierre Comte–Offenbach, a great–grandson of Jacques, who entertained me in an up–market arrondissement of Paris. I felt that Comte–Offenbach liked to think he owned a monopoly of Offenbachiana. He gave me some valuable information, but professed to have no detailed knowledge of the English branch of descendants of whom Tony Almeida had told me. One of them, possibly named Buckley, who might have gone into shipping, was the farthest Comte–Offenbach would go in giving me information. I later discovered that he knew all the details, but wasn't telling me. 'Shipping,' I thought, 'ho hum.' Assuming my best private investigator persona, I decided , 'you've got to start somewhere.' I rang the Cunard Line, unlikely as they were to have any clue to a dead composer, and was lucky to be answered by a human being rather than a machine. After some delay while he delved in the archives, a polite young man told me that they once had a James Buckley, (in a very junior position, I gathered, albeit more than a cabin boy). Buckley, my informant thought, might have gone to the Dart Container Line in Southampton.

With small hope I mustered up confidence and rang the Dart Line. 'May I speak to Mr James Buckley please,' I said boldly, doubting that they would know any such person. 'I'm sorry, sir,' replied a nice sounding young woman, 'Mr Buckley is not in his office at the moment; can I get him to ring you?' My spirits rose. So James Buckley existed!

It was the beginning of a long collaboration and friendship with the Buckley family that led, after four years, to a party at the Royal Opera House.

James Buckley did indeed exist, as did his beautiful wife Sabine and their two daughters. I was to be guest at both girls' marriages, one in Winchester, one in France; but not before I had received a great deal of help in my research on Offenbach, from both James and his French cousin Michel Brindejont. James and Michel were both in possession of several of the original manuscripts of Offenbach full scores. They gave me access to these, James in England and Michel in France. On one occasion James insisted on my taking away one score to study at home. I was so nervous at being in possession of such a priceless document that when I went on holiday I put it on safe deposit at my bank, with full instructions re its rightful ownership.

James and Michel both possessed villas at Etretat in Normandy. Before I knew the two cousins I visited Etretat accompanied by my sister Harriet. We sailed on the ferry from Southampton to Le Havre and drove east along the Normandy coast to discover, nestling among the cliffs, the pretty little town, since the days of Napoléon III a popular holiday resort for the élite. Two parallel streets, the rue Jacques Offenbach and the rue Guy de Maupassant, form the town's main thoroughfares. Adjoining one of these, Offenbach built a large villa on the hillside, the *Villa Orphée*, on the proceeds of his first massive success, *Orphée aux Enfers*. Three weeks after the completion of the house it burnt down. Offenbach immediately had it rebuilt on the strength of his continuing success: a far cry from a later point in his life when he fled from the bailiffs to Brussels, before resuming much subsequent success.

Harriet and I continued on our trip, driving to Paris, via the pleasant but relatively down–market resort of Fécamp, delaying for one evening of gastronomic excellence in Rouen. In Paris we stayed in my usual small hotel on the right bank; I resumed my research at the Bib. Nat. with valuable help from Harriet, who made happy use of any free time in Parisian sightseeing and Parisian shopping.

On my second visit to Etretat I was the guest of Michel and Mme Brindejont. I was allotted a room in their villa where I could write and study scores, apart from which I enjoyed their superb hospitality. The whole Buckley/Brindejont clan were in the town for the wedding of the second Buckley daughter. I remember little of the ceremony. The bride, like her recently married sister, was the attractive daughter of good–looking parents. The groom, like his recently acquired brother–in–law, was a personable young man, with what I dared to imagine was going to be a prosperous future.

The highlight of my sojourn, however, was my visit to the Villa Orphée. The Offenbach descendants no longer owned the villa, but it was in the possession of close friends who were more than happy to show it off to the Buckleys' visitors. I was fascinated to see that each bedroom door bore the title of an Offenbach operetta — *Orphée aux enfers, La Belle Hélène, La Vie parisienne, etc.* My mind filled with visions of Maupassant, Meilhac, Halévy and the composers, singers and literati of those days.

On Friday 19th December 1980, a group of six people occupied the centre of the stalls circle in the Royal Opera House, Covent Garden: James Buckley and Michel Brindejont, great grandsons of Jacques Offenbach and their wives; myself and my sister, Dr Harriet Rhys–Davies, who had contributed a medical essay to my centenary biography of the composer.

The occasion was the opening night of the centenary performance of *Les Contes d'Hoffmann*[6], with Placido Domingo as Hoffmann. In the interval we were entertained to champagne by Sir John Tooley, the General Administrator of the Royal Opera, who had, many years before, been my boss when I conducted the Royal Ballet. We were later taken backstage, where my guests were introduced to Domingo. They were duly impressed by the whole evening, and topped it off by taking Harriet and me back to the Dart Line's elegant suite in Piccadilly. There they produced a whole salmon, caught, I think, by James; it was our turn to be impressed.

That was my last significant contact with the Buckley ménage. James and Sabine moved to the south of France. A few years later I heard the James had died in his fifties of a heart attack.

I wrote above of my excitement at the discovery that James Buckley existed. He exists now in my memory as one of the kindest and most generous helpers in the course of my career.

---

6 LES CONTES D'HOFFMANN — Libretto: Jules Barbier & Michel Carré after E.T.A. Hoffman; Music: Jacques Offenbach; Producer: John Schlesinger; Conductor: Georges Prêtre.

Incidental

Misheard

My hearing is not as good as it was. I note that I hear the vowels correctly, not the consonants — lack of "top" on the sounds. I decipher men's voices more clearly than those of women.

The reception of my bedside radio is not as good as I would like; hence I sometimes mishear fragments of the news, e.g. on the occasion of Cardinal Hume's death a woman announcer told me, as I thought, that the sad event would be remembered in Westminster Cathedral by a wrestling match.

A what?

A requiem mass.

Again:

When King Hussein of Jordan died I heard a reporter announce, 'The King will be succeeded by his half–witted son Abdullah.'

Surely not. Libel.

His half–British son. True.

On *Farming Today* the interviewee seemed to say, 'For hill farmers today most of our income comes from selling bathing suits.'

I doubt that but I don't know the answer.

Hard Day at Drury Lane

Originally published in the New Statesman 17 October 1975, reproduced by kind permission

*S*aturday midday. My local is opposite, and I mean opposite, my flat in Primrose Hill. The social weekend drinking is beginning, and is the warning signal for me, as musical director of *Billy*, to leave for Drury Lane and face the prospect of two performances today, the 586th and 587th of the run. This is the long day's journey into night that is my working Saturday in the theatre. The compulsive time–watching has gripped me. I resist until 12.20 and then walk to the tube.

Chalk Farm is a station which nowadays has a widowed appearance, the forlorn air of a woman who no longer has anyone to tart up for. Change at King's Cross (12.31), out at Covent Garden. The Opera House is advertising *Siegfried*. I play my sub–titles game: *The Ring* — An Everyday Story of River Folk; *The Flying Dutchman*, or *The Lass that Loved a Sailor*[7].

Bow Street, Catherine Street, and lunch in a local trattoria. Four ladies with wedding rings but no husbands are at the next table. A splinter group from the Ambridge WI, I dare say. Audience for *Billy*? Audience for *Oh! Calcutta!* Not the cast of *Oh! Calcutta!* surely, cela serait trop bizarre. To what green altar, O mysterious ladies, have your husbands gone on this soccer–playing Saturday?

1.15 p.m. Back stage, to despondent greetings of some actors and musicians, all looking as weary as I am at the thought of the two shows to come. And yet half an hour later the trumpeters will be trumpeting and the dancers will be dancing, and Michael Crawford, whose mind–bending energy would in any case shame the dead into working hard and loving it, will have begun again to exercise the magic that has filled the theatre for 18 months.

2.25 p.m. They call 'Beginners' on the intercom. Call–boys are a thing of the past. How they managed in loveable, rambling old Drury Lane I can't imagine. It must have taken 15 minutes to get round all the dressing–rooms. (Mind you, I seem to remember that they just yelled from the end of the corridor.) I go to the

---

7 Subtitle of HMS Pinafore.

prompt corner to await the stage manager's word to begin. The actors are drifting on stage. As they see each other in costume and make–up they seem to slough off their previous grey reluctance and become animated, colourful creatures. There is that inexplicable birth of excitement, heightened by the uniquely emotive sound of the orchestra tuning up, out there, beyond the curtain.

2.29 p.m. 'Will you go through, please, Mr Faris,' says the deputy stage manager, a courteous Scots lad called Willie. Willie always says 'through'. They usually say 'in' or 'down'. But 'through' is good. Through the glass doors I go, through the frontier that divides the cast from the audience, an envoy from one to the other, a Kissinger sent to soften them up with an overture before the curtain goes up on the big show.

2.30 p.m. Performance No 586. Matinee. In a long run there is the perennial problem of how to maintain concentration. Inevitably much of the mechanics of the performance is pure reflex. The mind is not fully occupied. Every performer has experienced the moment when the brain switches over to the automatic pilot. This may be all very well for a few lines of dialogue or a few bars of music, but the conductor must wake up in time for the next change of tempo.

During the dialogue scenes the musicians, temporarily redundant, can stave off boredom by reading, and a surprising variety of literary taste is evident in the orchestra pit. Today I find the tuba player deeply involved in The Peloponnesian War of Thucydides. The double–bass, on the other hand, favours Moravia's The Two of Us, the book which, according to the blurb, 'starts where Portnoy left off'. Every orchestra has its Guardian reader (bassoon, younger generation, liberal). And, heavens, the harpist is reading the *Tatler*; I didn't know it still existed.

5.15 p.m. Final curtain. Screams of rapture from the teenagers. During the play–out music I catch a smile from the girl who today has seen the show from the front row for the 90th time. At a cost of £270.

5.30 p.m. Leave the stage door fighting my way through the fans, Crawford's, not mine. One down, one to go.

Feeling rather tense, I take my tea in the café round the corner (a Librium and a poached egg). Then lie down in my dressing room to hear Robert Robinson Stopping the Week on Radio Four. A soothing programme, in that the conversation, while entertaining, reaches no demanding conclusions, but evermore comes out by the same door as in it went. Reflecting that hypotheses are more relaxing than conclusions anyway, I drift off to sleep, and wake up to hear Lord Carrington on his desert island requesting Irene Dunne and *Smoke Gets In Your Eyes*. A good choice too; what a tune, what a lyric.

7.30 p.m. No 587 gets off to a good start. A packed house at Drury Lane, with even the boxes full, is a fine sight. Then word gets around that Bing Crosby is in front, with Henry Fonda's mother. It doesn't have to be true; the rumour, the names are enough to get the adrenalin going. We hear later that the Old Groaner was indeed present, with or without Mr Fonda's mother.

9.05 p.m. The second and last act for the second time today. Keep going, men, we only have to survive 90 more minutes of melody, romance and laughter. When we finally make it, I feel as if I have been in the theatre for 100 years.

10.15 p.m. Curtain calls. The orchestra plays on like a horse turned for home. Conducting seems simple again. I am redundant. Michael Crawford is the unredundant one. The man they come to see, a superstar who earns his money the hard way. At the end of the longest day he could still do a midnight matinee.

Once the two shows are over you would think that the musicians wouldn't want to play another note, but you would be wrong. The next five minutes in the band room are bedlam. Most of the boys are packing up their instruments to get off home, but for some reason the trombonists always go on tromboning for a bit, and the first horn has a worrying tendency to keep playing the opening of *Till Eulenspiegel*. But they calm down and the serious members of the orchestra concentrate on their serious drinking.

11.15 p.m. Homeward bound. On Saturday nights London Transport is a dead loss (in accordance with its policy of making Saturday night like every other night). There are no taxis. Just as I am about to order a minicab the first trumpet offers me a lift. It's out of his way, but he always pretends it isn't.

Midnight. Home to four large Scotches. I put on the ending of *Rosenkavalier* until the man upstairs makes his ritual complaint. I switch off, leaving the poor fellow to his sleep as I drift off into my own, wondering what the part of Octavian would have been like if Strauss had written it for a tenor instead of a woman.

My D-Day at the London Palladium

The Observer, 16 November 1975, reproduced by kind permission

*W*e all have our D–Days. My first one brought news of the Normandy landings, (read by John Snagge), as I was playing croquet on the lawn of the officers' mess at Pirbright. I was 23, a subaltern in the Irish Guards. I felt like Sir Francis Drake on Plymouth Hoe, but it was two months before I flew to France on a metal seat in a Dakota to join the tanks and the dust and the dead cows.

My second D–Day was on Monday night at the London Palladium: the Royal Variety Performance. I was to conduct for Michael Crawford in an excerpt from *Billy*. We had moved over from Drury Lane for the night. I had a haircut in the morning, then, late and jumpy, was delayed in Regent Street by one of the great bores of the musical profession. Every time we say hello I die a little. I got rid of him with a cunning untruth and made it to the theatre for the rehearsal. Security pass. Luggage check.

Sir Bernard Delfont had promised an international cast. He's a man of his word. The place was full of Welshmen and Zulus. The Zulu girls were topless. Harry Secombe wasn't. We greeted each other as old friends but were overwhelmed by the topless Zulus. Harry vanished.

The cast were called to rehearse the finale, the only part of the show when the company of 350 appeared together on stage. This worked as long as nobody breathed. Something seemed slightly wrong. The girls in *Billy* were all dressed as Ginger Rogers, the rest were in sweaters and jeans. Someone had blundered. But I recall the efficiency of the supreme command who mounted this massive operation. For Ike and Monty read Delfont and Nesbitt. I was excited to find myself between Charles Aznavour and Count Basie. Nearby were Telly Savalas, Dame Vera Lynn, Harry Secombe, Kris Kremo, Larry Parker, Arthur Lowe, John Le Mesurier, Clive Dunn and the rest of *Dad's Army*. Behind us, the Rhos Male Voice Choir.

The company was lined up as if on parade. I muttered, 'Haven't stood still so long since I was in the Army.' The black face of Count Basie, with its grizzled sideburns, turned and beamed at me.

Lunch at The Shakespeare's Head. An upstairs room had been reserved as a waiting–room for *Dad's Army* and *Billy*. Bar open all day. cautiously under–patronised by both groups until their big moments were over. Later, trade became brisk as tasselled–and–embossed programmes were handed round for autographs.

Dressing rooms at the Palladium were too few for the occasion. A bussing operation brought the companies of *Billy*, *Dad's Army* and *Kwa Zulu*, already in costume and make–up from. Drury Lane, the Shaftesbury and Piccadilly Theatres, which were closed for the occasion.

The first Royal Variety Performance was attended by King George V and Queen Mary at the London Hippodrome in 1921, less than a week after their return from the opening of the first Northern Ireland Parliament. Last Monday Mrs Annie Agustin, described as 'a resident of Brinsworth House, 94 years of age, one–time Acrobatic Barrel Jumper,' presented a bouquet to the Queen.

The orchestra pit was so full that the five conductors had to climb in from the stalls. When my turn came, I trampled on a mink coat.

Bruce Forsyth ran the show as usual, with superb technical finesse. Even the stars depended on him; even Vera Lynn. At the end of the show, microphone in hand, he called the roll. 'The *Billy* Company!…The *Dad's Army* Company!… *Kwa Zulu*… The Musical Directors to the Stars!' We strode on in front of the Zulus. Two of us were Oxford MAs; the others hadn't found it necessary. Blinding heat and light. The actors are used to it, I'm not. As we sang the National Anthem, the lump in the throat made it hard to keep a steady voice.

On the way to my dressing room I was introduced to my favourite Zulu, a happy but exhausted boy of four who turned out to be a fan of Michael Crawford. I was still humming *Rose of England*, Ivor Novello's great war–time anthem, which we had heard earlier, sung in the slow–slow *tempo di nostalgia* that only works in times of war or for Vera Lynn. She was the Forces Sweetheart and I was the Forces. Memories of the blitz, ITMA, Anderson shelters, Churchill. Dead Oxford friends.

Tommy and the Prince

*I*was standing in the moat of the Tower of London when Prince Charles, shaking my hand, said to me with a smile, 'It was all very well for you.' If this sounds like the beginning of a dream, read on.

The occasion was the opening night of a season of performances of *The Yeomen of the Guard*, part of the 1978 City of London Festival, starring Tommy Steele. I was the conductor.

Tommy Steele may have seemed eccentric casting in a Gilbert and Sullivan opera, but he was already emerging from his pop stardom to prove himself a fine legitimate actor, and his singing voice was well up to Sullivan's demands. He was due to rehearse in my flat, and I received a telephone call from his car where he was on one of those new mobiles, (very trendy then), asking the way.

We began to rehearse, and had reached the patter song, *I've wisdom from the East and from the West*, with its comic lyric set to neatly classical music. Tommy began to 'bend' the tune slightly, evincing his pop background. 'Tommy', I said , 'if you sing it like that, the critics will tear you to shreds.' Professional that he was, he took me seriously, and never again departed from the straight and narrow. He was an unusual and effective Jack Point, and was well received.

A wooden stage had been built up against the Tower wall. A flight of steps led from the stage to the battlements, beyond which could be seen the spire of St Peter ad Vincula, the church that stood on Tower Green, scene of the executions of many famous prisoners, including Anne Boleyn.

Tower Hill, rising from the moat, provided a perfect auditorium, seating over a thousand people in the newly–built rows of seats. The orchestra pit was in the moat, below and in front of the stage. In case of rain it could be covered by horizontal roller–blinds to protect the musicians and their instruments. As conductor my podium consisted of a kind of rainproof perspex sentry–box. This elevated position resulted in my being landed with one unwelcome duty: I was charged with the onerous decision; if it should start to rain during a performance, of deciding if I should stop the music, sending the audience away to claim refunds or vouchers for a future performance.

The Yeoman of the Guard
at the Tower of London 1978

On the first night, in the presence of H.R.H. The Prince of Wales, it did indeed start to rain, the royal presence adding greater anguish to my pressure for a decision. I was told later that the Prince had gallantly refused the loan of an umbrella — it proved only to be a light shower — and I continued stubbornly, fearful of royal disapproval; but an eventual princely rebuke was delivered in a friendly spirit. The occasion included a celebration of some kind, with fireworks on the Thames after the show, which went by unspoilt by a threatening sky. After the show the Prince met a line—up of the cast. Referring to the rainfall, he said to me, 'It was all very well for you!'

The production boasted two notable moments. The performance began in full daylight, but, as darkness fell, the stage lighting gradually took hold with, among other effects, a searchlight picking out the spire of St Peter's. This happened during the moving funeral march at the end of Act I of *Yeomen*, the church bell tolling in synchronisation with the music. No—one on our staff was permitted to toll the bell, which had by law to be rung by a real life Yeoman of the Guard.

A second dramatic tour—de—force accompanied the hero's reprieve at the end of the story. From far away around the corner of the moat came a crowd of Londoners led by a messenger on a white horse carrying the message of mercy. These two moments added a lustre to Anthony Besch's brilliant production; as did the superb cast, including Alfred Marks, Anne Collins, David Fieldsend, Dennis Wicks and Della Jones.

Vienna and Bad EMS

*I*t was in the Österreichische Nationalbibliothek that Sir Charles came to my rescue. I was searching for the score of Offenbach's only "grand" opera, *Die Rheinnixen*, and was experiencing some linguistic problem with a young would–be helpful librarian. 'Sprechen–Sie Deutsch?' he asked. 'Nur ein wenig', I apologized, conjuring up one of my three WWII phrases, (the others being 'Hitler kaputt', and 'Noch ein Mal' when I wanted another drink). It was at this moment that I spotted Charles Mackerras, an old friend and colleague, at a distant desk. He returned my wave and came to help.

Die Rheinnixen is a maverick in the Offenbach canon. Many Offenbach devotees have no knowledge of it. A *Times* critic once denied the existence of any Offenbach "serious" opera, and I had the gratification of a published acknowledgement of my erudite contradiction. The opera in question was never successful. Offenbach, true to his economical nature, plundered its pages to supply the barcarolle in *The Tales of Hoffmann*. Charles Mackerras and the librarian unearthed the score from some dark vault, leaving me with a valuable piece of research, and an opportunity to say boo to *The Times*.

After Vienna I visited Bad Ems, where I was joined by my sister Harriet. In spending summer days in this pretty spa, we were following Offenbach's habit of going there for his health, (gout), his gambling and his summer productions. Earlier writers have remarked that his Ems pieces never had a cast of more than three or four characters; I suspect that they had not visited the town or its "theatre", which is not a true theatre but a sort of banqueting hall with a small, low platform at one end — no normal stage. There being no orchestra pit, the orchestra must have been a small one, positioned on the floor.

The librarian at the Stadtsmuseum was a bespectacled middle–aged frau, who was only too glad to give us much relevant information, backed up by photocopies.

The weather was fine; Harriet and I stayed in an elegant nineteenth century spa hotel, and had time to wander along the wooded river bank with its Victorian mansions. We sent no Ems telegrams to Bismarck or anyone else.

Savoy

Frederic Lloyd was the long–standing general manager of the D'Oyly Carte Opera Company. He invited me to lunch at the Savoy Grill. Richard D'Oyly Carte had built the Savoy Theatre in 1881 to house the Gilbert and Sullivan operas, and the company had since had its home in the Savoy buildings.

The meal, as one might expect, was excellent, but the purpose of the meeting painful. At this time, the D'Oyly Carte Company was the object of severe criticism. And the musical director bore the brunt.

Fraser Goulding, the conductor in question, was half my age. He was a good conductor, but as yet no disciplinarian. He received no adequate backing on tour from the touring company's weak orchestral manager. Musicians, for instance, were not reprimanded for returning late to the pit after their interval drinks, nor for similar delinquencies. The management, stuck in London, were frankly clueless. Hence my lunch at the Savoy. Fraser was to become an associate, I was invited to succeed him in the top job. I had worked with him once before and liked him. I was reluctant to take his place, but somebody was going to do so anyway.

Freddie Lloyd arranged a meeting between us at the Garrick club. (Nothing but the top venues). Fraser and I had a conversation which was distressful to both of us for opposite reasons. It was forever to his credit that he never did anything to undermine my new position or make my job difficult. We have remained good friends to this day; while Fraser has gone on to make his reputation in other fields.

The plan was that I should take over as musical director for the forthcoming crucially important autumn season at the Adelphi Theatre. The success or otherwise of this season would determine the company's future. I was given extensive powers in all musical matters, including funds and permission to re–floor the awkward Adelphi orchestra pit, to employ my colleagues Alan Franks and Charles Norton, (no–nonsense men), as orchestral managers, and to appoint a new orchestra if I so desired. The members of the existing touring orchestra, knowing this, became extremely nervous about my decisions, and I quickly made it clear that no musicians would be sacked, but that extra, well–established London players would be added to the strength.

I was allowed the choice of opera with which to open the London season, and chose *Ruddigore*. I had had my fill of *Mikados* and *Iolanthes*, much as I admired them. *Ruddigore* is one of the best of G. and S. pieces, and possesses in addition a fine new overture by Geoffrey Toye, ideal for our enlarged orchestra at the Adelphi.

The opening night went well, the *Guardian's* critic commenting, 'At least the music has taken a turn for the better.' Fraser and I conducted alternate performances, which went smoothly until one night when I thought it was to be Fraser's performance and not mine. Fortunately, I rang up to check and was told that I was due in half–an–hour. In a panic, I recruited my neighbour, who, bless him, rushed me to the theatre in his Aston Martin, to arrive only five minutes late. On the way I said, 'I don't know whether it's *Iolanthe* or *The Mikado* tonight, but it doesn't matter, I know them both backwards.' It was *Iolanthe*. My heart beat faster all through the first act. The deputy conductor had been given his one night off in the whole season, to allow him to conduct some family performance in Wales. A night impossible to forget.

The season proceeded uneventfully apart from one welcome and cheery visit from Sir Charles Mackerras, (Charlie to us all), who had been invited for some celebratory occasion to conduct a guest performance. Otherwise, alas, we were on a downslide. Hopes that the company might be rescued financially faded. On the last night, the director, Wilfred Judd, pulled off a dramatic coup de théâtre. After the final curtain call, the curtain rose again to reveal a stage empty of all scenery. It signified the end of a century–old company.

As I left the theatre, I was politely accosted by a well–spoken elderly lady. 'Are you Mr Faris?' she asked. 'Yes,' I replied. 'I must tell you,' she said, 'my sister and I have attended nearly every performance, and we have been hearing the music *through new ears*.' For the second time I felt justified in having accepted my appointment. I joined my friends in the pub for a farewell drink, sad that the episode was over.

Happily, a new D'Oyly Carte company was later formed, with my friend John Owen Edwards as musical director, who launched it on a successful progress.

Priest of Love

*I*n 1981 I was invited to an office in Hill Street, off Berkeley Square, to meet Stanley J. Seeger, an American millionaire, and a composer, James Brown. Stanley Seeger was planning a film about D.H. Lawrence to be called *Priest Of Love*. Seeger was the producer and financier; he and James Brown, under the pseudonym Joseph James, were joint composers of a piano score which they were asking me to arrange for a huge orchestra. Once more I had no idea who had recommended me for this remunerative task — I no longer had an agent. I accepted their offer with alacrity.

We recorded the music, a lengthy effective score, at Olympic Studios in Barnes. The film starred Ian McKellen, Janet Suzman, Ava Gardner, Penelope Keith, John Gielgud, James Faulkner and Sarah Miles; an impressive line–up!

When we finished filming shortly before Christmas, Stanley distributed generous presents to the company, mine consisting of bottles of wine and many other goodies.

Early in the New Year my phone went. 'Oh, Mr Faris,' a lady said, 'you haven't received the rest of your Christmas present.' What could she mean? I had already enjoyed a lavish gesture of gratitude. The lady asked if I would be at home on such–and–such a day to receive a further gift.

I was touched by the answer to my puzzlement. Stanley Seeger had apparently spent Christmas in Paris, where he had attended an Offenbach performance at the Théâtre du Châtelet. There he saw for sale a picture of the proscenium as restored in the style of the Second Empire of Napoleon III. The restoration was the inspiration of Jacques Chirac, the future Mayor of Paris. Stanley Seeger, knowing of my reputation as an Offenbach conductor and biographer, bought this exquisite work of art, done in ink, watercolour and gouache. This kind, thoughtful and valuable present now adorns my flat.

My hours on the podium at Olympic aroused the memory of a legendary practical joke, the perpetrator being Keith Grant, Director of the studios and a brilliant sound recordist. On one occasion, after a trying morning's recording, where a weary orchestra trudged out to lunch, Keith decided to enliven the afternoon session. The leader of the orchestra played on a Stradivarius. During the break he and Keith went to a junk shop and bought a crummy old violin for a fiver. Shortly after the next session began Keith pretended to be furiously angry with the violinist. Seizing the instrument from his hands he threw it on the floor and stamped on it. The players, thinking he had destroyed a Strad, reacted with horror. A pause... then the whole studio, orchestra, engineers and all, burst into laughter. Adrenaline surged.

The Girl in the Middle

'**W**endy!' I said firmly, 'Let's don't talk shop!' my unwonted American lingo witnessing that I was in the middle of an American thriller. We were both at supper in an Ankara hotel, and were both reading.

Wendy and I had been spending long tiring days rehearsing at the Turkish National Opera; she as director, I as conductor, in what we were told was an atrocious translation of *The Mikado*. We had made a pact not to talk about it at meals. Wendy had just broken the pact:

'Darling Sandy, I can't hold it in any longer. I spent all yesterday afternoon choreographing the girls in "Three Little Maids from School", and today they couldn't remember which of them stood in the middle.'

I calmed her down and returned to Raymond Chandler.

Wendy and I began our long association in a tour of the Vivian Ellis musical *And So To Bed*[8]. This story about Samuel Pepys starred Leslie Henson, Keith Michel and now Anne Ziegler and Webster Booth. In the cast too was the young Stella Chapman, later Mrs Stella Quilley, wife of the inimitable Denis, a pair who, with their family, became my life–long friends. I first met Denis in Nottingham where Stella, Denis and I were staying chez the famous Mrs Breckenridge. Stella and I were performing at the Theatre Royal; Denis at the Playhouse.

Ankara is a city of contrasting delights and demerits. Kemal Ataturk wished the capital of Turkey to be in Asia rather than Europe. In contrast to the beauties of Istanbul, he chose for its location a smog–ridden valley, choked by a ring of hills. From high up in the British embassy, where we were lucky enough to be entertained, the city has the aspect of a bowl of brown Windsor soup, the desert dust being unable to escape from the enclosing uplands. Against that there are worthwhile sights; the tomb of Ataturk has a solemn grandeur, the guards who

---

8 Book, music and lyrics by Vivian Ellis; adapted from the play by J. B. Fagan
Original London cast: Leslie Henson, Jessie Royce Landis, Keith Michel, Betty Paul, Dudley Jones, Hazel Jennings, Stella Chapman, Alan Duffy; Musical director: Mantovani

mount duty there have a smartness of appearance and military discipline that struck a thrill in my Irish Guardsman's heart. Against that again, I was less than thrilled to see the entire wall of a bookshop occupied by the works of Barbara Cartland. W.S. Gilbert and Cartland — an impossible pair of candidates for Turkish translation.

When our project was completed, happily with considerable success, I set off home, flying to Istanbul to begin with. There I spent a day contemplating the Bosphorus from the comfort of the Hilton Hotel, then taking to the train for the glorious trans–European journey to the Hook of Holland, stopping to sleep in Milan, where I a night porter robbed me of £50.

Two ferries arrived at the Hook simultaneously, providing the customs officers with about 2,000 passengers to deal with. Of these, 1,999 it seemed, went through the green channel; I, having no chance of getting off scot–free, chose the red. I was greeted by a senior officer who was training a young woman in the job. (The girl in the middle, I privately echoed.) The officer seemed amenable. After paying a modest amount of duty, and packing my bags, I set off for the train, when I was called back. I thought, 'Here comes the body search', trembling. 'By the way,' said the officer, 'what were you doing for two months in Ankara?' 'I was conducting a production of *The Mikado* for the Turkish National Opera, in Turkish.' 'That's the first thing you've said this morning that I don't believe.' He let me go. After all, I considered, in the circumstances his incredulity was understandable.

Bedsitter Images

Al Stewart is a folk singer, currently enjoying a distinguished career in the United States.

A disciple of Simon and Garfunkel whose influence is evident in his work, though he is certainly no plagiarist, he performed in many popular folk venues, backed by George Butler, a drummer, and a bassist. It was the music producer Roy Guest, Al's agent, who was determined to supply him with the backing of an orchestra, and Roy asked me to do the orchestrations. I got on happily with Al, and we eventually made an album, recorded at IBC Studios in Portland Place. It bore the title of his best song, *Bedsitter Images,* a vivid account of his way of life.

Roy Guest then decided to promote Al in a concert in the Royal Festival Hall. I duly supplied larger orchestrations, including an overture involving the Festival Hall organ. This piece was received with loud applause, but sadly, when Al came on stage, he said to me, 'How can you follow that?' And he was right; but he gallantly put up a good show. However he typically resumed his performance with his small group, which showed him at his best, and before long he departed for America and a bigger career. I have never met him since.

Scoring for Pavarotti

I walked into the Savoy Hotel as one in a dream. Thirty years earlier, in the "Fiona era", I was on the point of turning down an offer to orchestrate a musical show on the grounds of my imagined incompetence. Here, I was being greeted by Anna–Maria Verde, the delightfully buxom secretary of the great Luciano, once the young footballer, now the greatest tenor of the twentieth century. Who had recommended me for the job of arranging an album for the great man? Sir Charles Mackerras? Sir Humphrey Searle? I'll never know. It was inconceivable that the Decca company would have come to me as their first choice to write for Pavarotti. Somewhere I must have had a friend or admirer. Some things you win.

The project in hand was to create an L.P., as they were then called, consisting of seventeenth, eighteenth and nineteenth century songs that had originally been written for piano, harpsichord or clavichord, and were now to be enlarged for a full orchestra. LP stood for "Long Play"; discs which we put on the gramophone at 33½ revs per minute; these already succeeded "78s".

We ran through a few numbers, but the big man was not too well. This was not the first time that I had found him unsure of the quality of his voice, often without reason. He arranged for Anna–Maria to cancel his performance of *Tosca* that night and book him on a flight home to Italy. As I left the Savoy and drove up the Aldwych in a bus, I passed a long queue looking forward to his appearance that evening at Covent Garden, little knowing that he was already homeward bound.

After another couple of Savoy sessions, I got down to work, and before long was proud of a substantial pile of scores, hoping for approval of those in high places. As the date of the recording sessions approached, the conductor turned up. Piero Gamba, for it was he, had been known in London as the boy prodigy Pierino Gamba, conducting at the age of eleven, in short pants, at the Festival Hall. Now it was the middle–aged conductor of the Toronto Symphony Orchestra whom I met over coffee at the Piccadilly Hotel. He was agreeable and approved from then on of my work.

Before the age of computers, the orchestrator's work existed in silence, in pen or pencil on the page. When the Philharmonia Orchestra assembled for their first recording sessions in the Kingsway Hall, I had naturally a mild tremor of nerves about the potential sound of my writing. But I *knew* that it would all sound good; the old unconfident self was a creature of the past, justified on the final recording day when Pavarotti inscribed one of my scores: '*ad Alessandro con tutta la mia stima ed ammirazione*' — Luciano Pavarotti. This compliment now hangs, framed, on my wall.

The three–day recording sessions were not without incident. Hence the following exchange when something had gone slightly wrong:

The producer, James Mallinson:

'Sorry, Luciano, we'll have to do an edit.'

L.P: 'Where from we go?'

J.M: 'We go from letter "G".'

L.P: 'No, we go from letter "J".'

J.M: 'It's impossible to edit from "J".'

L.P. (reluctantly): 'O.K.'

The conductor and orchestra stood by to start from the letter G.

L.P. (suddenly): 'No! We go from where's impossible to edit!'

So we did.

On the evening of the final recording session, Pavarotti was suddenly smitten with a bilious attack. The orchestra was already in place, awaiting the outcome; record or go home? Doctors were summoned, one from the Royal Opera House, one from the Savoy Hotel, an *embarras de richesses*, one might have thought. Anna–Maria produced a kettle of boiling water. The spectacle of Pavarotti lying back on a couch with the kettle on his large stomach added a touch of farce to the poor man's suffering. I handed Luciano a cup of hot water. He said, 'Thank you Sandy', then, 'Cancel the doctors, Anna–Maria, I'm dying!' came the agonised cry. Nobody paid any attention to the exaggeration. Before many minutes passed, the great man seemed to recover, and soon declared himself ready to record. He entered the studio. I looked up. 'How are you?' I asked, concerned. 'How are *you*?' was his friendly reply. He then sang the three scheduled songs; sang them beautifully in everyone's opinion.

Except his own. He refused to believe that his singing was up to his own high standard; refused to agree to Decca's issuing the album with these three recordings. The argument continued for years. Decca re–mixed the recording several times, played him the new mixes in London, in Milan, in New York; to no avail. After eight years, Decca were persuaded to re–record these numbers, again with the full Philharmonia Orchestra, still with my orchestrations, but with a different conductor. I never thought Pavarotti really liked Piero Gamba as a conductor, and nor did I; I could have done the job more sympathetically, I was sure, but I could not have done both that and the orchestrations.

Throughout the sessions Pavarotti never made any criticism of my work; a boost for my self–confidence.

Present at the recording sessions at Kingsway Hall was David Llewellyn, then living at no.8 Rothwell Street and acting as my secretary and helper in my daily life. He was later to marry my niece Hilary and to become a well–known writer on Rugby and Cricket on *The Independent*. David helped with handing out music to the Philharmonia players, not to mention procuring a cup of tea for Luciano, whose plight when suffering gave David some amusement.

Eight years later, the album *La Mattinata* was issued in its new form. My orchestrations and my inscription from Pavarotti survived the changes.

Missing for Ustinov

After my modest success as a conductor of operetta at Sadler's Wells, I decided to try my hand at writing an operetta myself. In the early 1970s I teamed up with Julian More. He was keen to write the lyrics and I wrote the music for an adaptation of Peter Ustinov's *Romanoff and Juliet*. Julian and I completed a script and score, which we titled *R Loves J*, and which met with Peter Ustinov's approval. We played it to him in my flat on Primrose Hill and he joined us afterwards for dinner in The Queen's.

Peter then invited Julian and myself to stay with him for a week or two in his delightful house outside Geneva. He was a generous host and took us for a weekend to the ski resort Les Diablerets. We also visited his son Igor at the famous international boarding school Le Rosey.

After this memorable visit the story had is ups and downs. A German producer, Peter Goldbaum, offered to mount a German version of the show in Munich. It transpired that the German translation of the lyrics was highly unsatisfactory and the reviews were less than enthusiastic.

In 1973, John Clements, then the director of the Chichester Festival Theatre, offered to mount the production that summer, starring Topol, with whom Chichester had a standing contract at the time. Topol was by no means an ideal casting for a Ustinov part, and was also persistent in demanding rewrites of some of the numbers.

The show received cool revues, but despite this Harold Fielding, at that time London's premiere impresario, was enthusiastic and would have put the show on in the West End had it not been for further demands from Topol for rewrites.

I suspected that Peter was seriously unhappy with Topol in his own original part. In retrospect, too, I felt that my own style of music was perhaps out of date for the age. Whatever the troubles Ustinov made no mention of either Topol, Julian or me in his autobiography *Dear Me*. Dear me.

Later, my music for several television shows met with considerable success, indeed, the theme music for *Upstairs, Downstairs* won an Ivor Novello award in 1975.

Brent Walker G&S

After a hundred years the Gilbert and Sullivan operas were as popular as ever. George Walker, brother of Billy, the boxer, was not familiar with them, but had the sense to see them as a commercial proposition, and planned a video series.

On a New York visit, George was impressed by the talent of Judith de Paul, a young former opera singer, now a producer. He invited her to produce his English series. Judith descended upon us, one dynamic lady.

If George Walker knew little of the Gilbert and Sullivan operas, Judith de Paul knew, if possible, less. She faced a tough challenge, but she was an apt learner. She began with a list of possible conductors, headed by Herbert von Karajan. I couldn't see Karajan and G & S as bedfellows, and he would undoubtedly have refused the assignment. I was not yet on the list of candidates myself, being merely a recommended consultant. We came to Sir Charles Mackerras, who was either unwell or unavailable for some reason, and after one or two other suggestions, it came to me.

I was interviewed by George W. He asked me if we could use Roger Daltrey for a certain part. I have never heard Daltrey perform — he belonged to a different world. George sent out for his latest album. I listened and said, 'No!' I think it was my categorical answer that gave George confidence in my advice from there on. He gave me his home telephone number, saying that if I had any problems I could call him there if necessary. He was as good as his word. In the course of eight months I called him twice, and the problem was solved with a boss's authority. In that respect I was more fortunate than Fraser Goulding had been in the D'Oyly Carte fiasco.

We were to begin with a stint of five operas, to be filmed at Twickenham in the course of one week. Five operas involved the casting of about fifty artists. Judith had a list of available singers and actors, but no clue to their suitability for the G & S characters in question. We solved this over coffee sessions in The Grosvenor House, where she was luxuriously ensconced, while I accepted the excellent suggestions and rejected the ludicrous ones. She later told George Walker, 'The best thing you ever did was to employ Sandy Faris.' I like to think that she was right.

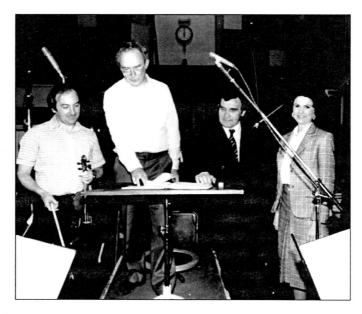

Brent Walker G&S Group
(Left to right) Michael Davis (Leader LSO), Author, George Walker, Judith de Paul

In the *modus operandi* proposed by Judith de Paul, the orchestral tracks would be recorded first *in the absence of singers*, leaving: (1) the conductor to guess how the singer would perform each passage of recitative, and (2) leaving the singer to follow an already recorded orchestral accompaniment, not knowing when he or she might suddenly be interrupted by the orchestra.

At Abbey Road studios we recorded one opera a day for a week. The orchestra was the London Symphony Orchestra. No singers. The first day, a Monday, was allotted to *The Gondoliers*. I knew this opera well, (as I knew most of the others), having played the rôle of the Duchess of Plaza–Toro at my preparatory school. Even with such familiarity as I had, it was a nerve–wracking task, guessing how the absent singers would eventually perform, and allowing spaces of silence for them to fill with their recitative. After lunch that day, we devised a new system: the all–knowing Jeremy Sams stood in a box, his recorded voice audible to me only, singing *every part*. Only with the help of Jeremy's incredible talents could we have done this.

Our second stint of recordings, some months later, took place at Shepperton. Again, we had a variety of directors; some good, some bad, some awful. No names, no pack drill.

I had to stay overnight in Shepperton one Saturday night. A telephone call came from my friend and neighbour, well known film editor Teddy Darvas in London:

'Don't worry Sandy, but a van has just broken into your kitchen.' I arrived back on Sunday to find the wreckage. The van, whose brakes had failed, had crashed through my railings and into my kitchen. I claimed insurance for both railings and kitchen damage, .'so for five free–range eggs, size two.

After the G & S recordings we made a successful *Orpheus In The Underworld* and an unsuccessful revue–type hotch–potch, *A Night On The Town*, in which a galaxy of stars each sang a well–known number. In spite of wise advice from Ned Sherrin, it was a mess. I met Ned a year later at the interval of a Denis Quilley first night at the Barbican. Ned was in good form as usual. He recalled our experience at Shepperton, 'I think, Sandy, that that episode marked the nadir of both our careers.'

For all Judith's superficial toughness, people came to appreciate her. On several occasions I was one of the last to leave the studio and Judith would give me a lift in her hired Mercedes. She would then unburden her problems, revealing an otherwise unusual softness. I was sorry when the day of parting came. I liked her and hoped we might meet and work together again.

As with the directors, some of the performers were superb, some mediocre, some unmentionable.

Barbican and the L.S.O

As a result of my work for Brent Walker on the Gilbert and Sullivan operas, I acquired a new and fruitful association with the London Symphony Orchestra.

I was engaged to conduct a series of concerts at the Barbican. I found the Barbican something of a warren and had difficulty finding my way to the back stage area, the band room and my dressing room. It was not long however before I found a cunning exit route through the underground garages which led directly to the nearest pub.

On one of these concerts, Alfred Marks, the Master of Ceremonies, made a delightful joke at my expense, having previously kindly asked me if I minded. He had already introduced the principal singers at the concert, and had embarrassingly forgotten the name of the leader of the orchestra. Then came my turn: 'Our conductor tonight is Alexander Faris, the best conductor in the country, [pause], not so good in the town.'

The last concert of the series was a Christmas celebration, ending with the standing packed audience singing *Hark, The Herald Angels Sing*.

Sirmione and Venice

*I*n the post–war years, when I was stationed north of Hamburg in a place called Plön, Admiral Dönitz's last headquarters after Hitler's death, my friend Tony de Lotbiniere was stationed nearby in Hamburg.

The two of us wangled a leave which we used to visit Venice. This was, in fact, illegal, because it was forbidden by the army to travel to another theatre of war. However, we sojourned in Paris for a few days where the father of one of our friends was the British Military Attaché. He kindly gave us a document saying: *"To all this may concern to give to these two officers all help they may require."*

And, sooner or later, we arrived in Venice. At this time, the Danieli Hotel had been taken over by the combined British and American forces. We stayed there for a week at the Army price of 1/6^d, (one shilling and sixpence – now seven and a half pence). Over and above this modest charge we could spend our savings on Italian food and wine.

Moving forward in time, I travelled again to Venice in the course of a visit to Sirmione on Lake Garda. Sirmione was the home of Catullus, where, among the olive groves he wrote some of his poems, including, *"Vivamus, mea Lesbia, atque amemus"*. Beneath the cliff, where he wrote the poem, we used to swim in the waters of the lake.

Sirmione was also the centre of Mussolini's rule over the northern section of Italy, before he was captured and shot by the Germans. He and his wife were later grotesquely hung, upside down, from lampposts in Milan.

On this second visit to Venice, in 1968, the cost of one meal at the Danieli Hotel was the equivalent of one at The Ritz or Claridge's. I was accompanied this time by my sister Harriet and her husband, both of whom I greatly admired. They were later sadly to be divorced. Their daughter Hilary, my beloved niece, now a distinguished GP, remains one of my fondest friends.

Melbourne Hall

*D*uring the war I made new friends and lost others; some tragically killed; some temporarily far away. The reunion with the latter after the war brought relief and pleasure. Foremost among my returned friends was Peter Lothian, my Oxford roommate. He invited me to visit him and his wife at their home in Melbourne Hall on the outskirts of the city of Derby. It was my first of several visits.

The present Hall, a late 17th century rebuilding of an older manor house, faces onto extensive gardens. From the terrace the view is of a lake beyond which a wide tree–lined avenue rises to the hilltop. Below the hill, spreading from one side of the lake, lie gardens comprising a parterre, a beech wood tunnel and, dotted here and there, pieces of archaic statuary. To one side of the house stands the chapel, where I attended a service more than once over the years. Peter and his wife Toni

Melbourne Hall

(Antonella) are devout Catholics; a room in the house has become a small chapel; but my two good friends are broadminded enough to join their guests and household at an Anglican service.

Toni is a saint; a beautiful saint with a sense of humour; the latter being a trait that I regard as a sign of sensitivity, beyond the mere ability to appreciate jokes. Peter has this too; he is incidentally, a good jazz pianist (more than I am). Toni's humour is exemplified in her labelling the bedrooms "Lord Palmerston's bedroom, Lord Melbourne's bedroom" and so on. She says, 'I haven't a clue who slept where, but it fascinates the summer tourists.'

I slept in "Lord Palmerston's bedroom"; perhaps so did he.

I was proudly introduced to Peter and Toni's firstborn, the one–year–old Michael, Earl of Ancram, who was later to sit in the Commons as Mr Michael Ancram, a notable figure in the Tory party. If I ever met him (unlikely) I shall say, 'You won't remember me, but I think we once met.'

Tinker

$\mathcal{C}$aptain Vivian Taylor, MC, known since his Downside schooldays as "Tinker", became adjutant of the 2nd Armoured Battalion Irish Guards while we were still in Germany after the end of World War II.

The adjutant is responsible for discipline, which Tinker observed impeccably, although surprisingly, since Tinker was a paradox; a kind, gentle being, albeit with a core of toughness, whose qualities earned him a loyalty and respect that bore fruit in discipline.

There was little indiscipline within the battalion itself; I have written earlier about our problems with the D.P., (displaced persons), camps in our charge[9]. There were frequent raids of D.P's, (Russians and others), breaking out at night to plunder the local villages.

Coming as I do from a strife–torn Ulster, with forebears in the south, the Irish Guards have a particular importance for me. The regiment is recruited, not only from the north and south of Ireland, but from Liverpool and London. We were Protestants and Catholics, with padres of both persuasions. During my four years in the army, I was never aware of any hostility between North and South Ireland, or between Catholic and Protestant. Would that our respective homelands were as peaceful.

After my demobilisation, when I had settled in at the Royal College of Music, my only contact with Tinker was at the annual dinner of the Quis Separabit Club, an exclusively officers' institution. We met firstly at Claridge's, (white tie and tails, medals), then for some years at the Savoy, (black tie, no medals), finally at the Cavalry and Guards Club. At the Savoy we were honoured more than once by the presence of the Grand Duke of Luxembourg, who, as Prince Jean, had been one of my young contemporaries, and was now the Colonel of the Regiment; and on one occasion by Elizabeth, the Queen Mother, who graced me with her smile and a charming comment.

It was not until fifty years after the end of the war that a group of us decided to assemble a volume of reminiscences, collected from those veterans who were still alive, that I joined Tinker as co–editor of the project , and, over several visits to his

---

9 The Armoured Micks, Farewell to Armour p.134
10 The Armoured Micks. Published by The Regimental Headquarters Irish Guards.

Tinker

home in Wimborne Minster, became a friend of his wife, children and grandchildren. For these last, Liam, "PJ", (Patrick James), and Jessica, I used to write personal limericks to accompany the Christmas chocolates.

Apart from the occasional trips to such places as the Bovington Tank Museum or the gardens of Kingston Lacey, Tinker and I worked hard morning and afternoon on '*The Armoured Micks*'. There was a mass of contributions from old friends of all ranks in the battalion, these varying from the literate to the near–illiterate, and from the amusing to the boring, so that we were landed with an extensive editing job. My own articles, '*Battle Music*', and '*A Farewell to Armour*' are reprinted in this volume. After our daytime labours we would sometimes attend a show at the little local theatre, where we would enjoy seeing a variety of touring performers, including sometimes an old friend and colleague such as Keith Michel. Tinker's wife Heather, our delightful hostess, joined us in these visits.

Tinker had a weak heart, which finally gave up on him. Harriet drove me from her home in Milborne Port to the funeral, and I later attended Tinker's memorial service in the Guards Chapel where I was not ashamed to shed a tear. Heather asked me to keep in touch, so as not to make a complete break from such a valuable part of our lives.

The Young Visiters

The Piccadilly Theatre, December 1968, was the scene of a new musical, *The Young Visiters*, drawn from Daisy Ashford's classic written when she was nine years old; a love story imagined by a child, hilariously funny, with idiosyncratic spelling and a child's uniquely imaginative conception of upper–class romantic goings–on.

The book was published with an introduction by J.M. Barrie. In case some thought he had written the book himself, he quashed that suggestion by producing Ashford's pencilled manuscript, part of which is now reproduced in a new edition with witty illustrations by Posy Simmonds.

Of all my West End shows *The Young Visiters* was by far the most charming. Not only that; the cast of stars became a cast of friends. With happy memories I name them: Alfred Marks, Tom Chatto, Clive Morton, Frank Thornton, Barry Justice, Vivienne Ross, Anna Sharkey, Jan Waters. Music and lyrics by Ian Kellam, with additions by Richard Kerr and Tom Maitland.

The Young Visiters was well received, in particular by Harold Hobson, the revered drama critic of *The Sunday Times*. Sadly, the show did not attract a large public, lasting only for sixty–three performances. Perhaps the title was not a money–catcher. Again, the Piccadilly Theatre was *not quite* on Shaftesbury Avenue, the great theatre vortex, London's Broadway, where passers–by could see the front–of–house publicity, with enticing photographs and favourable notices displayed — all the box office allure.

Critics can sometimes be supportive. Knowing that we were not doing too well, Harold Hobson wrote a second review urging the public to flock to the theatre. Alas, to no avail.

Eighty–seven year–old Daisy Ashford attended the First Night, proving that she herself had written this childhood masterpiece. I think.

Bar Mitzwah Boy

*J*ule Styne used cheerfully to describe himself as "America's greatest composer". In terms of show composers, Jule *was* great, as witness *Gypsy*, *Gentlemen Prefer Blondes* and other winners. But greater than Gershwin, Cole Porter, Richard Rodgers, Irving Berlin, Frank Loesser? "Greater" and "greatest" are meaningless classifications. Was Mozart greater than Beethoven?

Anyway, when we came to rehearse *Bar Mitzvah Boy,* there were a few greats around: Jack Rosenthal, author of the original TV play; Don Black, the lyric writer; Irwin Kostal, the orchestrator and arranger; Peter Gennaro, the choreographer, and the overall director, Martin Charnin.

The "creative team" was housed for the five week prior–to–London tour in the Midland Hotel in Manchester. High class digs, and we needed them. The show was continually being altered. Every single day *Bar Mitzvah Boy* was changed radically, every day there was a completely new or partly new musical number. Jule Styne would sit up all night composing a new number that demanded a new lyric from the ever–patient Don Black. The resulting music had then to be orchestrated during the night by the not–so–patient Irwin Kostal. The orchestral parts had then to be copied in the dawning light by my indefatigable colleague, the copyist David Redston.

I derived one unusual pleasure during rehearsals. Though I have many good Jewish friends, it was the first time I had worked in the midst of a Jewish community. A highlight for me was when one of the actors had a birthday, and the cast celebrated by breaking off rehearsals for a party with much Jewish song and dance, all of which I found more than a little moving. And I learned the meaning of "lox and bagels".

Jule would turn up at morning rehearsals, but at midday he would disappear — off to put money on that day's horses, his favourite hobby.

The first full dress rehearsal for the London opening took place in the afternoon. David Redston and I were sitting with Irwin Kostal in the front row of the stalls at Her Majesty's Theatre, hoping that at last there would be no more changes. Irwin, who was a very tall man, suddenly spotted Jule, (who was, incidentally, a small man), coming in through one of the stalls doors. Irwin crouched down, trying to keep out of sight of Jule. 'What's the fucking little monster want *now*?', he exclaimed. But Jule had no more changes.

We opened at Her Majesty's Theatre to a lukewarm reception and ran for a few weeks only.

Clouds, Sunshine

After two stints at the Theatre Royal, Drury Lane, with first of all *The Great Waltz* and secondly *Billy* with Michael Crawford, I spent four years travelling and researching for my forthcoming biography of Offenbach, which was published successfully on the centenary of his death.

I returned to find that my conducting career had taken a moderate downturn. My place had already been usurped for some years by Ray Cook, an aggressive Australian who had adopted the West End as his own territory. I took over musical directorships, firstly of *Showboat* where I had the pleasure of working with Cleo Laine and later with Jan Waters, and the company of John Dankworth. Then came a stint with *Oklahoma*, where I was warmly received by Jamie Hammerstein, son of Oscar. Ray Cook sadly died early, and I attended his funeral in a friendly mood with only faint memories of resentment. The West End became the scene for a younger generation of Musical Directors, including the talented Ian McMillan.

Meanwhile, back in Primrose Hill, I made new friends. Among these were my former agent Annie Clough, with whom I used to drink too much whisky and Alan Cooper who is, as I write, helping me compile this book. There were four good pubs where I became a well known figure. The Queens, the Queen's Tavern, The Princess of Wales and the Enterprise. The latter boasted two enormous open coal fires on either side of the pub and in those days I didn't drink before conducting but in the weeks or months between shows I would go to The Enterprise in the evenings to join my companions. I would sit in front of the fire, mentally composing my next opus.

During the Primrose Hill era I have made many friends. I gave parties on my 60th, 70th and 80th birthdays; the last of these was a specially memorable occasion. I invited 150 old friends and colleagues and took a lot of trouble in advance, buying fire extinguishers and ladders in case there should be a fire in that crowd. Irish Guards Headquarters supplied me with an excellent barman, one Peter Taylor, a charmer who became a great success with the assembled company. Annie Clough was a guest at the party; during the course of the evening Annie, dressed in pink chiffon, insisted in helping the "dishy" barman.

It was many months before I heard from her again, when she telephoned to tell me,

70th birthday party
Bill Drysdale and Paul French

80th birthday party
(Left to right) Terry Mitchell, Author, Cynthis Morey, Alan Spencer, Grant Hossack and ?

among other things, that she had made an unsuccessful suicide attempt. After that sad episode her friend and former assistant Alexandra Wagstaff invited her to live nearby.

Towards the end of the evening I uncovered the Broadwood grand and three guests, all excellent pianists, took it in turns to play. Their services would have cost a packet if I had had to pay them, but they were eager to contribute, (and show off). The three virtuosi were: Stefan Bednarczyk, actor and diseur in the Noel Coward tradition; Paul French, classical/pop composer; Kate Bergman, ebullient American with an encyclopaedic repertoire of Broadway musicals.

After an hour or two of sleep I awoke to find two unopened bottles of champagne near the bed. Feeling somewhat hungover after my party of the century I decided that a walk would do me good; it was a June morning and the sun was shining. I took the bottles round to Alan Cooper's flat where he and his partner Gill joined me in continuing the party.

The Flat

At the time of writing I have been in my flat for nearly half a century. When I came back to London from Down Under I was given a hospitable refuge by my friends Michael Jackson and John Armstrong in their Hampstead flat. I spent the days searching for a place of my own. I considered buying a flat in Victoria Park, south London, until I realised that it was too much out of the way for friends to visit me after the show at nights or on Sundays.

Eventually I spotted a house in Regent's Park Road that had been damaged in the Blitz and was now being converted into flats by one Paul Ridgeon, a dynamic young developer. We got on well — his wife once entertained me on a trip to Glyndebourne, Paul not being interested in opera — but I disagreed with him about his designs for the basement flat, which I had chosen as a good place for a musician like myself since it was positioned somewhat apart from neighbours who might be disturbed by my musical noise. In the event, only one neighbour ever complained; he was promptly put down by his wife, who said, 'You're out all day, I *like* Mr Faris's music!'

At school in the thirties I had revealed an unexpected talent for woodwork, under the tuition of Mr Andy McKim. I now made use of this experience in redesigning my new flat, at first undoing Paul Ridgeon's half–finished work. I made detailed drawings of a wall of bookshelves and installed a large mirror — 5ft x 7ft — a present from my friend Tony de Lotbiniere who already possessed more mirrors than he needed for his new home in Shepherd's Bush. This made the flat seem larger and lighter.

I have written of two renovations. Renovation no. 3 was a new bathroom with a walk–in shower, necessary because at eighty I could no longer safely climb in and out of the bath, plus a restored bedroom. I paid what I could, but received a generous subvention from the Musicians' Benevolent Fund, whereupon I left an appropriate amount in my will to help future musicians over hard times.

For the décor I went Italian; on the floor large square terra cotta tiles, on the walls a two–tone belt of soft–coloured marble. On one tile a craftsman inscribed the legend *D G balnea Faris fecit MMI;* (David Gloster created the Faris bathroom 2001).

Hampstead Afternoon

Left to Right: Christa Ardito, Stella Quilley, Jane Wenham, Carlo Ardito, Denis Quilley, David Quilley, John Armstrong, Eddie Marsh, Gwen Marsh

In all, a showpiece.

The rest of the flat is as lovely as ever, but there is no room for more books, and no wall space for more bookshelves; the bedroom having already absorbed the overflow. So now, when I have finished a crime paperback, I discard the volume onto a pile which Alan later takes to the Community Centre to be sold for charity. Yielding to my addiction, I return to the bookshop.

Canada

I have made three visits to Canada. One; in 1957, the occasion of a Guards anniversary dinner in Montreal. I drove there from New York with three friends, former guardsmen. I remember little of the dinner other than of returning well-oiled to a luxurious hotel. On the following night's return journey we ran over a skunk. The smell of the wounded animal, an odour new to me, lasted in the car and on my clothes for days. No wonder the term skunk is always pejorative. Perhaps 'drunk as a skunk' is what I was after that dinner.

Two; in spring 1972 I was engaged to conduct a musical TV programme in Toronto. I forget what the music was – maybe an Offenbach offering. However, owing to a strike of technicians we didn't record anything for a week, during which time I relaxed in the plush Sutton Place Hotel, was invited twice to good restaurants by old friends from England, and saw the sights of the city.

On the way home my plane touched down at Montreal. Canadian police came aboard asking for a Mr Faris. I was summoned into the covered gangway leading from the aircraft to the terminal, experiencing unsurprisingly a *frisson* of anxiety. I was interrogated in some detail by two Canadian policemen (good guy, bad guy, I thought, knowing my American crime thrillers). After a ten-minute ordeal I was dismissed with apologies as a case of mistaken identity. Somewhere another Mr Faris was in for trouble.

A large scotch-and-soda calmed me down and I slept to Heathrow.

Three; in 1985/6 I was engaged to conduct a Christmas season of *The Mikado* in Toronto, with a cast from the Toronto Opera headed by four well-known British stars, all old friends; Marilyn Hill-Smith, Yum-Yum; Anne Collins, Katisha; John Ayldon, Pooh-Bah and Donald Adams as The Mikado.

Our British contingent was accommodated in a small hotel used to theatrical folk. John and I occupied adjoining flats, where a friendly routine developed, John cooking the after-show supper, both of us enjoying the late-night whiskies.

During our rehearsal period I had to give an afternoon talk to a group of opera-lovers. A trying chore, but it went down well.

The fine production, directed by Lotfi Mansouri was a success except for one critic's comment after the first night, taking an exception to *The Mikado's* over-long overture. A justifiable comment; this overture, like those of most of the G & S operas, was cobbled together by a musical director. Sullivan himself composed only three of the overtures, those for *Patience, Iolanthe* and *The Yeoman of the Guard. The Mikado*, without the overture, has a striking orchestral introduction to the opening chorus. After that first night we omitted the long-winded prelude, to good effect. I have never used the piece again and have advised other conductors to do the same.

Came two joyful encounters, one with an old school friend from Belfast, now living in Toronto with his wife. The couple drove me along Lake Ontario to Niagara Falls; I can't well describe the majesty of Niagara; better not try. Days later a potent memory was revived by the appearance of Pat Kern. Twenty-odd years earlier Patricia Kern had played Iolanthe in our famous Sadler's Wells production. I treasure forever her rendering of Iolanthe's moving plea to the Lord Chancellor in the aria 'He loves ... he dies'. A heartrending performance from a unique voice; Patricia in real life a lovely person.

During that Canadian season I suffered some psychological misery with an almost obsessive anxiety about my health. I found relief in more than one transatlantic call to my friend Hujohn Ripman, 'Rip', our wartime Medical Officer, a wise and affectionate counsellor.

John Ayldon and I returned home happily. I was not interrogated by the Canadian police.

Alan Gout

Sandy's Last Stand

"Is that Mr Alexander Faris?"

Yes, I said.

"I've been trying to find you for six months. My name is Stephen La Rivière. My production company at Pinewood is making a series of DVDs concerning the creation of the TV series *Upstairs, Downstairs*, would you be prepared to give us an interview about the origin of the series?"

I agreed willingly, thinking that this would mean a half hour chat. In the event Stephen arrived in my flat with a cameraman and camera tracking equipment plus Stephen's pretty blonde assistant Sylvia and another young man with beauteous eyes

Sandy's Last Stand
Recording Session, Pinewood Film Studies 15th November 2005

and a degree in mathematics. I was asked to play the theme tune of the series on the piano which worried me because I was, by then, becoming arthritic. However, it all went comparatively well, and ended with Stephen's suggestion that we should do a new orchestral arrangement to be included on the DVD.

I recommended that this should be done by Alan Gout, an old friend and colleague, and a brilliant musician and organiser. A few weeks later, Alan had engaged an orchestra and done a new orchestration faithful to my original conception, and before long twenty–five musicians turned up at Pinewood studios and played the arrangement splendidly.

After a glass or two of wine at lunch I conducted, standing up for most of three hours. Once I got onto the podium, my former lack of confidence left me.

However, towards the end of the session I was wilting, and said to the orchestra, 'I think we had better call this session "Sandy's Last Stand"'. This got a friendly round of applause. Stephen, who expressed his delight at the success of the afternoon, had my gag printed on the cover of the DVD.

Fine.

The Author
… al Fine

Appendices

Appendix A — Memories
HARRIET EMILY
Dr Harriet Rhys–Davies

MEMORIES

Belfast Trams

I remember these with great affection. The old ones were red and the others were blue and more streamlined. Both were double–decker. I favoured the top but couldn't carry my cello up. There was just room to stack it next to where the conductor stood. During the morning rush hour, when we were going to school, they came at five minute intervals, starting with the red ones on the hour. Usually Sandy started for school early and caught the blue 8.25. Mother and I caught the twenty five or twenty to nine.

Cinema Trips

At one stage, when we were teenagers, Sandy and I frequently used to go to the Classic Cinema on a Saturday afternoon. There we saw a series of splendid films including *Sabotage, A Hundred Men And A Girl,* (Deanna Durbin and Stokovsky), *Fantasia, The Lady Vanishes,* (Margaret Rutherford), and *Mr Deeds Comes To Town,* (or *Goes* — I'm not sure which). This was my first introduction to the tuba. We also saw *Gone With The Wind* at the Ritz. It lasted for four hours and was the first film we had encountered with an interval. The entertainment also included the delights of Joseph Seal playing the organ which rose, majestically, under a spotlight from the floor of the auditorium.

Sunday Afternoon Walks

These usually took us to Shaw's Bridge, a pretty spot beyond the end of the Malone Road. We very often met members of the Boyd family and sometimes Maurice Gibson.

Music with Mother

When I first learned the cello, the three of us used to play simple trios — I think with Mother on the violin and Sandy on the piano, although as he was learning the viola at the time, I may be wrong about this. I have clearer memories of singing Gilbert and Sullivan with Mother; in particular *Strange Adventure*. We coped with just three voices.

Music at Blairbank

These lively sessions were conducted in the dining room, usually on a wet afternoon. Dennis Harriman played the violin and I on my cello was usually responsible for any breakdown of ensemble. One of our favourite pieces was *Eine Kleine Nachtmusik*.

The Nutcracker Orchestra

We rehearsed at Rosebank on Friday evenings. Mother and I made piles of sandwiches beforehand. A popular filling was sliced apple with golden syrup. Sandy conducted and Geoffrey Simmonds was Leader. Molly Mellon, a school friend of mine, was another violinist. Mother played the viola and was sometimes supported by Miss Loughrey. Jeanette Llubera was a fellow cellist; her father had the chair of Spanish at Queen's. Our pianist was Ian Moss, and when Vincent Acheson wasn't away at Rugby School, he brought his clarinet. We used to play for charity and I particularly remember playing at the League of Pity Tea Shop which was run by some of the good ladies of Belfast every year just before Christmas in Wellington Place.

The Audition

In June 1939 Sandy skilfully persuaded the conductor of the BBC Northern Ireland Orchestra – Mr B. Walton O'Donnell – to audition us, (The Nutcracker Orchestra). It was very exciting and took place at the BBC. We played a movement from the Mozart G Minor Symphony and one from Bach's Suite No.3 in D. He listened sympathetically and said we were "good – very good", but if he was going to broadcast a children's orchestra for the first time, he would want us to be a little bit more polished. He then conducted us himself and pointed out a few areas for improvement: "Go away and practise hard over the summer and I promise to put you on in the autumn." Then the war came so it never happened.

Portballintrae Reminiscences

Walks over the common to the farm at Lisanduff where we were given glasses of warm buttermilk.

Going to the little nine–hole golf links at Bushfoot. Here Sandy and Dennis Harriman chatted up a lady who owned a lively pointer dog. She was glad to let them walk him. They soon found that he could easily find all the lost balls and set up a profitable business selling these to members in the clubhouse. I think Mother stopped this 'nice little earner' for moral reasons!

Bathing daily before lunch in the blue pool whatever the weather, and diving from 'top rock'.

The long walk to Dunluce Church.

Fishing for mackerel or dabs in the Pearl with Uncle Edgar.

Tennis tournaments organised by Cousin Jimmy on the Blairbank tennis court.

Going for walks with Agatha to look for caterpillars on the common.

Getting up at 6.00am to go salmon fishing in the cobble with Jimmy Skelly in charge. Sometimes, if a storm blew up, I had to walk on my own all the way from the far end of Runkerry Beach.

Picnics at Ballintoy.

Trying to be brave enough to walk across the rope bridge at Carrick–a– Rede.

Going to Runkerry House market garden to buy tomatoes. Sometimes we would encounter Lord Macnaughten of the "Macnaughten Rules".

Buying sweets and touristy presents from Mr MacConnaghy in his little shop with the corrugated iron roof.

Annual trips to the Giant's Causeway with Aunt Anna, (and Uncle Tom while he was alive), where we were treated to tea at one of the two hotels.

Annual trips to Portrush with all the cousins at the end of August for the firework display.

The excitement of rushing up to the Blairbank attic with its worn linoleum when we first arrived on holiday to see if our buckets and spades were still safely where we had left them under the eaves. Also the delights of Golden Shred marmalade and Hovis bread which we never had at home.

Equihen and Paris 1937

In 1937 Mother took Sandy and me to France for a month. John had remained up at Oxford to work on his thesis for his B.Litt. and Katharine was in Germany with Aunt Molly, staying with Frau Eckhardt, whose family had been penfriends of the Acheson girls in the early part of the century and had stayed in touch ever since. We shut up the house in Belfast and sailed from Folkestone to Boulogne. I had never heard native French spoken apart from our school mademoiselle, and I remember my excitement when we berthed at Boulogne and all the porters rushed on board crying, "*Porteur, Madame! Porteur, Madame!*".

From Boulogne we travelled west by bus along the coast of the *Pas de Calais* for about eight miles to the little fishing village of Equihen. We stayed in a very modest *pension* with bare boards for flooring. Mother and I shared a room with a bay window on the corner looking out on to the little square with the church and a *boulangerie*.

It was all spotlessly clean and the food was excellent, simple French cuisine.

A short walk from the *pension* brought us to the top of the cliffs and to a wonderful view of the beach – miles and miles of golden sands and a gentle surf rolling in. A white mist often rose over the water in the late afternoon, but on a clear day we could see the coast of England. I remember the sea as always being blue, but I don't suppose it really was.

Every day there was a slow procession of elderly peasant women dressed in black making their way down the steep cliff path to collect mussels on the rocks at low tide. They filled sacks with these and then toiled slowly up to the top again bearing this heavy load on their backs. Most of them looked very old and wizened. We felt sorry for them and thought that the men folk who went out fishing had a much easier life.

Once or twice we visited the little seaside resort of Wimereux, a few miles along the coast. It was more upmarket than Equihen and had an attractive seafront with brightly painted boats bobbing about and plenty of pavement restaurants. Very French. On another occasion we ventured farther afield to Le Touquet – which liked to call itself *Paris Plage*. We looked into the expensive shop windows full of jewellery and designer clothes and sat in the grand marina, watching the rich French prancing about in the swimming pool. We preferred Equihen.

Two important events took place during our stay at Equihen. The first was the *Fête des Pêcheurs*. This was said to occur only once every hundred years. I wondered how they knew how to organise it. It went on for the best part of a week, and consisted of endless processions of floats, carts and other vehicles, draped with fishing nets and coloured streamers. Most of them were bearing a fishing boat filled with excited and noisy participants dressed in bright colours, singing and waving to the crowds of spectators who had come in from the surrounding neighbourhoods. There was a great deal of drinking and revelry which went on well into the night. And the little square was not quite so peaceful as before. We were rather relieved when it was over.

The other memorable event was the state visit to France of King George VI and Queen Elizabeth fresh from their recent coronation. They sailed across the Channel in the royal yacht *Victoria and Albert*. To the delight of the local French people the vessel was open to the public for part of the time when their Majesties were not on board. We went to Boulogne to avail ourselves of this opportunity, and I remember how wonderful the ship looked dressed overall in the harbour. We were welcomed on board by the crew – the ratings immaculate in their white bellbottoms. They were obviously relishing the chance to show off to the French. The interior of the ship was very grand – befitting royalty with beautiful carpets and lots of highly polished mahogany.

On our last day in Equihen we bathed in the late afternoon. Sandy dived into the surf with his glasses on and they disappeared. We searched for ages with little hope of success. On our way back to the pension we went into the village post office and put up a notice in our best French appealing to any finder to send them to our Paris address. The next morning we strolled along the beach at low tide and suddenly I saw them gleaming in the wet sand! What a bit of luck, we thought. A month later he lost them – this time forever – in the blue pool at Portballintrae.

AUNTIE NAN
Dr Harriet Rhys–Davies

Early in the first world war Auntie Nan with several of her student friends became a volunteer at the Surgical Requisites Association which had been founded in June 1915. Its object was to supply bandages, dressings and appliances of all kinds for treatment of wounded soldiers in war hospitals at home and abroad.

Branches were established all over the country. The London one attended by Auntie Nan was at 17, Mulberry Walk, Chelsea. Many of the women who worked there were wealthy aristocrats and they became known as the "Ladies of Mulberry Walk".

While she was there she helped to fold bandages, make dressings of sphagnum moss and pine, and prepare slings, crutches and leg cradles. It was when she visited patients in hospital that her artistic mind was appalled by the sight of straight rigid wooden splints being applied to the curved limbs of the wounded soldiers and she realised that if moulds could be made of the distorted limbs and casts applied, the results might be much better.

She set to work preparing a special papier maché consisting of nine layers of paper cut in strips, dried and polished. The paper used was blue sugar bag paper willingly contributed by local grocers. The process was lengthy and complicated. It was difficult to complete without damaging the cast.

So the papier maché splint was invented. It was an unqualified success and years later was succeeded by plaster of Paris now universally used. For this invention Auntie Nan was awarded the CBE which she received from King George V in November 1919. Her decoration is now in my possession.

Alexander Faris

My first significant memory of Auntie Nan was when mother took Harriet (then called Hilary) and me to visit her in London in 1934. I was thirteen, Hilary ten. Auntie Nan was, I think, fifty–one. She lived in King's House Studios near the

World's End pub, where the 11 bus turns left then right again, still on the King's Road. She had a close friend and helper in one Bill Baker, who was probably in his sixties.

We had travelled from Belfast on either the Liverpool or Heysham ferry, I can't remember which. It was the first journey outside Ireland for H. and myself; an exciting adventure — to a dream city. A routine developed. In the mornings Bill would take Hilary and me to see the sights of London; Buckingham Palace, the changing of the guard, St Paul's, Westminster Abbey and so forth. Bill would always buy us an ice cream, so often that Hilary developed a severe distaste for that commodity. In the afternoons mother and Auntie Nan would rest. One day I was given the fare for a journey on the no. 11 bus; there and back to St Paul's. On another day we all went to the Open Air Theatre in Regent's Park to a matinee of *The Tempest* starring the famous Nigel Playfair and, I think, Leslie French as Puck. Many years later I was to work with Leslie when he played the dame in a pantomime for which I was the Musical Director.

LILI MARLEN'

Hans Leip, 1915

Vor der Kaserne
    Vor dem großen Tor
Stand eine Laterne
    Und steht sie noch davor
So woll'n wir uns da wieder seh'n
    Bei der Laterne wollen wir steh'n
Wie einst Lili Marleen.

Unsere beide Schatten
    Sah'n wie einer aus
Daß wir so lieb uns hatten
    Das sah man gleich daraus
Und alle Leute soll'n es seh'n
    Wenn wir bei der Laterne steh'n
Wie einst Lili Marleen.

Schon rief der Posten,
    Sie blasen Zapfenstreich
Das kann drei Tage kosten
    Kam'rad, ich komm sogleich
Da sagten wir auf Wiedersehen
    Wie gerne wollt ich mit dir geh'n
Mit dir Lili Marleen.

Deine Schritte kennt sie,
    Deinen zieren Gang
Alle Abend brennt sie,
    Doch mich vergaß sie lang
Und sollte mir ein Leid gescheh'n
    Wer wird bei der Laterne stehen
Mit dir Lili Marleen?

Aus dem stillen Raume,
    Aus der Erde Grund
Hebt mich wie im Traume
    Dein verliebter Mund
Wenn sich die späten Nebel drehn
    Werd' ich bei der Laterne steh'n
Wie einst Lili Marleen.

Tommie Connor, 1944

Underneath the lantern,
 By the barrack gate
Darling I remember
 The way you used to wait
T'was there that you whispered tenderly,
 That you loved me,
You'd always be,
 My Lilli of the Lamplight,
My own Lilli Marlene

Time would come for roll call,
 Time for us to part,
Darling I'd caress you
 And press you to my heart,
And there 'neath that far—off lantern light,
 I'd hold you tight ,
We'd kiss good night,
 My Lilli of the Lamplight,
My own Lilli Marlene

Orders came for sailing,
    Somewhere over there
All confined to barracks
    Was more than I could bear
I knew you were waiting in the street
    I heard your feet,
But could not meet,
    My Lilly of the Lamplight,
My own Lilly Marlene

Resting in our billets,
    Just behind the lines
Even tho' we're parted,
    Your lips are close to mine
You wait where that lantern softly gleams,
    Your sweet face seems
To haunt my dreams
    My Lilly of the Lamplight,
My own Lilly Marlene

Alan Franks and Chick (Charles) Norton used to turn up at the theatre in similar formal overcoats. I quote Patricia Routledge: 'What are Rosencrantz and Guildenstern doing here?' She was right, for all the world they looked like a pair of diplomats.

"Parson's Pleasure" was the nickname for an enclosed meadow area on the banks of the river Cherwell, a pretty tributary of the Isis, (Oxford's name for that reach of the Thames).

P–P was an exclusively male precinct. Here dons could lie nakedly and discreetly sunning themselves. On one occasion, however, a punt–load of women had strayed into this sacred area. One don hastily threw a towel round his middle. His companion wound *his* towel round his head, leaving his lower parts exposed.

'My dear fellow, what do you think you're doing?'

'I am happy to say, Dundas, that in Oxford I am known by my face and not by my genitals.'

Robin Dundas, my tutor, was a regular at Parson's Pleasure.

Dundas was a nice Scotsman and a distinguished Greek scholar. He was well–known to have an eye for pretty young undergraduates (male). A randy old so–and–so, but likeable and popular with it. His career had a sad, almost tragic, ending when he left the manuscript of his life's work, a Greek history, on a train at Didcot. It was never found. No copy.

REVIEWS

SULLIVAN : THE MIKADO

John Holmes (bass) *The Mikado*; John Wakefield (tenor) *Nanki–Poo*; Clive Revill (baritone) *Ko–Ko*; Denis Dowling (baritone) *Pooh–Bah*; John Heddle Nash (baritone) *Pish–Tush*; Marion Studholme (soprano) *Yum–Yum*; Patricia Kern (mezzo–soprano) *Pitti–Sing*; Dorothy Nash (soprano) *Peep–Bo*; Jean Allister (mezzo–soprano) *Katisha*.

IOLANTHE : EXCERPTS

Elizabeth Harwood, Elizabeth Robson, Cynthia Morey (sopranos); Heather Begg, Patricia Kern (mezzo–sopranos); Stanley Bevan (tenor); Eric Shilling, Denis Dowling, Julian Moyle (baritones); Leon Greene (bass); Sadler's Wells Opera Chorus and Orchestra / Alexander Faris.

Reviewing recent new recordings and reissues of *The Mikado,* I have regretted the continuing absence from the catalogue of what I and others still consider the best recording of the work. Well, here it is at last! Sensibly combined with the *Iolanthe* highlights that likewise resulted from Sadler's Wells Theatre's burst of enthusiasm for G&S following the expiry of Gilbert's copyright, it makes a remarkable bargain. At the core of the performances are some of the finest British singers of 30 years ago, all of whom were chosen not just for their singing but for their sense of the theatricality and humour of Gilbert and Sullivan. Just listen, for instance, to how John Heddle Nash gives full expression to every word of Pish–Tush's "Our great Mikado". In both works Denis Dowling, as Pooh–Bah and Mountarat, is a tower of strength, as is Patricia Kern as Pitti–Sing and Iolanthe. Here, too, is Marion Studholme's delicious Yum–Yum and Elizabeth Harwood's joyous Phyllis. If one singles out Clive Revill for special mention, it is because his Ko–Ko is uniquely well–judged and imaginative, combining superb comic timing, verbal clarity and vocal dexterity. His "little list" is hilarious, and one can almost feel one's hand gripped at the words "shake hands with you *like that*".

At the helm in both works is Alexander Faris, who was equally at home in the pit at Sadler's Wells or the West End theatre, and, whether in Sullivan or Offenbach, knew supremely well how to capture the lightness and sparkle of operetta. "Now please you sirs", for instance, goes like a dream. The new Overture put together for *The Mikado* by Stephen Dodgson may come as a surprise, but it is apt and cleverly done. The sound is inevitably dated when compared to more recent recordings, but it scarcely mars the enjoyment. Who could fail to be captivated by these performances?

AML

NEWPORT HOUSE

The First Convoy and U–Boats
From "An Indian Chequerboard", vol. II, by Sir James Acheson, (c. 1969)

It was then, in early '39, that Vio and I went home on long leave, our last. Jimmy was now at Christ Church, Oxford. He was. an ardent member of the University R.A.F. Volunteer Reserve Squadron; and also did a certain amount of reading. Vio was then living with her mother in a comfortable flat in Gloucester Road; it was the beginning of the Easter holidays, and Anthony from Wellington and Kitty from Victoria College, Belfast, were also there. Vio managed to fit me and then Jimmy in also, how I cannot tell. Jimmy had an old but powerful, (and very noisy), car called Baby, in which I careered happily round London with him and Anthony. I remember his taking us all to two plays; one was The Beggars' Opera, with Edith Evans, then magnificent in her prime, and the other Synge's Playboy of the Western World, where we had a foretaste of the ripe racy speech of Co. Mayo. I had taken a house at Newport in that famous County, from July on.

But before we went there I took Anthony in a new Wolseley, thrillingly delivered at the door of our flat on the morning of our departure, for a week's holiday fishing at Alford Bridge on the Aberdeenshire Don. I caught one salmon, and Anthony lost one, and both caught some good trout; it is a very likeable river in a pleasant, agricultural Scots countryside. Then the whole family, except Mrs. Field, found their way by divers routes to our holiday home on the shores of Clew Bay with its 365, (or, as the locals never forget to add, in a leap year 366), islands.
The house was a large and beautiful, but sadly dilapidated one, eighteenth century, at the mouth of the Newport River. I had leased it for the season from the widow of the last of the O'Donnells, a family of renown in Irish history; St. Columba was one of them, and they used to maintain that it was an O'Donnell and not an O'Neill who smote off his own hand and threw it ashore so as to be able to claim to have been first to touch Ulster soil; whence the "Red Hand of Ulster".

The house had its little park, including a chapel at one side and a special entrance to the principal public house of Newport on the other – the sacred and the profane. There was a long gate–house at the entrance from the main street, and when we entered it for the first time, there stood the entire old O'Donnell household staff, all re–assembled in front of it with bows and wreathed smiles outside, headed by the housekeeper May Burke, delighted to see the house occupied once more, even for only two or three months. May was a very capable person and a personage in the little town. She had no difficulty in recruiting a couple of "girls dragged out of the bog", as she described them, to take a hand with the cooking and cleaning up and mopping necessary, when the multitude descended on Newport House.

We had all our children there, also Edgar and Molly and Grace and Harriet, Grace's daughter and Kitty's school–friend, and Michael Patton–Bethune, a Wellington friend of Jimmy's. Leslie Plant, the boy's old Prep. School Head, (an old T.C.D. friend of mine), and his wife Phyll came later, but unfortunately just after I had been recalled, a few days before the beginning of the war. Peter Williams, our nephew from Sherborne, was also there, with his young sister Eve.

Even the great house could scarcely hold all these visitors; they ebbed and flowed, loike, (as they would, say in Mayo), but most of them were there most of the time. The black shadow of war was over us, but we managed to forget it and be happy until the last week or so when it seemed certain, though even then we hoped against hope as we got the news from the radio and telephone at the pub by our gate. Irish Republicans, ex–I.R.A., and English and Ulster visitors were all one in their detestation of Hitler and also their hopes that somehow war would be avoided.

We fished and bathed and sailed to our heart's content. Our boat was a redoubtable heavy open fishing boat called the *Tope Queen*. Tope was the local name for the small basking sharks which abounded in Clew Bay, and it was for the debased, but highly popular sport of catching these harmless and inedible fish that the *Queen* was, built.

She was guaranteed not to upset in any wind; we had a delightful lad called John Meany, the son of a local ex–policeman, as boatman and general handyman; he was much liked by all the family and I wonder what became of him in later life. The *Queen* was easily the slowest sailor in those waters, and that is saying a lot. They had a tremendous regatta in the estuary, and the *Queen* was out of sight of all the rest as they entered the estuary from the starting post some miles out in the Bay among the islands. But Peter Williams retrieved the honour of Newport House by stolidly winning, one after another, all the swimming races, against a large and showy field.

Our little chapel was the only Protestant church in the parish. It was Church of Ireland, as this was the Protestant branch of the O'Donnells; and the parson was a remarkable character, a slim, silver–haired man called Canon Shea. There were, by this time, only two families in his congregation. It was no fault of the Canon's, as he was a genial and able man and an excellent preacher. He was well–known to the local folks, and full to the brim of good stories. One I particularly remember, (not told from the pulpit), was about a worthy R.C. priest who was a strong advocate of temperance. He did his best to eradicate the vice of poteen–drinking from his flock, and one Sunday he followed up his sermon on this subject by handing out pamphlets containing terrifying details of the ingredients, (e.g. sulphuric acid), of various prescriptions for blending the noxious potation. After Mass the next Sunday a prominent member of the congregation came up to him and said he wanted to thank him for the gift. "Indeed, I'm glad to hear you say it, Mr. O'Flaherty, for to speak plain you are inclined to be overgiven to strong drink yourself". "Well, it's like this, Your Riverence, thim thracts contain the swatest little ricipe for potheen that iver I clapped me eyes upon!"

The House was indescribable, paper hanging off the walls and worn out carpets and ragged curtains. However, the ponderous plumbing — which required all hands to the old pump in the stable–yard, daily — never let us down.

And in the evenings we settled down round the sweet–smelling turf, (Anglice peat), fire, in the only elegant and undilapidated room in the house, the drawing–room–cum–library, and chattered and forgot about the squalor without. In short, we were supremely happy.

But the pub radio became more and more depressing. Gloom settled on little Newport as on the rest of the British Isles. Discussion of the prospects of a good September run of sea trout was forced and unreal. Cheerfulness would keep breaking in, but never for long, and when towards the end of August I received my recall telegram it was a kind of relief. I had to report immediately at Chester for further orders.

I bade farewell to Vio, and Jimmy and Anthony took me in the Wolseley to Belfast. I said good–bye to Grace and her children there, and gave my blessing to our two boys and went on board the steamer for Liverpool en route to Chester.

After a few days in that never very exhilarating city, then deep in gloomy apprehension, I, with about 150 others, Indian Army Officers, and men of the various Civil services, a number of men on leave from key posts in mining and other occupations of defence importance, and a few belonging to these classes whose jobs were in Gibraltar, Malta and Egypt, clambered at dawn on to a special train at Chester Station. We were not told our port of embarkation, and consequently had no notion when we were due to arrive there. But from the stations we passed through it gradually became obvious that our destination was a Scottish port, and at last we climbed out on to the platform of Greenock, on the Clyde.

There we were transferred on board the *Britannic*, a large White Star liner lying in the roads. She was one of a convoy of five, the others including the *Duchess of Bedford*, the *Reina Del Pacifico*, and a small fast freighter. This latter vessel may not have been "built in th'eclipse", but could fairly be described, as "Rigg'd with Curses dark"; for she sailed throughout the voyage, or at any rate as far as Port Said, in the exact middle of the square formed by the big first–class liners; and she was generally, and probably justly, suspected of being packed to the gunwales with H.E. The consequence to all and sundry in the convoy should one of the torpedoes directed at its midst unfortunately slip past the liners and find its billet in the mystery freighter, did not bear thinking of. The *Britannic* was an aging White Star liner built for the Atlantic passage, i.e. for cold wintry weather and not for one of the hottest runs on earth, namely the Red Sea in mid–September. She even had sheet iron instead of open deck–rails so as to shelter the passengers and crew from the wind. She had very incommodious cabins, and fans were not a standard fitting. Add to this that she was grossly over–crowded and that there was a shortage of crew and stewards, and you may well say 'What a floating hell!'

Surprisingly enough she was nothing of the kind. The shortage of staff was in fact our saving; it kept us occupied, and therefore contented. Everyone on board regardless of seniority had to join a labour squad first of all to shift and stack mountains of baggage, boxes and crates. Then to distribute cabin trunks, and throughout the voyage to act as cabin and table stewards in aid of the skeleton staffs recruited at the last moment and rushed on board.

INDEX

Nurturing Success

Helen Sonnet

...ission to photocopy

This book contains materials which may be reproduced by photocopier or other means for use by the purchaser. The permission is granted on the understanding that these copies will be used within the educational establishment of the purchaser. The book and all its contents remain copyright. Copies may be made without reference to the publisher or the licensing scheme for the making of photocopies operated by the Publishers' Licensing Agency.

Acknowledgements

I should like to thank Liz Stokes, head teacher of Hayesdown School, Frome, for sharing my vision and for having sufficient faith to allow me to establish Sunflowers, our nurture group. Thank you too to all the staff of Hayesdown School for their good-natured tolerance of my requests and their enthusiasm.

I am grateful to Simon Bishop, who runs a nurture group at Christchurch School in Frome, for his help and for the valuable resources he has allowed me to include in this book. I should like to thank Caroline Hawkes, The Nurture Group Network co-ordinator for Somerset, for her encouragement and advice and for the examples of good practice she shared with me.

Finally, I am grateful to Clare Kennedy, my co-worker at Hayesdown, for her patience, boundless enthusiasm, creativity and sheer hard work. It is a joy to run Sunflowers with her.

MT10773
ISBN-13: 978 1 85503 429 7
© Helen Sonnet
Illustrations © Mike Phillips
All rights reserved
First published 2008
Reprinted 2011, 2012, 2013

Printed in the UK for LDA
Pintail Close, Victoria Business Park, Nottingham, NG4 2SG, UK

Contents

Foreword

Nurture groups offer a well-established model for working with children who struggle with school, and for whom coping with the expectations of classroom behaviour is just too much. Such children are often labelled as having 'behavioural problems', and may face a bleak prospect in terms of their future schooling. A central message of the nurture group approach is 'growth, not pathology'. In other words, such children should not be dismissed as inherently 'bad'. Instead, much thought should be given to the origins of their difficulties and to possible remedies. A number of these children will be found to have missed out on key early learning experiences, the context for which is the secure attachment relationship most children have with their parent figures.

In a nurture group the focus is on providing stable daily routines and developmentally appropriate activities. Through these experiences, and especially in their relationships with the staff, the children rediscover the essential security of early attachment. The nurture room itself provides a secure base from which the child can begin to engage in the processes of learning and develop the self-confidence that enables them to find their place in the wider school community.

And, of course, there are potentially serious long-term consequences if these children do not successfully engage with school at this early stage. In later childhood they will be more vulnerable to mental health problems, and perhaps be drawn into anti-social and delinquent behaviours.

I am pleased to write a foreword to this important and useful book that tells the story of one nurture group, and provides such an interesting and comprehensive set of activities. As the author emphasises, the children are given unconditional warmth and acceptance. These are the essential qualities for nurture-group practice and for achieving the outcomes for which nurture groups strive. I commend this book and congratulate the author on its publication.

Jim Rose
Director
The Nurture Group Network

Introduction

I have worked in education for over thirty years, and during this time I have become increasingly concerned that being in school is a deeply unhappy experience for some children. Their academic difficulties or inappropriate behaviour may prevent them from achieving success in the classroom, resulting in their feeling marginalised.

By the end of their second year in primary education, it's likely that a number of children will feel unable to cope with the work they are given, even if it is at an appropriate level. As the gulf between their capabilities and what a child of their age is expected to achieve widens, these children experience failure on a regular basis. As a result, their self-esteem is eroded and their confidence plummets. They become less willing to take on new challenges, and instead tend to develop avoidance strategies.

I had been working for some years as a classroom assistant and was dismayed at how regularly some children were excluded from an activity or even a classroom. As I looked at one boy in his all-too-familiar position of sitting on the floor facing the wall, I felt sad that the system could often do nothing more positive for such children. I imagined myself in his shoes and thought what an unfulfilling and negative picture of school this child must have. I resolved to try to do something to offer such children an opportunity to enjoy success, feel the positive regard of others and look forward to their lessons with eager anticipation. I felt that if children in this situation were presented with a timetable and a curriculum that was appropriate to their needs, they would respond in a positive manner.

At this time, I was taking small groups of children out of their classrooms once a week for activities designed to enhance their social skills. This was good practice in so far as it went, but at just an hour a week for half a term this programme was not enough for many of the children. For there to be any real and lasting benefit, I felt that these children needed more input in several areas over a longer period.

I began to explore how I might use my skills and experience to have a positive impact on this situation. I had worked with Jenny Mosley, founder of the Quality Circle Time model, for over fourteen years and co-authored several books with her. Through this work I had gained considerable understanding of the powerful influence of circle time in raising the self-esteem of children. The social skills sessions that I already ran utilised much of the good practice and activities that we had shared in our books. I felt that there was more that could be achieved if we had more time.

At this point, I also became interested in the concept of nurture groups developed by Marjorie Boxall during the 1970s in London. For more details see *Effective Intervention in Primary Schools* by Marion Bennathan and Marjorie Boxall (details of books mentioned are in the Resources chapter on pages 96–7). These groups were intended to be an intervention for children who showed signs of deprived early childhoods, manifested in the classroom through either disruptive behaviour or extreme withdrawal. The rationale for nurture groups suggests that adequate care in the early years is essential for healthy development of a child's emotional, cognitive and social skills. If children are deprived of this care, they are likely to be unable to respond in an appropriate manner to the demands of the classroom.

I began to think that such a group, utilising my other experience, might be a way to help those children who were of concern to me. I was aware of a nurture group that had been running for several years in a local school. I knew the teacher who had set up the group and had enjoyed several conversations with him about his work. He was very positive about the impact of the group and I was keen to see the approach in action. I arranged to visit the group with my social skills co-worker. We were impressed by what we saw and heard, and felt that the children we worked with would benefit from such an approach. So, armed with our knowledge, experience and enthusiasm, we arranged a meeting with our head teacher to talk about our thoughts and to explore the benefits of running a nurture group for the children involved and the school as a whole.

We explained that we wanted to set up and run a group which provided a modified curriculum aimed at raising the self-esteem of struggling children. This curriculum would be based on a programme of work that was engaging, provided a suitable learning experience, guaranteed a successful outcome and encouraged a positive identity for the children. We wanted them to understand and appreciate that they had useful skills and competencies. Alongside these aims, we wanted children to experience warmth and acceptance from the adults in charge and to feel that they were liked and valued. We also wanted to equip them for their return to the mainstream classroom.

When we spoke to our head teacher, the government had just published *Every Child Matters* (DfES 2003). Our aims reflected this document's observation that 'pupil performance and well-being go hand in hand'. The document also encouraged schools to offer 'a range of extended services that help pupils engage and achieve'. This climate and the fact that our head teacher shared our views meant that she was happy to offer her support to our proposal to set up a part-time nurture group.

We felt that a part-time group was the way forward for our children. I had some experience of children who had been completely removed from their classes and, while it may have alleviated certain problems, in my opinion it caused others. The children became estranged from their peer group and a sense of being part of that group was lost. It often led to the excluded child trying to regain their status aggressively when they were reintegrated.

After our meeting with the head teacher, she consulted with the school management team and governors. As a result of this, she informed us that we might go ahead with a group that would meet on four afternoons a week from the following September. The children would remain in their classes on Friday afternoons, when Golden Time – a celebration of each class's ability to keep the school's golden rules – took place. (For more information on Golden Time see *Better Behaviour through Golden Time* by Jenny Mosley and Helen Sonnet.) That gave us a term to prepare!

What follows is the story of the setting-up, running and evaluation of our nurture group. I shall share with you the successes and struggles that we encountered, the lessons that we learned, and the progress that we made. I'll also provide a wealth of resources for you to use in your group sessions. By doing this, I hope to guide you as you set up your own group and help you to enjoy its benefits for yourself, your children and your school.

1 Preparing the ground

Thinking through your pedagogy

As with any new project, there is a far better chance of success if the groundwork is well prepared and thorough. It is important to spend time prior to setting up your nurture group in clarifying exactly what you intend to do and why. A set of clear aims and specific success criteria will help you to keep on track and will inform others of your intentions. These details can be used as the basis for a policy document for your group. Although such thinking may be time-consuming, it is a valuable exercise in helping to ensure the validity of your group, both for yourself and for use when outside agencies are concerned.

To help you with this process, there is a sample policy on pages 98–103. In addition, The Nurture Group Network, the national charity for promoting nurture groups and supporting those who work in them, have over a thousand groups registered with them and you may find a group near you that will be willing to share their policy documents. Contact details may be found in the Resources section (pages 96–7).

Deciding on your aims and criteria

The sample policy on pages 98–103 includes a set of aims. Deciding at an early stage on what your group's aims will be will help to inform all the work that follows.

Having aims such as these clear in your mind and agreed with staff will help you to set up an effective nurture group, run it well and evaluate its success.

In a similar way, it is good to develop an agreed understanding about the sorts of children who might be considered for inclusion in the group. For example, any of the following might be accepted for referral:

- ✪ Those who appear to be emotionally insecure, which could present itself as lack of self-acceptance, low self-worth or a lack of trust.
- ✪ Children who are withdrawn and unresponsive.
- ✪ Children with poor social skills, who cannot share, are demanding or uncooperative.
- ✪ Those with a poor attention span.
- ✪ Children who demonstrate immature behaviour.
- ✪ Children who behave aggressively, impulsively or inappropriately in other ways.
- ✪ Children who find change upsetting.
- ✪ Children who appear to be unable to integrate into a mainstream classroom.

In Chapter 2 I provide guidance on how to assess such referred children and decide if they will benefit from being a member of the group.

Our group caters for up to twelve children, selected from years 1 to 4 using the criteria above. Twelve felt like quite a large number at the beginning, and you may want to start with eight. While some educators recommend choosing children from two year groups only, we have never found that a broader age range presented a problem. Older children quickly become gentler in their play to accommodate the younger members, and model more mature behaviour for them to aspire to.

Our group includes children who have shown signs of a deprived early childhood and who are therefore failing to make satisfactory progress at school. In addition, there are children who are simply unable to cope with the academic side of school and have gradually become marginalised; others whose behaviour is symptomatic of disorders on the autism spectrum; and children whose development is delayed for other reasons. All of the children are, for one reason or another, deemed unable to engage satisfactorily in the normal routines and activities of the classroom.

Such children should benefit from the unconditional acceptance, warmth and level of care a nurture group can offer. Co-operative, supportive behaviour needs to be modelled consistently by the adults running the group, with an emphasis on positive behaviours such as sharing, taking turns, playing gently, being considerate, resolving differences in an acceptable manner, and taking good care of the group's facilities and equipment. More than anything, such children need to be shown that they are liked and valued by the adults as they may have had little experience of this elsewhere.

The children chosen for the group need to be those who will benefit from a modified version of the National Curriculum, delivered using predictable activities and familiar routines. Activities should be chosen to enhance a child's social skills, improve their self-esteem and develop the skills necessary for learning – such as concentration and processing skills. We use circle-time activities to focus on the basic skills of looking, listening and speaking, areas that are often underdeveloped in these children. An emphasis on enhancing language skills enables children in a nurture group to communicate their ideas and feelings more fully and with greater confidence.

We seek to give children tasks that increase gradually in terms of difficulty, helping to create an upward spiral of success. Initially we pitch activities at a fairly low level to ensure that all the children can achieve satisfactory end-products. Affirmation and praise are crucial to a child's sense of success.

Particular attention should be paid to developing positive relationships between the adults and children, and between the children themselves. You could use a different theme each half-term as a means to look at such issues as feelings, friendship, resolving conflicts and working co-operatively. The DfES Social and Emotional Aspects of Learning (SEAL) materials include some resources for small-group work that are helpful, although we often shorten or modify the sessions for our children. We also focus on activities that will develop a positive dynamic and promote team-building and a sense of belonging. We want the children to have a sense of ownership of the group.

We have found that the adults who work in a nurture group can best facilitate change by incorporating a parenting role alongside their educator's approach, showing a greater tolerance – not to be confused with acceptance – of a child's idiosyncrasies.

Informing the staff

Having gained agreement for setting up a group in your school, and having spent some time exploring the aims and ethos of this group, you will then need to share your vision with others, starting with the school staff.

In our case, once the decision had been taken to go ahead with the group, a meeting was held to share what was going to happen with the staff. As is likely with any group of teaching professionals, some were in favour and could see the benefits of providing an alternative and modified curriculum, while others raised objections.

One of the main concerns related to the loss of classroom help as two teaching assistants would be running the group. A second concern was that it might appear that children who misbehaved were having their misbehaviour rewarded with the 'treat' of going to the group. A further worry was that by grouping some of the most troublesome children together, we would be creating a sin-bin that would create more problems than it was attempting to solve.

The strongest argument against the first objection was that many of the teachers would benefit from the removal of disruptive and challenging children from their classrooms for four afternoons a week, making the job of teaching much more comfortable. Some of the challenging children needed constant supervision, monopolising the help available. Once these children were removed, classroom assistance would no longer be necessary and could be used elsewhere. The adults and the children remaining in the classes would enjoy more opportunities to work together, with fewer disruptions.

We explained that the intervention we wanted to introduce should be seen as an investment. By helping the children to view themselves in a different and more positive light, and see themselves as capable and competent, we believed that their behaviour would improve, and that their passage through the school would be happier for both themselves and the adults who worked with them. In order for this to happen, the children needed to be offered a modified curriculum in different conditions from those of the classroom. This would set them on the road to success. While a nurture group is not an initiative that will necessarily bring immediate benefit to the staff, the benefits for the future may be considerable.

As for the second and third objections, there was, in our opinion, a very logical argument against them. This is based on the notion that the human race is sociable. There are benefits to people living in communities and therefore a need to develop the social skills that will make them effective members of such communities. From an early age, emotionally healthy children begin to develop these skills in order to get on with those around them. By the time children reach school age, most of them have made sufficient progress and are able to interact with other children and adults in a generally positive manner.

The children who do not possess these skills or the requisite skills for learning may become gradually aware that they are not always held in high esteem by their fellow pupils, and possibly by some of the adults in their school. They may believe that they are 'naughty' or 'stupid'. They may have even had this view reinforced by those who cared for them before they came to school.

At the same time, they will also be aware of children who seem to be more popular, and of the successes they enjoy. If, at this time, the struggling child were capable of being any different, it is likely that they would change their behaviour of their own accord in order to gain popularity and feel happier about their position in the school society.

We all want to be liked and praised. However, as adults we know how difficult it can be to change aspects of our character or habits, even though we have the advantage of being older and more capable. We know, as well, that we often don't react well to people who don't appear to like us or who may be angry with us. If it is not easy for experienced adults to respond in a positive manner in some circumstances, how can we expect children with difficulties to do so? Such children have probably become locked into negative behaviour patterns, are subject to self-fulfilling prophecies and are unable to change without intervention.

The aim of the nurture group, we explained, was to provide a forum for intervention to take place. It was not our intention to reward difficult behaviour or create a sin-bin. We wanted to find an effective way through praise, personal affirmation and caring warmth to help children to release themselves from established, negative responses and to find more positive ways to view themselves and life, so that they were able to be successful – in all senses of the word – in the classroom.

It is probably hard for us to imagine the conditions which some of the children that we work with have to endure in their home lives and the devastating impact these may have on them. To label such children as 'naughty' and therefore undeserving of a potentially effective form of help is to do them a great injustice.

While we may not have won over every member of staff, the meeting was helpful. It was evident that the hope was that the group would have a beneficial effect for the troubled children in our school, and for the school as a whole. It is important to have such support for a nurture group as an adult's attitude towards the group will be clear to a child asked to attend it. The child's peers will also pick up such messages. If a nurture group's value in highlighting the root causes of inappropriate behaviour and then taking a proactive approach to alleviating them is appreciated by all members of the staff, they will help to shape the positive way in which the rest of the school community will view it.

At the end of the meeting, the teaching staff were given two hand-outs relating to the group. The first outlined the aims of the group and the second explained the criteria for referring children for assessment for inclusion in the group. The hand-outs may be found on pages 104 and 105.

Finding and equipping a venue

Once we had the endorsement of the staff for the group, we turned our minds to where we could meet and what we might need in terms of equipment and resources to get started.

With regard to a venue, we were fortunate. There was a separate unit in the school grounds that was sometimes used as a spare classroom. It was used for music lessons, a place to use audio-visual equipment, and as an occasional function room. It had toilets, a kitchen and a small side room. It was ideal for our purposes.

You may not have the luxury of such a space. If at all possible, try to use a separate space, away from other children. You may be able to negotiate the use of a room that is used only occasionally, such as the hall or library.

You will need sufficient space to accommodate three or four classroom tables and leave room for a circle of chairs. The chairs from the tables can be used for the circle when needed, with the tables moved to one side to provide enough room, if necessary. You will also need something to write on; a whiteboard would be ideal but a flipchart will suffice. Storage for your equipment would also be helpful. In addition to chairs, we have some large brightly coloured floor cushions that the children sit on at story time.

In terms of consumable resources, we were able to order paint, brushes, glue and scissors from a school supplier. Paper, card, pencils and pens were donated by family and friends, as were painting shirts and cooking aprons. We were given an initial budget of £150 to buy toys and games for the group. After several visits to car-boot sales and charity shops – where you can often find toys in excellent condition for a fraction of their retail price – some cut-price store purchases and many donations from members of staff, friends, parents and the parent teacher association (who allowed us to select a few items whenever they held a fair), we were able to assemble the following items:

- a toy garage and a selection of small cars, plus a floor mat with a road layout marked on it;
- a box each of Lego® and Duplo®;
- a farm and a set of farm animals;

- ✪ a toy doctor's set;
- ✪ two picnic hampers, containing plastic crockery, cutlery and food;
- ✪ two doll babies, a doll's cot and a pushchair;
- ✪ several Barbie® and Action Man® toys — minus weapons;
- ✪ dressing-up clothes;
- ✪ a box of small toy dogs;
- ✪ a doll's house with furniture;
- ✪ a selection of board and card games, including Bingo;
- ✪ some jigsaw puzzles, books, and a variety of soft toys.

Having prepared as much as we could, we began to think about the children who would benefit most from time with us in the group.

2 Selecting children to join a nurture group

It is helpful to have an agreed and systematic process by which children who may benefit from time in a nurture group can be assessed. Such a process needs to be both thorough and workable for those administering it.

Initially, we asked the class teachers to refer to us any child whom they thought should be included in the group. The choice was based on the criteria that we discussed in the staff meeting to launch the initiative.

Goodman's Strengths and Weaknesses Questionnaire

We asked each teacher to complete a Goodman's Strengths and Difficulties Questionnaire (SDQ) on each child in their class whom they had suggested as a candidate for the group. The SDQ is a well-regarded, easily available and validated questionnaire developed by Robert Goodman. It is a concise behavioural screening questionnaire created as an objective means to identify those children in need of support.

The questionnaire features twenty-five psychological attributes, ranging from positive to negative. It explores the areas of emotional symptoms, conduct problems, hyperactivity and inattention, peer relationship problems and pro-social behaviour. Once a questionnaire has been completed, the scores for each area are compiled to generate an overall score.

There are different versions of the SDQ for various ages, which is helpful. These can be found at www.sdqinfo.com

Boxall Profile

The SDQ provides a lot of useful information on which to base your decisions regarding a child's inclusion in a nurture group. If a teacher arrived at an abnormal result for a referred child, we asked them to complete a Boxall Profile for the child to help us assess whether inclusion in a nurture group was the best way to address their difficulties.

The Boxall Profile is a diagnostic tool devised by Marjorie Boxall and colleagues to assess the emotional and behavioural needs of a child so that a suitable intervention programme can be planned for them. It is very user friendly. It may be found in *The Boxall Profile: Handbook for Teachers* (No. 7) by Marion Bennathan and Marjorie Boxall. The book provides photocopiable templates of the profile and detailed guidance on how to administer it.

In brief, the profile consists of two sections to be completed by the child's teacher or another designated staff member. Each section includes thirty-four statements. The adult carrying out the assessment scores each statement from 0 to 4, with 4 indicating that the child usually acts in the way mentioned, and 1 that the child virtually never does. Zero means that the statement cannot be assessed. Two histograms are then created from each set of scores, enabling comparisons to be made between the child and a competently functioning child of a similar age. The first section of the profile, called 'Developmental Strands', consists of statements that focus on the early personal and social development of a child from 3 to 8 years old. They show the levels of engagement that a child has with the world, their stage of personal development and their awareness of others.

The second section of the profile is the 'Diagnostic Profile'. The statements in this section are divided into three clusters focusing on self-limiting features, undeveloped behaviour and unsupported development.

The results of a profile will help to highlight the areas of concern that give rise to the inappropriate behaviours a child may be exhibiting in the classroom. In other words, the profile's results should help you understand what lies behind a child's behaviour and what you might do to improve the situation. The Boxall Profile can also be used to assess a child who has been given additional support to see if they have made progress.

In our school, once the profiles for the children with abnormal SDQs had been completed, we were able to chart their responses and compare their behaviour to that of a competently functioning child of the same age. That enabled us to identify those children with the greatest needs and what those needs were. These findings are a key aspect of choosing the children who will make up your group, or who will join it when a place becomes vacant.

Making the final selection

It is important to try to have a mix of children with a range of needs, and both boys and girls if possible in your group. Avoid a single-sex group made up entirely of aggressive or withdrawn children – an extreme example.

When choosing the children who would attend our group, we looked at the SDQs and profiles of the various candidates, spoke to their teachers and discussed them with the SENCo and the head teacher.

Two girls were submitted whom we felt would benefit from the group, so we accepted them for two of the twelve places available. Of the remaining ten places, five were given to challenging, disruptive children and five to quiet or withdrawn children. The twelve children came from the following year groups: year 1 – one child; year 2 – five children; year 3 – four children; year 4 – two children.

This was the range of children for our first group, but it may vary considerably over time. Our present group consists of four children from year 1, five from year 2, one from year 3 and two from year 4. When a child or children leave the group, we invite teachers to put forward new candidates to take their place. Any such children are assessed as outlined previously.

Informing parents/carers

It is important to keep parents and carers fully informed if their child has been selected to be involved in a nurture group. Our head teacher writes a letter telling them of this decision and explaining the purpose of the group. She explains that, using carefully considered criteria, their child has been chosen as someone who would benefit from attending the group. She also states that the group will provide their child with an alternative, modified curriculum for a fixed period of time each week so that, in time, they will be able to access the full curriculum with the rest of their peers. A sample letter is provided on page 106.

After a letter has been sent out, my co-worker and I make contact with the parents/carers through the relevant class teacher. We then arrange a convenient time to meet them with their child to show them where we shall be working, explain the nature of the work and answer any queries they might have. This is a valuable part of the child's induction into the group.

During this meeting, we ask the parents/carers to complete a parent/carer interview form (see page 107). This is a useful document that informs us of details about a child before we start to work with them. It helps to forge links between home and the group. It also gives us a shared reference point when we review a child's progress with their parent/carer. In addition, we give the parents/carers a leaflet about the group to take home and read with their child. It outlines the group's aims, and details where and when we meet, and what we do. It includes information on when parents/carers can come and visit the group, or discuss any questions with us.

We did have parents/carers who had initial reservations about their children missing out on the learning taking place in their classroom. If you have parents/carers with similar reservations, you may need to explain tactfully that the children have been selected to attend the group because they are failing to access the curriculum satisfactorily in their classroom.

It's also reassuring for parents/carers to know that the group offers a modified curriculum with a particular focus on key learning skills – such as listening, maintaining concentration, working co-operatively, carrying out verbal instructions and using expressive language. As a child shows improvement in these and other important learning areas, they will be able to access the curriculum more successfully in the classroom. In practice, many of the curriculum areas covered in the afternoons in the classrooms are included in a modified form in a nurture group's timetable – examples being music, art, drama, science, physical education. Other subjects such as history, religious education and geography often arise in general conversations during refreshment times.

Some parents/carers may have the same fear that our teaching staff initially had, which was that the group would become a sin-bin for children considered to be naughty. Others may not like the idea of their child being singled out from their peers. For the most part, in our experience, once we had an opportunity to describe in detail the work we did, the range of children who attended and the benefits that their children would gain from being in the group, the parents/carers accepted the situation happily.

Keeping clear channels of communication

We decided that unless a major incident occurred, our policy would be to give parents/carers only good news. This is an important strategy to help them to have a positive perspective on their children in the school setting. Some of the parents/carers whose children come to a nurture group may have consistently heard negative reports about their children. Such comments will doubtlessly influence the parents'/carers' views of the school and of their children. We felt that showing the parents/carers that we liked, understood and cared about their children made it easier for them to approach us with an open mind.

To start with, parents/carers may be wary, but as time passes they usually begin to respond well to the positive approach employed in the group and the attention their children are receiving, becoming more open to talking about their children and sharing good news. The children can be the best adverts for the group in terms of their development and the good reports they give about the group at home.

In addition, group members are encouraged to invite their parents/carers to visit the group each term to view their work, enjoy a drink and snack, and join in some of the activities. These occasions are usually very positive. We find that the majority of parents/carers attend such sessions, including those who do not come for their child's normal parents' evenings.

In order to formalise parents/carers' involvement, it's a good idea to ask them to participate in the ongoing development of the group. This can be done by asking them to complete a questionnaire regularly in order to assess their views on the group and to highlight ways in which it might be improved (see page 108).

We also provide an after-school session one afternoon a week, when parents/carers can come in to see their children's work, discuss their progress and chat about any concerns they have.

3 Establishing the structures and routines of your nurture group

It is important that you apply as much rigor to the daily routines of the group as you do to establishing its ethos and promoting it in the school community. This chapter is intended to guide you in such matters, and will provide you with a wealth of activities to use within the structure you create.

Finding a name for the group

We felt it was important that our group had a name. The name needed to be one that could be the everyday means of referring to the group. It needed to be something that was easy for the children to remember and that reinforced the positive and optimistic image we wished to promote.

I like our group's name, but these badges are heavy.

After discussing various options, we decided to call our group 'Sunflowers'. This has proved a popular name and one that is firmly embedded in school usage. Having a name for your group can do much to help it to be positively accepted by the school community.

Establishing ground rules

Before our first group met, my co-worker Clare and I met to discuss what ground rules we felt were needed for the group to work effectively. We decided that rules needed to be clear and easy to enforce. We settled on the following rules to inform the children of the behaviour required in the group:

- ✪ We play gently.
- ✪ We take turns and share toys.
- ✪ We talk politely to people.
- ✪ We take care of our equipment.

We made posters displaying these rules and put them up in the group's room so that they could be easily seen. We discuss them with children who join the group so that they feel a sense of ownership of them, agree on their fairness and commit themselves to abiding by them. Having clearly displayed rules means that they are easy to refer to if an infringement occurs. It is a good idea to say these rules with the children at the start of each session for a few weeks whenever a new child joins or a new group begins. It also helps to do so after a holiday.

Devising a timetable

The timetable that you create for your nurture group should incorporate the approaches and strategies that have been noted by Marjorie Boxall as essential for the effective development of children involved in such a group. These approaches and strategies are as follows.

- ✪ Clear expectations of the children.
- ✪ Consistent rewards and sanctions systems.
- ✪ Clear behavioural limits and boundaries.
- ✪ Activities with clear routines.
- ✪ Plenty of contact between co-workers and children.
- ✪ Simple instructions.
- ✪ Plenty of individual attention.
- ✪ Frequent praise.
- ✪ The development of trusting relationships.
- ✪ Frequent opportunities for success.
- ✪ Celebration of individual and group success.
- ✪ Opportunities for children to act responsibly.
- ✪ Encouragement of the children so that they feel secure and valued.
- ✪ Calm and caring adult role models.

The timetable that you devise should include activities that involve the group working together, and others that allow for children working or playing on their own, in pairs or smaller groups.

As well as the curriculum subjects of science, art, drama, PSHE and PE, the timetable for our group includes circle-time activities, games, singing, clapping rhymes, story-telling, cooking, gardening and free play.

We plan each session so that it includes a drink and snack break, which takes place with all the children and adults sitting round a table. The children take turns to clear away the toys beforehand, set the table, hand out the drinks and snacks, and clear the table and wash and dry the plastic crockery afterwards.

If your timetable follows the same format for each session – with special activities such as cooking, art and gardening on the same day each week – the children will feel safe with the predictable format.

As a guide, the format we use for our group is as follows:

- ✪ greeting ritual;
- ✪ circle-time activities;
- ✪ designated activity of the day;
- ✪ free play;
- ✪ set table and tidy up equipment;
- ✪ refreshments;
- ✪ washing-up and story time;
- ✪ clapping rhyme or song;
- ✪ ending ritual.

We view beginnings and endings as very important. We particularly want the start and finish of a session to be positive experiences that involve all of the children.

We believe that this timetable provides well-balanced content for the children, keeping them engaged, occupied, interested and working within their capabilities. We found that by providing a timetable that is suited to the children's needs, we reduced the incidence of inappropriate behaviour. By building on their successes, we helped them move towards a more positive identity.

Each day we display the session's timetable in a visual format, so that when the children arrive they can look at the timetable that is on display to see what is happening. We use a visual timetable as this is easy for the children to interpret. Pages 109–11 provide you with a range of images that can be used in your visual timetable. 'Activity of the day' has been left blank for you to draw an appropriate image for the day in question if one has not been provided.

Some detailed comments on some of the activities that make up a typical day in our nurture group follow. In Chapter 5 we offer a programme for a complete term that you may decide to use.

Greeting ritual

We recommend that you start each session with a greeting ritual that helps to promote a positive group dynamic. A selection of ten of our favourite greetings follows. Once the children are familiar with these, we allow a different child to choose a greeting to start each session. We place the names of the children and adults in a bag, take one out each day and put it on the side until everyone has had a turn. Page 111 includes a sign for the visual timetable for each of the greetings. With all these greetings it is good if you and/or your co-worker are able to join in.

Bean and Gone

You will need a beanbag for this game.

The children sit in a circle. Give one of the children the beanbag. They choose someone in the circle to throw the beanbag to gently. As they do so, they say 'Hello, . . .'. The child who receives the beanbag repeats this action with another child. They then fold their arms to indicate that they have been greeted. The ritual continues until everyone has had a turn. The final person to receive the beanbag tosses it into the middle of the circle and says 'Hello, everyone.'

Clap and Call

The children stand in a circle. Choose a child to begin. They call a greeting to someone else in the circle and clap their hands twice after they have done so. The other children repeat the greeting and action. The named child then chooses another child to greet in the same way, which the group then repeats. This continues until everyone has been greeted once. The final person can say 'Hello, everyone' before clapping their hands. This is repeated by the group to end the ritual.

Children who have been mentioned should sit down to indicate who still needs to be greeted.

Clap and Greet

Sit in a circle. Choose a child whose name will be the focus of the start. Instead of speaking a greeting this time, the children are going to clap one. For example, 'Hello, Rachael' will involve four claps, one for each of the syllables in the greeting. Continue round the circle in a clockwise direction until everyone has been greeted.

Go and Greet

You need a circle of chairs for this game.

The children stand in a circle, one in front of each chair. Choose a child to begin the ritual by crossing the circle to greet another child. They must give a verbal greeting along with an action, such as shaking hands, bowing or giving a high-five or another appropriate greeting. The first child returns to their chair and sits down, and the greeted child greets another child. This continues until one child is left standing. This child can choose any of the seated children to greet before they too sit down.

Mingle

You need a tambourine or other sound source for this game.

The children walk about the room. When you make a sound with your musical instrument, the children stop, shake hands with and say 'Hello' to the person standing nearest to them. You can develop this greeting by asking them to share further information with the person they greet. They could tell each other their favourite food, something they did the day before or something they are looking forward to doing. Play several rounds of this ritual, asking them to try to greet a different person each time.

Pass It On

The idea of this game is to send a clap round the circle as quickly as possible. Sit or stand. Choose a child to start. They turn to the person on their left and say that person's name, followed by a clap. The greeted person tries to say the name of the person on their left and clap as quickly as possible. This continues round the circle until everyone's name has been spoken.

Shaky Circle

The children stand in a circle. Choose a child to begin the greeting. They turn to the child on their left, shake their hand and greet them by name. The greeted child returns the greeting and then does the same with the child on their left. This continues round the circle until everyone has been greeted. The High-five Circle on page 81 is a variation on this; a gentle high-five is passed round instead.

Speak from the Centre

You will need a beanbag for this game.

All the children except one sit in a circle. The remaining child stands in the centre of the circle with the beanbag. This child throws the beanbag gently to someone in the circle, greeting them as they do so. The child who receives the beanbag greets the thrower before throwing the beanbag back to them. This continues clockwise round the circle until everyone has been greeted.

Whom are you Calling?

For this game you need a circle of chairs, one for each participant.

The children stand in a circle, one in front of each chair. Choose a child (Child A) to begin the ritual by naming another child (Child B) using the following chant. The children clap the syllables of each line as they chant:

> Who is [Child A] calling?
> Listen out with care.
> [Child A] is calling [Child B]. *Child A inserts a name at the end*
> *of this line.*
> Now, sit down on their chair.

Child A then sits on Child B's chair. The chant is repeated with Child B calling another child. This continues until one child is left standing. When this child gets to line 3 of the chant, they call 'everyone' before sitting down on the chair Child A vacated initially.

Who's Calling?

Sitting in a circle, the children use the following chant to greet someone. Choose a child to be the caller (Child A).

> 'Ring, ring' goes the phone
> in a cheerful way.
> [Child A] is calling [Child A names another child in the circle]
> So that he/she can say
> [Child A says] 'Hello, [Child B], it's [Child A], have a lovely day.'

Circle-time activities

The games and activities that we use for this part of a session have four main aims. These are to:

- ✪ promote positive group dynamics, a sense of belonging and a desire to claim ownership of the group;
- ✪ enhance the children's social skills;
- ✪ develop the skills necessary for learning;
- ✪ raise self-esteem.

In addition to these main aims, we select games that allow the children to practise such valuable skills as:

- ✪ turn-taking;
- ✪ waiting patiently for a hesitant child to participate;
- ✪ looking and listening;
- ✪ expressing feelings appropriately;
- ✪ learning from others;
- ✪ feeling confident to try something new;
- ✪ participating actively;
- ✪ forming positive relationships;
- ✪ using agreed codes of behaviour;
- ✪ initiating activities with other children;
- ✪ choosing activities for the whole group;
- ✪ abiding by shared rules;
- ✪ considering their own and others' needs.

Circle activities are an excellent way of encouraging participation. The activities we use are designed to be non-threatening. A circle also makes it easier to keep the children on track. The children can see everyone else in the circle, which encourages even the shyest to become involved. Choosing activities that are fun and engaging helps this. By doing so, you will find that the children have responded before they have had time to worry about 'joining in'. We have found that even the most withdrawn of children soon participate. Because we repeat the games frequently, they quickly learn what to do and want to be part of the fun. To start with we allow withdrawn children to use non-verbal signals until they have the confidence to use their voices. We aim to have a mix of physically active and calmer activities in each session, with a weekly focus on team or group games to promote co-operation.

We include daily rituals as part of our circle activities. You will find that the children really enjoy the anticipation of these activities. On Tuesdays, for example, we play Hunt the Toy, using a small toy dog instead of a thimble. Every Thursday we play Spot the Additions. This is an activity based on a simple line drawing that I produce each half-term. It is of a scene such as a playground, park or classroom. Every Thursday, I add two small details to the picture that the children have to find. I very rarely manage to add anything that they are unable to find. To increase the enjoyment, I award the group a point for each detail they see and myself a point if they fail to spot one of my additions. By the end of each term, I have earned very few points.

The following comprehensive selection of activities should give you a good collection to get going with. You will find hundreds more in the collections of 101 games mentioned in the resources section on page 96.

Afloat in a Boat

You need a soft ball for this game.

The children sit in a circle and say the following verse as they pass the ball round the circle in a clockwise direction:

> *[Number in the group]* children
> were afloat in a boat.
> They gave a loud shout
> and one fell out.

The child who is holding the ball at the end of the verse is out and must go and sit in the middle of the circle. They are given an opportunity to guess who will be out next. If they are right, they can rejoin the circle. Don't forget to adjust the number each time someone is out or rejoins the circle. Continue the game until there are too few left in the circle to make it viable.

All Change

Ask the children to stand in a circle, facing clockwise. Tell them that you will call out a way of moving, such as skipping, hopping, crawling, bunny jumps, walking sideways, heel to toe, and so on. They need to move in a clockwise manner round the circle in the way you describe, being careful not to injure the person in front of them.

Baked Beans

Ask the children to find a space to stand in. Explain to them that you are going to call out different beans, all of which have a different action. You will need to demonstrate the following when you play this game for the first time:

- Baked bean — crouch into a ball on the ground.
- Runner bean — run on the spot.
- Broad bean — stretch arms and legs wide like a star.
- French bean — say *Bonjour*.
- String bean — stand on tiptoe and stretch arms up high.
- Jumping bean — jump on the spot.
- Jelly bean — shake arms and legs.

Body Language

This activity is useful for calming children after an energetic game.

Ask the children to lie down on their backs and close their eyes. As you read out the following script, the children will concentrate on each body part in turn.

Concentrate on your right foot, feel the weight of it. Think of each toe in turn and then imagine the shape of your ankle and the bones in it. Do the same thing with your left foot. Now imagine a line from your left foot to your knee. Think about the shape of your knee. Now think about your spine, feeling how it presses against the floor. Think about how strong and flexible it is. Concentrate on your shoulders now. Think about their width. Think of your right arm. Imagine the shape of your elbow and how it can move. Think of your wrist and how it can bend and swivel. Now think of your fingers and all the things that they can do. Finally, think about your head – how heavy it is, its shape and features: your eyes, ears, nose and mouth. Lie quietly for a while and think about what a marvellous piece of work your body is.

Body Watch

This is a follow-my-leader game. You touch a part of your body and then clap your hands twice. The children have to try to keep up with your movements. When the children are familiar with the game, allow them opportunities to lead it.

Button and Key

You will need a blindfold, a key and a button for this game.

Ask one child to stand outside the circle. Place the blindfold on them. Choose a second child to give the button and key to two different children in the circle. While they are doing this, the children say:

> Down came *[name of child giving out the objects]*.
> Down came *[name of child giving out the objects]*.
> *[Name of child giving out the objects]* is hiding the button and
>   the key.

By this stage, the objects should have been safely distributed. The children in the circle ask 'Who has the button?' The appropriate child responds 'I have the button', disguising their voice. The other children then ask 'Who has the key?' The appropriate child responds in a disguised voice. The child wearing the blindfold must try to guess the identities of the two children holding the objects. Change the roles for a new round.

Categories

Think of a category – such as countries, books, pets, colours, football teams, flowers, makes of car, television programmes, historical figures and vegetables – and ask the children to think of six items that belong to it. This can be done on an individual or group basis.

Clockwork Toys

Put the children in pairs. Tell them that they are going to pretend to be a clockwork toy. One child will be the toy and the other child will wind them up. The child who is the toy needs to move round the room in an appropriate manner, slowing down gradually as their spring unwinds. The children then swap roles.

Dice Game

This game requires a large 1 to 6 dice.

Ask the children to sit in a circle. Number them 1 to 6 in a clockwise direction. Place the dice in the centre of the circle and choose someone to roll it. Any children that have the number shown swap seats.

You can play the game using two 1 to 6 dice to create two numbers each turn. Another alternative is to number the players 1 to 5, with 6 indicating that everyone changes places.

Duck, Duck, Goose

You need some space for this game.

The children stand in a circle. Choose one to walk round the outside of the circle. As they do so, they tap the others on the shoulder and say 'Duck' or 'Goose'. If they tap someone and say 'Goose', that player has to leave the circle. The child doing the tapping must then run in a clockwise fashion round the circle while the tapped child must run in an anti-clockwise direction. Each child is to try to get back to the vacant space first. The one who loses becomes the next child outside the circle. Try to ensure that all participants have a turn outside the circle.

Express Yourself

The children are asked to make an appropriate facial expression to show how they would feel in a given situation. Situations could include:

- they are going on holiday tomorrow;
- they have accidentally broken their mum's favourite vase;
- they are about to eat their favourite meal;

- their best friend has called them an unkind name;
- their friend has the new toy they have wanted for ages;
- they've lost something that was important to them;
- it's raining and they can't go out to play;
- their teacher has praised their work.

Farmyard

You need a circle of chairs for this game.

Give each child in the circle the name of one of three farm animals. When you call out one of those names, the relevant children stand up and swap seats. Try calling two names close together. When you call 'farmyard', all of the children stand up and swap seats.

Fishes in the Sea

Ask the children to find a space to stand in. Explain to them that you are going to call out different things, all of which have a related action. You will need to demonstrate the following when you play this game for the first time:

- Low tide: walk towards the back of the room.
- High tide: walk towards the front of the room.
- Killer whales: lie flat on the floor.
- Trawlers about: crawl on hands and knees in a zigzag fashion.
- Sharks ahead: walk backwards slowly.
- Coral reef: jump forwards with feet together.

Fruit Bowl

You need a circle of chairs for this game.

This is a variation on Farmyard (see above). Give each child round the circle the name of one of three fruits. When you call out one of the fruits, the relevant children stand up and swap seats. When you call 'Fruit bowl', all of the children stand up and swap seats.

Holiday Destinations

Put the children in pairs and ask them to take it in turns to tell their partner where they would like to go on holiday. Each child then reports their partner's choice back to the group.

Get Packing

You will need two travel bags and two sets of items often taken on holiday, such as two tubes of sun cream, two pairs of sunglasses, two towels, and so on. Collect enough items to have one for each child.

Put the children into two teams with an empty travel bag each. Put each set of items in a pile at the other end of the room. On your command, the first child from each team runs to the other end and collects one of the holiday items from their team's pile. They then run back and place it in their bag. As soon as they have done this, the next child in their team sets off. When a team has collected all their items, they zip up their bag and sit down in a line behind it. The first team to do this is the winner.

Giant's Garden

You will need a blindfold and some painted flower templates created by the children.

Choose a child to crouch in the centre of the circle wearing the blindfold. They are the giant. Lay the flowers on the floor around this child. Choose two children to enter the circle and try to collect as many flowers as they can without being tagged by the giant. The giant listens for any sounds they make and tries to tag them. Once a child has been tagged, they must return to their place, taking with them the flowers they had collected up to that point. When both the children have been tagged or all the flowers have been collected, the two children each count up their flowers to see who has more.

In the Driving Seat

You need a circle of chairs for this game.

The children pretend to be sitting in various seats, miming actions that are relevant to the one you have called out. You could try a seat on a train, a piano stool, a seat on a roller coaster, a swing seat, a saddle on a horse, a dentist's chair, a seat in a pedal car, a deck chair, a seat in the London Eye, and so on.

Lead On

You will need a blindfold for each pair of children in the group.

Set up a simple obstacle course in the room using chairs, tables, and so on. It doesn't need to be elaborate. Give each pair a blindfold – a strip of material is fine, or the children can use one of their jumpers. One child in each pair needs to wear the blindfold. The other child leads their blindfolded partner through the obstacle course by hand. They then swap roles. You can reverse the route through the course for variety.

Look at the Dragon
You will need a blindfold and a bell or musical shaker.

Choose a child to be the dragon. They must put the blindfold on and crouch down in the centre of the circle. A noisy object, such as a bell or musical shaker, is placed by the dragon's head. Everyone in the circle joins in the following chant:

> Look at the dragon resting its head.
> Look at the treasure close to its bed.
> See the brave warrior enter the den,
> Capture the treasure and creep out again.

During the chant, walk round the outside of the circle and tap a child on the shoulder. They are the warrior, and they have to try to creep into the circle, pick up the object and return to their seat as quietly as possible so the dragon does not hear them.

If the dragon hears them and points directly at them, they become the dragon for the next round. If they get back to their place without being heard, they hide the keys behind their back. The other children also put their hands behind their backs.

The dragon is then invited to sit up, remove the blindfold and try to guess the warrior's identity. If the warrior is identified now, they become the dragon next time.

Magician's Cloak
You will need a cloak.

Choose a child to be the magician and wear the cloak. Choose another child to be their apprentice. Tell the children that the wizard needs to create a potion to help someone to feel happier.

The wizard then points at children in the circle in turn. The apprentice asks them what they think should be included in the potion.

Encourage the children to think of imaginative ingredients, such as a joke book, a cuddly toy, a game, a smile. If the potion was to help someone feel well, it might include a hot-water bottle, a bunch of flowers, a teddy bear, a get-well card.

The magician pretends to stir the ingredients in an imaginary pot, while the children say together, 'Stir it up and mix it thick, our magic potion will do the trick.'

Mirror, Mirror

Put the children in pairs and ask them to stand facing each other. Each pair must choose who will lead and who will follow. With their arms and hands the leader makes slow movements, which their partner attempts to mirror. After a couple of minutes, ask the pairs to swap roles.

Musical Islands

You will need a carpet square or sheet of newspaper for each child. A CD player and some music are also necessary. Avoid this game if your room has a slippery floor.

Place the carpet squares round the room randomly. Tell the children to move slowly around the full space while the music plays. When the music stops, they must find an island to stand on. Before starting the music again, remove one of the squares. The children are not out if they cannot find an island to stand on in this version of the game. They can share with someone else. A child is out only if they fall off one of the islands.

Musical Mimes

You will need a CD player and a music CD.

This game is a version of Musical Statues. Each time the music plays, tell the children a mime to perform – such as hanging out the washing, digging the garden, driving a car, jogging, painting a picture, and so on. When the music stops, they must freeze. If they move, they are out.

My Object

You will need a box with a lid and a collection of distinctly shaped objects, such as a toothbrush, a can opener, a pine cone, a shell.

Put one of the objects in the box and invite a child to look at it without the other children seeing it. This child then needs to describe what the object is like to the others, without naming the object. The children try to guess what it is. Repeat this procedure with the other objects you have collected.

Pass It Along

The children sit in a circle for this game. Chose a child to start. Tell them an item to mime handing to the person on their left. Their actions need to match the object. The game ends when the imaginary object completes its circuit of the circle.

Ideas for objects are a fragile vase, a hot potato, very sticky paper, a very heavy weight, a wriggly kitten, a tiny screw.

Pizza Parlour

You need a circle of chairs for this game.

This is a variation on Farmyard (see page 31). Go round the circle naming each child one of three pizza toppings, such as tomato, cheese, mushroom. When you call out a topping, the children given that topping name have to stand up and swap seats. Try calling two toppings. If you call 'Pizza parlour', all the children have to stand up and swap seats.

Preference Pairs

You will need a set of pictures cut in half, so that each child has a piece.

Give out the cut-up pictures and ask each child to find the other person with the half that completes their picture. When they have done so, they sit down. Ask the children to talk to their partners and find out one thing that they both like to eat and one thing that they both dislike to eat. Tell them that it does not have to be their favourite item, but they must both agree on the choices. Ask one child in each pair to feed back on their choices.

Rabbit's Ears

The children need to be sitting in a circle for this game. Call the name of a child, who then puts their hands up by each side of their head with each index finger raised, each signifying half of a rabbit's ear. To complete the left ear, the child on the left of the named child puts up their right hand with their index finger extended. The right ear is completed by the child on the named child's right putting up their left hand with their index finger extended.

The named child calls the name of another child in the circle, who makes new rabbit ears, aided by the children on either side of them. The game continues in this way.

Remote Control

Explain to the children that you have a remote control that tells them how to move. When you call out the name of one of the buttons on the control, the children must perform the correct action:

- Play — walk forward at normal pace.
- Fast forward — run on the spot.
- Rewind — walk backwards carefully.
- Pause — jog on the spot.
- Slow motion — walk forwards slowly.
- Stop — stand still.

Ring on a String

You will need a length of string that is as long as the circumference of your circle of chairs, and a curtain ring. Thread one end of the string through the curtain ring and then tie the ends of the string together.

Ask the children to sit in a circle, each holding part of the string loop. Choose a child to leave the circle and cover their eyes while those left in the circle pass the ring around the circle by sliding it along the string loop. On your word, they must stop moving the ring and the child who has it in their hand at that time must grasp it in their fist. The other children must grasp the string in a similar fashion.

The child with their eyes covered is invited back into the circle and allowed to look as the ring resumes its progress. The child in the centre has three chances to discover who has the ring at any point. The players can try to confuse the guesser by pretending to pass the ring when they don't have it. If the child in the circle guesses correctly, they swap places with the child they caught in the circle. If they use their three guesses up and don't find the ring, choose someone for them to swap with.

Send a Smile

Tell the children to sit in a circle. Choose a child to start the game by turning to face the child on their left and giving them a smile. This child then smiles at the child on their left, and so on round the circle.

Send a Squeeze

Tell the children to hold hands round the circle. Choose a child to start the game by gently squeezing the hand of the child on their left, who then passes it on to the child on their left, and so on round the circle. The children cannot pass on the squeeze until they have received it.

Shake your Body

Talk the children through a series of movements that start at their heads and end at their toes. For example:

head nods,	shoulders shrug,
eyes blink,	fingers wiggle,
nose twitches,	arms stretch,
mouth opens,	hips sway,
neck bends,	knees bend,
elbows lift,	feet jump.

Work through the sequence in order twice and then call out instructions randomly so that the children have to listen carefully.

Spin the Bottle

You need an empty plastic bottle for this game.

Tell the children to sit in a circle. Place the empty bottle on its side in the centre of the circle. Choose a child to spin the bottle. Whoever the top of the bottle is pointing at is asked to complete a sentence stem that involves expressing a preference, such as 'My favourite fruit is . . .'.

Tone of My Voice

Teach the children the following chant:

> We're the children of *[name of group]* group
> And we like to speak in this way,
> 'Hello, everybody, we hope you have a nice day.'

Once the children are familiar with the words, ask them to volunteer different ways of saying the chant, such as angrily, excitedly, quietly, loudly, with a bad cold, in a robotic voice. Try these out together to see how they sound.

Two-dice Lotto

Each child will need a small whiteboard and a pen for this game. You will also need two large 1 to 6 dice.

Ask each child to write down two numbers between 2 and 12 on their whiteboard. Roll the dice. Ask the children to add together the numbers shown on the dice. Ask one of them to tell you the answer. If a child has that number on their whiteboard, they can cross it off. The game then continues. The winner is the first child to cross off both of their numbers.

Walking a Tightrope

Ask the children to line up on one side of the room. Explain that they are going to cross to the other side, one by one, miming walking on different surfaces, such as:

- wet, sticky mud;
- a tightrope;
- hot coals;
- a thick sponge;
- the moon;
- a noisy marble floor;
- an ice rink.

What am I?

You will need a collection of pictures of familiar animals for this game.

Fix a picture of an animal to the back of a child. They need to try to work out what their animal is by asking the other children questions about it, such as:

- Do I have four legs / two legs / no legs?
- Have I got fur/scales/feathers?
- Do I live on a farm / in the jungle / in the desert?

Allow the other children to have a turn subsequently.

What Can I Take to . . .?

Ask the children to think of things for a given category, such as items needed for a party. Keep going until the children run out of ideas, then try a different category.

Who Can Think of Something . . .?

Ask the children various questions and choose a different child to answer each time. For example, 'Who can think of something soft/expensive/scary/cuddly/beautiful?'

Wiggle and Shake

Ask the children to find a space to work in. Starting with their heads and working downwards, ask the children to shake and wiggle different parts of their bodies. Begin with their head, then lead on to their shoulders, arms, hands, fingers, hips, legs and feet. Ask them to explore how many of the body parts you mentioned they can wiggle at the same time.

You Make Me Laugh

Put the children into pairs. Tell them to take turns to try to make their partner laugh by pulling funny faces or telling jokes. Their partner has to try to stay serious for as long as possible. Once they laugh, or after a suitable period of time, the children swap roles.

Zoom and Eek

Ask the children to sit in a circle. Turn to the child on your left and say 'Zoom'. This child repeats the action to the child on their left and so on round the circle. If all the children repeat 'Zoom', the round ends when it returns to you. However, if any child says 'Eek' on their turn, this reverses the direction. Each child should be allowed only one chance to say 'Eek' during the activity.

Games that need more space

Some of the games that we use need more space than our room allows.
This applies to some team games and some traditional playground games.

Team games

Beat the Bouncer

You will need two netballs for this game.

Split the children into two teams and ask each team to stand in a circle of
the same size. Choose one child from each team to stand in the centre of
their circle. Give them a ball each. On your word, each child must bounce
their ball to every child in their circle. When a child receives the ball, they
must bounce it back to the child in the centre of their circle. When all the
children in a team have done this, they sit down. The first team to achieve
this is the winner.

Pass Masters

You need two football-size balls for this game.

Split the children into two groups. Ask each group to form a line facing
forwards. Give the child at the front of each line a ball. Tell them that, on
your word, they must pass the ball over their head to the child behind them.
This movement continues down the line. When the child at the back of one
of the lines receives the ball, they run to the front of their line and begin the
action again. This continues until the child who was originally at the front
of a line works their way forward to that position again. The children in that
team then sit down. The first team to complete the sequence and sit down is
the winner.

There are many ways to play this game, by changing how the ball is passed.
Try passing it in the following ways:

- through the children's open legs;
- bouncing it from child to child through open legs;
- over heads and through legs alternately.

Ready to Relay

Divide the children into two groups. Ask each group to form a line facing
down the length of the playing area. On your word, the first child in each
team runs to the end of the playing area and back. On their return, they
touch the hand of the next child in their team, who then sets off. When all
the children in a team have completed their run, that team sits down. The
first team to do so is the winner.

This game may also be played with any number of other actions, such as hopping, skipping, heel-to-toe steps, bouncing a ball, balancing a beanbag on their heads, and so on.

Winning Weavers

Divide the children into two groups and ask each group to stand in a well-spaced-out circle. On your word, the child chosen by each team to begin leaves their place and weaves round their circle, in and out of the standing children. When they return to their place, the child on their left sets off. When all the children in a team have finished, that team sits down. The first team to do so is the winner.

Playground games

Cat and Mouse

One child is chosen to be the cat and another to be the mouse. The remaining children stand in a circle, holding hands. The cat begins outside the circle and the mouse inside. The cat must chase the mouse in and out of the circle, trying to catch them. The children in the circle can try to assist the mouse by blocking the path of the cat. Once the mouse is caught, or when the children are out of breath, choose two different children to take their places.

I Sent a Letter

The children stand in a circle. One child is chosen to walk around the outside of the circle. As they do so, everyone says 'I sent a letter to my friend and on the way I dropped it. Someone must have picked it up and put it in their pocket.'

The child on the outside of the circle then taps the children in turn on the shoulder, saying 'It wasn't you.' However, if they say 'It was you', that child races their accuser round the outside of the circle. If they catch them, the new child takes their place.

Peep Behind the Curtain

One child is chosen to stand at one end of the playing area, facing a wall. The other children stand at the opposite end. They must try to creep up on the child in front and touch the wall without being seen. The child facing the wall can turn round whenever they choose, at which point the other players must freeze. If the child facing the wall sees any child moving when they turn, that child must go back to the start. The first child to reach the wall takes over from the child currently guarding it.

Queeny, Queeny, Who's Got the Ball?

You need a small soft ball for this game.

One child is chosen to be Queeny. They stand facing the wall. The other children form a line behind Queeny, who then throws the ball over their shoulder for one of the children to catch. This child hides the ball behind their back. The other children also put their hands behind their backs. The group then says:

> Queeny, Queeny, who's got the ball?
> Are they short or are they tall?
> Queeny, Queeny, who's got the ball?

Queeny then turns round and tries to guess who has the ball. If they guess correctly, they throw the ball again. If Queeny guesses incorrectly, the child holding the ball takes their place.

Sheep, Sheep, Come Home

One child is chosen to be the farmer and stands at one end of the playing area. A second child is chosen to be the fox and stands in the middle of the playing area. The remaining children are the sheep and stand at the opposite end to the farmer. The farmer calls 'Sheep, sheep, come home.' The sheep reply 'We're scared of the fox.' The farmer tells the sheep 'The fox has gone to Devonshire and won't be back for seven year.' The sheep then attempt to reach the farmer without being tagged by the fox. If a sheep is tagged they return to their end of the playground and must be the fox in the next round.

Spider's Web

The children stand in a wide circle. One child is chosen to be the spider and stands in the middle of the circle. Number the other children 1 or 2 around the circle. These children are the flies. When you call either '1' or '2', the children with that number try to cross the circle to a vacated space. At the same time, the spider tries to tag as many flies as they can. Any fly that is tagged must stand still. Then call the other number. These children must try to cross the circle, releasing as many flies as they can by touching them without being tagged themselves.

Stuck in the Mud

One child is chosen to be the chaser. They try to tag the other children, who run around the playing area. When a child is tagged, they must stand with legs apart as they are stuck in the mud. They can be freed only when another child crawls through their legs. The game is over when everyone is stuck, or after an agreed time.

What's the Time, Mr Wolf?

In the traditional game one child is chosen to be Mr Wolf and the other children line up at the opposite end of the playing area. The wolf should have their back to the other children, facing a wall. The children call out 'What's the time, Mr Wolf?' Mr Wolf calls out a time without looking. The children take the same number of steps forward as the number of hours stated by Mr Wolf. This continues until Mr Wolf says 'Dinner time.' At this point Mr Wolf turns and chases the children back to the end of the playing area. If a child is tagged, they take over as Mr Wolf. If no one is tagged, the same child has to be Mr Wolf again.

If a child reaches the wall before Mr Wolf says 'Dinner time', they tap Mr Wolf on the shoulder and everyone runs back to the start with Mr Wolf chasing them in the same way.

Designated activity of the day

Our designated activities are always held on the same days each week so that the children know in advance what they will be doing. This sense of continuity and structure is important to many children who attend nurture groups.

Monday

On Mondays we alternate between cooking and gardening. We have a small budget that covers the consumables needed for cooking. We were able to obtain a donation for gardening tools and equipment from the local authority. It is worthwhile checking with your local authority to find out if there are any grants available for your group.

On days when we cook, we write up a list of ingredients and the recipe on a whiteboard for the group to read together. We lay out a bowl of warm water, soap and a towel so that we can wash our hands before we begin. The children work in four groups of 3, following the recipe with adult assistance.

Initially, we did not have a cooker in our room. The items that needed to be cooked had to be taken to another building. One of the adults would take a few of the children with them to put the items into the oven, returning later when they were cooked. Sometimes the children ate what they had made as their snack; sometimes they took them home.

During our third year, we received the donation of an electric cooker, which was very welcome.

We tried many different recipes, gradually dropping the ones that the children did not really like. Some of the children's favourite recipes are on pages 112–15.

We always use organic products and additive-free ingredients as some of our children have been diagnosed with a variety of food intolerances and are on special diets. Do make sure that you check on such matters before you begin to cook with a new group, and when a new member joins an established group.

Our gardening involves planning, preparing and maintaining a small plot of land in the school grounds. We sow seeds and plant seedlings, including lettuce, carrots, runner beans and strawberries, and a variety of annual flowers including sunflowers.

The group maintains the school's planters and tubs with summer and winter flowers, which is good for the group's profile. The children receive positive feedback from the school community.

At the end of a gardening session – if there is time – or on rainy days, we use the creative visualisations by Linda-Jane Simpson in *Into the Garden of Dreams*.

Tuesday

Having an attractive room is conducive to working, especially if the children have contributed to this. Each Tuesday we have an art activity which often results in eye-catching displays produced by the children. We sometimes tie the activity in with a theme for the term, such as animals, the seaside, or winter. You can gradually build up a display, adding items to it each week.

We also have stand-alone art projects that produce items to use in other activities, such as masks and puppets for drama.

Wednesday

On this day, we alternate between science and PSHE.

We particularly wanted the science we did together to be enjoyable and memorable, so we choose experiments for their 'wow' factor – such as making volcanoes using bicarbonate of soda and vinegar, and putting white carnations into coloured water to see the colour of the flowers change. Because the experiments we choose capture the children's imaginations, they engage the children effectively and are remembered by them. Two books that we refer to a lot are:

- *Dr Mark's Magical Science* by Dr Mark Biddiss;
- *101 Great Science Experiments* by Neil Ardley.

During the early part of the summer term, we send away for small tortoiseshell caterpillars from Worldwide Butterflies (www.wwb.co.uk). We look after these in an aquarium. They feed on stinging nettles and are easy to care for. The children are fascinated to watch how the caterpillars turn into pupae and then into butterflies, which we release.

We record the science we do as wall displays using models, drawings and photographs. One of the adults writes a brief and simple accompanying description, including comments that the children make.

The PSHE work that we do has a termly focus on a particular aspect of emotional literacy. We include such subjects as understanding our feelings, developing empathy and deepening friendships.

We have used photographs, comic strips and stories as vehicles to promote discussion. We also use sentence stems as a way to give children a structure to express their feelings and thoughts; for example, 'I was kind when I . . .'.

We have adapted aspects of the SEAL provision for small-group work in PSHE, shortening the sessions that we feel are too long for our context.

Thursday

On this day we hold a special games session. This may include some of the team and playground games mentioned earlier. We also use parachute games or have a PE session. On other occasions, we play board games or other group games such as Bingo. All these games give the children valuable experience of taking turns, working with others and learning to lose gracefully.

Each half-term, we hold a drama production on a Thursday. We base this around a traditional tale, which is read by a narrator with the children miming the actions or speaking short lines as appropriate. We perform these to a range of audiences – parents/carers, other school staff and the children's peers.

We feel that there is a lot of value in working on a single project as a whole group. It helps to foster a sense of community and to create a cohesive team. It will also give you valuable opportunities to see how the group members interact and to encourage those children who need support in this context.

There is a sample story on pages 116–18. It includes a number of spoken and non-speaking parts. You can perform it with a limited number of props, or make it a lot more elaborate, should you wish.

Free play

During free play, the children are allowed to play with any of the toys laid out around the room and to choose whom to play with. This is a really valuable time for you to observe the social interactions between children and to see how they put into practice the positive behaviour modelled by the adults in the group.

Independent play adds to the range of experiences that the children are presented with during a session. This part of the session usually lasts for about 20 minutes, depending on the time taken for the designated activity. This period is a good time for the adults to engage in conversation with the children as they play. It is also good for adults in the group to play with any of the more withdrawn children who are on their own, and spend some quality time with them. Sometimes we involve several children in role-play situations.

Set table and clear away equipment

Two children are chosen each day to help to set the table, serve the refreshments and clear away afterwards. This is done on a rota basis, the pairs changing each time so that different children work together.

We display a chart of the children's names alongside the visual timetable on which we indicate the helpers for that day. While these children help to get things ready, the other children clear away the free-play toys carefully. When this is done and the table is set, all the children are called together and allowed to sit down.

Refreshments

We offer the children a choice of water, milk or squash to drink. A snack may be something cooked that day on Mondays. If not, we normally offer a biscuit or some fruit. Make sure provision is made for any child on a special diet.

The day's helpers serve the refreshments while the other children wait, showing good table manners, until everyone has been served. We allow 15 minutes for refreshments, which allows time for eating and drinking, and some conversation. Any more and the children may become restless.

We consider this time a valuable part of the support fabric of the group. The coming together and sharing of food and drink is a satisfying experience for the children. Moreover, sitting together will give you an opportunity to talk to the children in a relaxed and low-key manner. Allow the children to set the agenda.

Washing-up and story time

While one of the adults supervises the clearing of the table, the washing- and drying-up, the other adult can call the remaining children together for a story. We allow the children to sit on large cushions that we have and to choose a soft toy to cuddle. You can use this time to praise those children who have shown good manners at the table by allowing them to choose their seats and cuddly toys first.

Less washing-up liquid next time, I think.

We display a selection of books on a shelf and a different child each day is allowed to select one to be read. We choose stories that fit with a current theme, such as showing kindness, or with an activity the children are involved in, such as growing sunflowers. Occasionally we use a story sack, which includes a story to read to the children, along with props and costumes that the children can use later to act out the story.

Clapping rhymes or songs and ending rituals

The children and adults always say 'Goodbye' to one another at the end of each day, using one of our closing rituals. Some examples follow.

Calming Rhyme

We teach the children this verse as a gentle way to bring the day to an end:

> We are sitting quietly to show that we all know
> That it is now our home time and we're ready to go.
> We are waiting quietly for *[name of group leader]* to say
> 'Goodbye, children. We've had a lovely day.'

Our Day is Nearly Over

You can use this positive verse as an ending ritual:

> Our day is nearly over and soon we will be done.
> We've worked and played together, and we've had a lot of fun.
> There is just time before we go and skip and walk and run,
> To look round at our friends and say 'Goodbye' to everyone.

Roll your Hands

This action rhyme begins with a burst of energy and then brings the children to a point of stillness:

> Roll your hands so quickly,
> Go fast and then go slow.
> Fold your arms and sit up straight
> Because it's time to go.

Sing Goodbye

We sit in a circle for this song. The adult leads by singing the following sentence to a simple tune of their own devising: 'Goodbye *[name of child]*, have a nice home time.'

The ritual ends when the adult has sung to each child in the circle.

Spoken round

The children sit in a circle and each child in turn completes the following sentence stem: 'One thing I enjoyed today was . . .'.

We are Ready to Go

This action rhyme draws the group to a close quietly and effectively:

> Sit on the floor as quiet as can be,
> As calm as a meadow and as still as a tree.
> Put your hands in your lap, rest them there just so —
> Now you have shown everyone that you are set to go.

We use a lot of songs and clapping rhymes in our group. They are good for building group identity and a positive atmosphere. We found that it was best to introduce these gradually, once the children were familiar with the group's routines and were able to sit for a long enough period of time.

The rhymes and songs were immediately very popular and the children always join in enthusiastically. Songs involving movement or responses from the children can be used to good effect. They often want to repeat such songs or rhymes several times. As they become familiar with the rhymes and songs, we allow them to use percussion instruments to accompany their singing occasionally as a special treat.

An extensive selection of songs and clapping rhymes may be found on pages 119–25.

4 Advice on how to make a good structure work

Starting a session well

In the previous chapter, I explained the structure that we use for our nurture group. I am aware that there is often a gap between such an ideal and how it works in practice. With this in mind, this chapter provides you with some additional advice that will help your group to flourish, avoiding some of the issues that we encountered.

As mentioned previously, a great deal can be achieved by making sure that you establish a positive atmosphere at the start of each session. Some of your children may come to the group in a bad mood, following unsatisfactory mornings in the classroom or difficulties in the playground. Make sure the room is ready before the children arrive so that you are free to welcome them in a relaxed manner, with warm words and a smile.

The greeting and circle activities often allow sufficient time and space for children to lose any ill humour and become involved in the positive and relaxed routines of the group.

The children will enjoy anticipating who will be choosing the greeting. You may find that each child has a favourite greeting that they choose every time they are asked. They never seem to tire of such repetition; the same greeting may be used for weeks until a new favourite replaces it. If this happens and you want some variety, you can use your turn to pick one of the lesser-used greetings so that the children do not forget them.

The repetition of activities is a positive feature of nurture groups, allowing children to feel secure through familiarity. This is particularly important for any withdrawn children as it may be several weeks before they feel confident enough to join in. We are careful to give such children plenty of time to make their contribution, and choose them after several other children have contributed, to avoid their feeling under pressure. We find that other group members become very considerate of withdrawn children and offer gentle encouragement patiently.

Use of incentives

The careful use of incentives is one way to help the smooth running of the group. We choose schemes that have personal and group rewards. These schemes are often shown visually in the room as this helps the children to monitor their progress. We change such schemes every term so that they maintain their novelty value.

Each term, we choose an incentive scheme to aid the smooth running of the group. It is important that the aims of such a scheme are realistic and attainable during the term. Children in our group talk about their progress amongst themselves regularly. Because we choose the incentives carefully, the children are always very keen to enjoy them and are motivated to gain their reward.

If the scheme for the group for a term is concerned with general behaviour, we often use a display entitled 'Trees of Kindness'. For this display, each child has to build up a picture of an apple tree. Each time they are kind, they collect a part of their tree – which is made up of one trunk, eight leaves and three apples. Each tree builds from the trunk upwards, and is mounted on a display board, with the child's name alongside their tree. Once a child completes their tree, they are allowed to choose a game for the group to play, enabling the group to share in that child's success. This motivates the other children and encourages an atmosphere of mutual support.

We use similar visual displays for other areas. For example, the children create a sunflower for the 'Good manners garden'. They also build up friendly fish and create sensible snowmen. The former are used to promote good table manners and politeness, the latter to encourage listening skills during circle activities.

The rewards we choose are designed to be empowering and to raise a child's status. Being able to choose something that benefits the group works well. In addition, we make sure that the child receives individual recognition, such as being commended in a whole-school assembly.

Another popular incentive we use is to allow a child to bring a friend to a session during the term when we are using the friendly fish scheme. To qualify for this, a child in the group has to make two friendly fish from laminated body parts. They earn a body part by being kind and friendly to other members of the group. It is a good idea to consult the children's teachers to ensure that they are happy to participate in the scheme.

In addition to these incentive schemes that focus on general group behaviour, the children also have specific individual targets that are reviewed every half-term. These targets are explained in detail in Chapter 6.

Maintaining discipline

While the use of incentives will go a long way towards helping with motivation and positive behaviour, you will need to think about the sanctions that you will use, should the need for them arise.

From the outset, we decided time-out would be the only sanction that we would use. We were fortunate to have a small room off our main room that we could use for this purpose. If such a space is not available, a quiet area of the room will be fine. Our time-out room contained a chair and a table with a one-minute sand-timer on it. We also included a large, soft toy dog that a child could cuddle, and a cushion in case they needed something to punch.

As a child or children join the group, we explain that the time-out room is a place where they may be asked to go to sit quietly, calm down and think about whether certain behaviour was inappropriate. This would include such things as fighting, swearing, spoiling other's games, damaging property, and failing to respond to an adult's request.

We are strict about maintaining clear behavioural boundaries as we feel this is necessary to keep consistent limits and provide a safe environment for all involved. As the time-out room is the only sanction that we employ, the children know what to expect if they transgress. On such an occasion, the child will be instructed to go into the room, sit on the chair for a specified number of turns of the sand-timer, and think about what they need to put right when they rejoin the activity. We ask them to remain in the room until we have spoken to them, if we feel this is necessary. If a problem occurs during refreshments, the child in question is asked to finish their snack and drink in the time-out room on their own.

You will probably find, as we did, that during the first few weeks of a new group you are using the time-out room repeatedly as the children test the boundaries.

We felt quite shell-shocked after some of the sessions by the behaviour we had seen. However, we persisted with a considered use of time-out, while making a concerted effort to praise and model good behaviour and remain positive and optimistic.

After a few weeks, we began to see the benefits and the tide started to turn. As the routines, games and activities became familiar to the children, the use of time-out decreased. The children were getting to know one another better and developing a sense of ownership of the group. With this, we noticed a gradual improvement in behaviour – fewer fights, less swearing, more co-operation and compliance with adults' requests, and so on. In turn, we were able to relax a little more and begin to have fun with the children. I reviewed the diary that I had been keeping of the first term's sessions and could see a steady decrease in the amount of time we spent managing the children's behaviour. We felt great relief that this burden had lightened and that we were able to share in more positive experiences with the children. As the behaviour of the more troublesome children improved, the quieter children felt safer and were able to join in and contribute more to the activities. By the third term, the time-out room was often out of service for days at a time.

We always behave in a manner that assumes a child will comply with our request to go to time-out. This assuredness nearly always engenders the required response. It helps that the children themselves feel that time-out is a fair sanction. Since the children are well aware of the behaviour expected of them, they know when they deserve time-out. Moreover, they know that once their time-out is finished, they are welcome to rejoin the group and enjoy the goodwill of the adults and children, with the incident forgotten.

I had wondered what I would do if a child refused to go into the time-out room, but this has only happened on one occasion. A boy who was new to the group refused to go to time-out. We responded by continuing the activity around him, without his participation. After several minutes of this, he went into the time-out room of his own accord.

Try to make a point of not entering into power struggles with the children as many of them are past masters at gaining attention in this way. One boy decided en route to the room that he was not going to come. I briefly tried to persuade him. When he resisted, I told him that if he refused to accompany me, I would have to leave him where he was and inform the head teacher. I did this, arranging for someone to observe him while I did so. The consequences of his decision not to go with me were sufficiently great to ensure that he did not behave in this way again. It is a good idea to have a plan for children who refuse so that it does not take you by surprise.

We also allow the time-out room to be used by children who are feeling sad, or who just want a few minutes of quiet on their own away from the bustle of the group.

We consider that, along with the positive influence of the incentive schemes we run, time-out is an adequate sanction to deal with all the behaviour issues that arise in our group.

The importance of play

Free play is pivotal to the success of a nurture group as it allows the children the freedom to play with toys and games at their own developmental level. We found that this was, at times, the most difficult part of a session. When we started, there were quarrels and fights as the children competed for certain toys. Sometimes children tried to hide their favourite toys so that nobody else could play with them. We found that any new toy that we introduced became the focus of intense rivalry for a few weeks until the novelty wore off. Don't despair, though, as we found that after a month or so children start to settle down and begin to play really well with the toys and each other.

Sessions involving playing games will allow you to get alongside small groups or individual children. We found it advisable to join in when the children wanted to play competitive games, such as Snakes and Ladders, as they often provoked arguments. During such sessions, you can encourage the participation of the more withdrawn children. Doing a jigsaw with a child provides a good opportunity for a friendly chat.

Getting the most out of drama

We particularly wanted to include drama in the timetable for our group as most of the children had not had positive experiences of this before. Either their poor behaviour prevented them from participating or they were too withdrawn.

Often a performance involves my reading the story while the children, dressed in costume, act it out. Those who are brave enough can also have words to speak, as when using the story on pages 116–18.

The first time we did a play with a group it was absolute chaos. The children were too excited, and many were silly and didn't listen to instructions. However, we persevered as I did not want to repeat the usual formula for these children, whereby their behaviour resulted in their being excluded from an activity.

While we thought the whole thing was a complete shambles, the children were thrilled with their performances and their involvement in a production. By the time the children performed their third play, they were wonderful. They were now old hands and no longer became overexcited. In fact, this production was so good that we invited the head teacher to watch a repeat performance. When you feel confident about your group's level of behaviour during a play, take as many opportunities as you can to perform their work in front of different audiences, such as their classes, other adults in the school, and their parents/carers. Take photographs of the children in costume so that you can make a display of each production for the rest of the school to see.

How to make art work

Our room is filled with displays of the art and craft work that the children have produced. It creates an affirming atmosphere. You may find that some of the children make very little effort over such work when they join your group. Many of our children were unused to producing anything that they expected praise for. Their approach tended to be slapdash and hurried, the idea being to complete the task as quickly as possible, with no thought about the quality of the end-product.

Because a nurture group is small in number of members, you can give each child more help and encouragement than they normally receive in their class. By carefully choosing art activities that can lead to fairly impressive end-products with the minimum amount of skill, you can ensure that all children achieve creditable results. When the children see their work on display and receive positive feedback from teachers and other children, who are impressed with what they have made, they will begin to pay more care and attention to other work they tackle. They will become proud of their achievements and delighted with their standard, which will empower them.

Telling a good story

We found story time quite an ordeal to begin with. Most of the children were unable to sit still for more than 5 minutes, and there were often jostling and petty squabbles on the carpet. The time-out room was used most often during this short time for the first month of our initial group. After this period, the children became more settled generally and adjusted their behaviour accordingly.

We also found that the children fought over the soft toys and cushions provided for this part of the session. We overcame this problem by selecting children, one at a time, to collect a cushion and a soft toy. Our selection was based on who was sitting well and showing good manners at the refreshments table beforehand. This avoided any scuffles on the carpet and ensured each child entered a settled situation when chosen.

The books that we read to the children are ones that are suitable for years 1 and 2. The older children in the group have never complained that they are too young – many have not progressed beyond this level anyway. We usually choose books with amusing stories or lively illustrations that will actively engage the children. To begin with, it is advisable to keep the stories short enough to complete in one session. As the children become able to sit for longer periods and pay more attention, you can choose longer stories that extend over several days.

An incentive that we use is to display a selection of books on a shelf, allowing a child who has been sitting well in refreshments to choose the story to be read that day.

Be flexible

Although you need to plan a timetable for the group, you can to a certain extent be flexible in following it, using your professional judgement as to when to adapt it. If, for example, you have planned a lively circle activity and the children are in an unsettled mood, you might be wise to replace it with something calmer. On the other hand, if you think that the children are really enjoying a games session and playing well, you might extend it by adding a few more games.

During the third term of our first group, some of the children stopped playing with the toys and started to play imaginative games. This would have been fine had we not felt that the violent themes of the games made them unsuitable. We wanted to discourage this sort of play as we also felt that it was unsafe in our setting – the younger children might have been hurt as the children involved became more boisterous and rough. We decided to adapt the timetable by increasing the circle activities and reducing the time spent in free play. After a few weeks we reintroduced free play and the children played with toys in more appropriate ways, the violent games forgotten.

At the end of the day we particularly want the children to leave in a calm frame of mind. If they are restless and silly, we may leave out the clapping rhyme or song. Be aware that on occasion you may need to change the atmosphere of a session by steering an activity in a new direction.

We have found that even when a group was well established, the sessions varied considerably, and we still experienced the occasional 'bad' day. Remind yourself that you will not always get it right, and that it does not take much to unsettle some of the children you will work with. It may be something that is completely outside your control, such as the weather, an eventful morning, a quarrel at lunchtime or a visitor to the group.

You may experience some unsettled behaviour when a child leaves the group and a new member joins. In our experience, new children soon become assimilated into an established group and peace returns quickly.

Maintain good relationships with the school community

Do your best to maintain good relationships with all members of staff. We talk to staff members regularly about the progress of any children from their class who are in our group. We are careful to show that we understand the additional influences and pressures that might prevent a child from behaving as well as might be expected in class. Where possible, we link our targets to those the children have in their classes. Where they are different, we make sure that we explain the reasons for this to the teacher.

The head teacher notifies all the staff and the governor for special needs that they are expected to attend at least one session of the group a year. This is a valuable exercise as it allows staff to see what really happens and shows them a more positive side to troublesome or withdrawn children.

We've only had one difficult issue with staff since our first group was established. This occurred when some teachers decided to use withdrawal from the group, for either a part or the whole of a session, as a sanction. While we understood their thinking, we were unhappy with this practice. We did not view attending the group as a treat; rather it was based on the children's designated timetable and was their entitlement. We also felt it important for the group that all children were involved in the opening rituals of each session. The head teacher explained to the staff that the use of withdrawal as a sanction could not continue. As an alternative, we agreed that we would be happy, on an occasional basis, for a child to bring some work from the classroom that they needed to complete, which we would help them with.

Towards the end of the third term of our first group, we felt brave enough to consider including parents/carers in part of a session. The head teacher approved this, but warned us that we might have very little success as traditionally many of the parents/carers of our children rarely came to review evenings or other school functions. However, we thought that it was worth a try.

The children were very excited about the prospect of their relatives visiting the group. We were careful to say that we would understand if they were too busy as we did not want children to be disappointed if nobody came. The children made cards inviting family members to join us for a drink and snack at the usual refreshment time on a Thursday.

Any chance of a second helping?

We all, children and adults alike, watched the clock anxiously that day. At the designated time, we were astonished to welcome three quarters of the parents of children in the group. Many of them commented on how much the children enjoyed coming to the group and praised the work on display around the room.

The afternoon turned out to be more successful than we had dared hope and we now formally invite parents/carers in every term to share in their children's success.

5 A suggested curriculum for the first term of a new nurture group

This chapter includes detailed plans for the first twelve weeks of a newly established nurture group. Each week includes plans for Monday to Thursday. They are for the autumn term. If you begin in a different term, some of the activities will need adjustment. These plans will give you an in-depth resource covering the content and structure that we consider provides a well-balanced nurture-group curriculum. You can follow them as closely as you wish. You may want to change or substitute activities to suit your group and your current focus.

If you find that you are struggling to fit in all the activities for a session early on, we suggest that you leave out one of the games and/or the clapping rhymes and songs at the end.

In the first week of a new group, it is a good idea to produce a positive display about the group members. Prepare a large display board with a bright background paper and border. Give the display a suitably affirming heading – we used 'Sunflower Superstars'. During the first week, try to take a digital photograph of each child. Print out the photos, along with a name label for each child, and stick these on coloured paper. Put these on the display. By the photograph of each child add some statements about things they like and are good at. We also include two speech bubbles per child in which we write any positive statements that the other children have made about them.

In the first session of a new group, begin by introducing the adults. Tell the children the name of the group and when it will meet. Show the children the visual timetable and explain the sorts of activities that will take place and the general routine of each session. Explain that each day the visual timetable will be changed to show what is happening that day. Tell the children that in every session two of them will set the table, give out the drinks and snacks and wash and dry up afterwards. This will be done on a rota basis.

Explain to the children that their teachers have decided that they would benefit from taking part in the group for a while. Tell them that because the aim of the session is to enjoy the activities and each other's company, there are very few rules. The rules that will be used are to ensure that everybody has a really good time. These are the rules:

- ✪ We play gently.
- ✪ We take turns and share toys.
- ✪ We talk politely to people.
- ✪ We take care of our equipment.

Tell the children that if they are having a bad day and things aren't going right for them, or if they get angry or frustrated, there is a special place where they can go and sit quietly for a while. Explain that sometimes one of the adults may ask them to sit there. If they need to calm down or think about something they were doing, they will have a sand-timer to help them.

Week 1

Monday

Greeting

Ask the children to sit in a circle. Give a child a small object, such as a cuddly toy. Explain that only the child holding the object is allowed to speak. Ask the child with the toy to say 'Hello' and state their name. They then pass the object to the child on their left, who does the same. This is repeated until the round is complete.

Play a second round using the sentence stem: 'My favourite toy is . . .'.

Circle game — Farmyard (*see page 31*)

Circle activity — Magician's Cloak (*see page 33*)

Activity of the day / Free play

As this is the first session, we don't advocate launching into some cooking or gardening. Instead, take the opportunity to introduce the group to the toys and games that are laid out around the room. Allow the children some time to play with the toys and to get to know each other. Remind them of the four rules to ensure everyone enjoys themselves.

Set the table and tidy up

Refreshments

Washing-up and story time

Ending ritual

Don't include a clapping rhyme or song on the first day, but make sure you say 'Goodbye' to each child by name.

 **Tuesday**

Remind the children of the group's rules.

Greeting — Mingle *(see page 25)*

Circle game — None

Circle activity — My Favourite . . .

This builds on the circle rounds of the previous day and lays the ground for the following day's circle activity. Use a range of sentence stems to help the children to get to know each other's preferences. All stems begin with 'My favourite . . . is . . .'. You could explore such themes as fruit, cartoons, sport, and so on.

Activity of the day — Art

You will need A4 paper or card and a range of art materials.

In this activity, each child will make themselves a place mat to use for refreshments, and a name plate for their coat peg. The children may stick a printed version of their name in the centre of their place mat. They could add a print-out of the digital photograph of themselves taken for the group display board. They can then create a decorated border around their name, using any of the art materials available. We've used potato printing, sticky-backed coloured shapes and finger or sponge painting. The name plates can be produced in a similar manner. Make sure you laminate both items before use.

Free play

Set the table and tidy up

Refreshments

Washing-up and story time

Ending ritual

Make sure you say 'Goodbye' warmly to each child by name.

 **Wednesday**

Remind the children of the group's rules.

Greeting — Mingle *(see page 25)*

Circle game — None

Circle activity — None

Activity of the day — PSHE

We based a lot of our PSHE activities for this half-term on the small-group work in the 'New Beginnings' SEAL booklet.

This activity explores starting back at school for a new term. Use the following two rounds to explore this subject:

- One good thing I did in the holidays was . . .
- I am happy to be back in school because . . .

You might want to explore possible answers with the children first.

Play Preference Pairs (see page 35) as a follow-up to this activity.

End the activity with a circle game. Choose a child to start the game by turning to face the child on their left and giving them a smile. This child then smiles at the child on their left, and so on round the circle until the round is complete.

Free play

Tactile play using materials such as sand, dough, finger painting.

Set the table and tidy up

Refreshments

Washing-up and story time

Ending ritual — Sing Goodbye

Lead this ending ritual by singing the following sentence to a simple tune that you make up: 'Goodbye, *[name of child]*, have a nice home time.'

Repeat for each of the children in the group.

 **Thursday**

Remind the children of the group's rules.

Greeting — Mingle *(see page 25)*

Circle game — Pass it Along *(see page 34)*

Circle activity — Spot the Additions

You will need a simple line drawing of a scene, such as a park or shop.

Show the picture to the children and explore what they can see. Explain that they need to look carefully as next week you will add two small details to the picture that they must try to find. If they find the details, they earn a point for the group. If they don't, you score a point.

Ask the children to tell you why the group rules are important. They should say to ensure that everyone has a good time and that the toys and equipment don't get broken.

Activity of the day — Group game

You will need a set of skittles and a ball. We use plastic bottles for skittles.

Set the skittles up and allow each child a turn to knock down as many as they can. We allow three throws per turn. Make a note of each child's score. Play a second game.

Free play
Set the table and tidy up
Refreshments
Washing-up and story time
Ending ritual — Sing Goodbye *(see page 47)*

Week 2

Introduce the Tree of Kindness incentive scheme this week. (See also page 49.) It is a good idea to have a prepared background on one of the display boards, such as a blue sky and green hills, with the title in place. Tell the children that whenever one of the adults sees a child being kind, they will award that child a piece of their tree. Once they have collected a trunk, eight leaves and three apples, they will be allowed to choose a game for the whole group to play.

 **Monday**

Greeting — Clap and Call *(see page 24)*
Circle game — Dice Game *(see page 30)*
Circle activity — Skills and attributes

In order to generate some positive statements for the group display board, use the following sentence stem as a round: 'One thing I am good at is . . .'. Make sure one of the adults records the children's statements.

Activity of the day — Cooking

Making Rice Krispies cakes – see page 114 for the recipe.

Free play

Tactile play.

Set the table and tidy up

Refreshments

Washing-up and story time

Ending ritual — Calming Rhyme (*see page 46*)

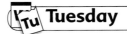 ## Tuesday

Greeting — Clap and Call (*see page 24*)

Play Hunt the Toy (*see page 27*).

Circle game — Two-dice Lotto (*see page 37*)

Circle activity — How Would you Feel?

Give each child a photocopy of page 126 and look at the emotions depicted. Tell the children that you will tell them a situation and ask them to point to how they may feel in that context.

You could use statements such as these:

- It is your first day at school.
- You are about to open a birthday present.
- Your teacher has told you off.
- Your best friend has called you a nasty name.
- It is a rainy day and you have nothing to do.

Activity of the day — Art

Use the art session to make a large sign advertising your group's name.

For our group we made a large sunflower. We painted a large piece of thick cardboard blue for the background, cut out and sponge painted yellow petals and green leaves, and made the centre of the flower by sticking sunflower seeds on to a disc of card. The petals and leaves were then arranged to create the flower. One of the adults cut out letters to spell out 'Welcome to Sunflowers'.

Free play

Set the table and tidy up

Refreshments

Washing-up and story time

Ending ritual — Calming Rhyme (see page 46)

Wednesday

Greeting — Shaky Circle (see page 25)

Circle game — Zoom and Eek (see page 38)

Circle activity — Preferences

Ask each child to complete the following sentence stem: 'One thing I like to do is . . .'. Make sure you note down what the children say so that the statements can be added to your group's display (*see page 57*).

Activity of the day — Science

You will need a plastic bottle with a lid, a darning needle and a bowl.

Before you begin this science experiment, use the darning needle to make a series of holes in the bottle approximately 7cm from its base.

When you are ready to begin, fill the bottle with water and screw the lid on. Hold the bottle over the bowl and unscrew the lid slightly. The water will begin to pour out of the holes. If you tighten the lid, the flow of water will stop.

After you have demonstrated this several times, ask the children why they think it happens. (When you unscrew the lid, the air that comes into the bottle pushes the water out through the holes.)

Give each child an opportunity to loosen the lid. You may need to top the water up as too much air in the bottle will make the flow continuous.

Children enjoy the apparent magic of this experiment.

Free play
Tactile play.

Set the table and tidy up

Refreshments

Washing-up and story time

Ending ritual — Calming Rhyme (see page 46)

 **Thursday**

Greeting — Shaky Circle *(see page 25)*

Circle game — Body Language *(see page 29)*

Circle activity — Spot the Additions

You will need your drawing introduced last week, with two additions made to it.

Ask the children if they can work out what you have added to the picture that you showed them last week.

Activity of the day — Board games

Use this time to play some board games with the children.

Many board games cater only for up to four players. We made some games of our own for six players, so that each adult could supervise a group.

Free play

Set the table and tidy up

Refreshments

Washing-up and story time

Ending ritual — Calming Rhyme *(see page 46)*

Week 3

 **Monday**

As it is the start of a new week, remind the children of the group's rules and the progress of the Trees of Kindness.

Greeting — Clap and Greet *(see page 24)*

Circle game — Fruit Bowl *(see page 31)*

Circle activity — Holiday Destinations *(see page 31)*

Activity of the day — Gardening

When we garden, we divide the children into two groups and take one group outside for 20 minutes, while the other stays inside and talks about an aspect of the growth and maintenance of plants, using illustrated books or actual samples. We also use the indoor session to discuss healthy eating and to taste fruits and vegetables.

If you have a garden space to use, we suggest you use the first session to weed and hoe the soil.

Free play

Set the table and tidy up

Refreshments

Washing-up and story time

Ending ritual — We are Ready to Go (*see page 47*)

 **Tuesday**

Greeting — Clap and Greet (*see page 24*)
Play Hunt the Toy (*see page 27*).

Circle game — In the Driving Seat (*see page 32*)

Circle activity — Look at the Dragon (*see page 33*)

Activity of the day — Art

You will need a piece of card 10cm square for each child, string, scissors, glue and spreaders.

Give each child a square of card. Show them how to wind the string to make coils and wavy lines. Ask them to make a pattern on their card by cutting lengths of string and gluing them down. Tell the children that next week they will make a print of the pattern they've created.

Free play

Set the table and tidy up

Refreshments

Washing-up and story time

Ending ritual — We are Ready to Go (*see page 47*)

 **Wednesday**

Greeting — Whom are you Calling? (*see page 26*)

Circle game — What Can I Take to . . .? (*see page 38*)

Circle activity — Mirror, Mirror (*see page 34*)

Activity of the day — PSHE

Explain that a wizard needs to invent a potion to create a kind group. Put the children in pairs to discuss what a kind group might be – how it would look, what it would feel and sound like. Bring their ideas back to the group. Think of suitable ingredients for the potion, such as kindness, sharing, caring, friendliness, smiles, taking turns.

Free play

Set the table and tidy up

Refreshments

Washing-up and story time

Ending ritual — We are Ready to Go (see page 47)

 **Thursday**

Greeting — Whom are you Calling? (see page 26)

Circle game — Shake your Body (see page 36)

Circle activity 1 — Spot the Additions (see page 64)

Circle activity 2 — Our Group is Special . . .

Put the children into pairs. Ask each pair to think of things that make the group special which they could tell a visitor about. Ask each pair to feed back their findings.

Activity of the day — Group games

Play a selection of team games (see pages 39—40).

Free play

Set the table and tidy up

Refreshments

During this time, discuss possible sandwich fillings for the next week. Have a vote to decide on the three most popular. You will need to consider health and safety concerns when choosing fillings.

Washing-up and story time

Ending ritual — We are Ready to Go (see page 47)

Week 4

 **Monday**

As it is the start of a new week, remind the children of the group's rules and the progress of the Trees of Kindness.

Greeting — Who's Calling? (see page 26)

Circle game — Baked Beans (see page 28)

Circle activity — Afloat in a Boat (see page 28)

After the activity, ask the children to talk in pairs about their ideal destination if they were 'afloat in a boat'. You can discuss possibilities first if you think this will be difficult for your children. Each child reports back their partner's choice.

Activity of the day — Cooking

The children make sandwiches using the fillings decided on last week. Store the sandwiches appropriately until refreshment time.

Free play

Set the table and tidy up

Refreshments

Washing-up and story time

Ending ritual — Spoken round

Each child in turn completes the following sentence stem: 'One thing I enjoyed today was . . .'.

 ## Tuesday

Greeting — Who's Calling? *(see page 26)*
Play Hunt the Toy (*see page 27*).

Circle game — Send a Squeeze *(see page 36)*

Circle activity — 'I' statements

The children make 'I' statements about themselves, such as:

- I am good at . . .
- I like . . .
- I can . . .

Activity of the day — Art

You will need the children's string patterns from last week, paintbrushes, paper and paint.

Give each child their string pattern, a piece of paper, a paintbrush and one paint colour. They paint over their string pattern and place the card paint-side down on to paper. If you have printing rollers, they can use these to roll over the back of their card. If not, they will need to press firmly down on the back. Remove the card to reveal the print.

Free play

Set the table and tidy up

Refreshments

Washing-up and story time

Ending ritual — Spoken round

Each child in turn completes the following sentence stem: 'One thing I found interesting today was . . .'.

 **Wednesday**

Greeting — Lead On *(see page 32)*

Circle game — Express Yourself *(see page 30)*

Circle activity — 'You' statements

The children make 'You' statements about someone they have been paired with, such as:

- You are good at . . .
- You can . . .
- You will . . .

Activity of the day — Science

You will need material for making nests with, such as shredded paper, straw, wool, leaves. You will also need a number of small glass bottles or jars with tops and a thermometer.

Create nests with the children out of different materials. Ask the children which nest they think would keep a mouse the warmest. Note their ideas. Make 'mice' from small glass bottles or jars partially filled with warm water and place one in each nest. Leave a bottle on the side as a control.

Take the temperature of the water in the containers at regular intervals to see which is the warmest nest. Discuss what you are doing with the children and ask them questions, such as 'Why did the water in the control bottle lose a lot more heat?', 'Which do you think will be the best nest and why?'

Free play

Tactile play.

Set the table and tidy up

Refreshments

Washing-up and story time

Ending ritual — Spoken round

Each child in turn completes the following sentence stem: 'One thing I learnt today was . . .'.

Thursday

Greeting — Pass it On *(see page 25)*

Circle game — Clockwork Toys *(see page 30)*

Circle activity 1 — Spot the Additions *(see page 64)*

Circle activity 2 — Act of Kindness

In pairs, the children take it in turns to tell their partner one kind act they have performed that week. Children report back to the group what their partner told them.

Activity of the day — Group games

Use this time to play a selection of group games, such as parachute games, Bingo, skittles, or some of the playground games that are described on pages 40–2.

Free play

Set the table and tidy up

Refreshments

Washing-up and story time

Ending ritual — Spoken round

Each child in turn completes the following sentence stem: 'One thing I enjoyed this week was . . .'.

Week 5

Monday

As it is the start of a new week, remind the children of the group's rules and the progress of the Trees of Kindness.

Greeting — Speak from the Centre *(see page 25)*

Circle game — Rabbit's Ears *(see page 35)*

Circle activity — Cooking comments

As Monday is the day for cooking or gardening, ask the children to use the following sentence stem to explore their feelings about these activities: 'I enjoy making . . .'

Activity of the day — Cooking

Making small sponge cakes – see page 115 for the recipe.

Free play

Set the table and tidy up

Refreshments

Washing-up and story time

Ending ritual — Our Day is Nearly Over (see page 46)

 **Tuesday**

Greeting — Speak from the Centre (see page 25)
Play Hunt the Toy (*see page 27*).

Circle game — Send a Smile (see page 36)

Circle activity — Understanding emotions
You will need enough copies of the expressions on page 126 for one per child.

Choose an expression and ask the children for examples of when they might feel like that. Explain that this doesn't have to be something that has actually happened to them. End with a positive expression.

Activity of the day — Art
You will need paper, pencils and colouring materials.

Ask the children to work in pairs to draw round each other's hands. The children decorate one side of their hand with a colourful pattern. On the other side, they write or draw kind things that hands can do. You can scribe for them if needed.

Free play

Set the table and tidy up

Refreshments

Washing-up and story time

Ending ritual — Our Day is Nearly Over (see page 46)

 **Wednesday**

Greeting — Clap and Call (see page 24)

Circle game — You Make Me Laugh (see page 38)

Circle activity — Animal Empathy
Use the following sentence stem with the children: 'If I were an animal, I would like to be . . . because . . .'.

Activity of the day — Science

You will need three different liquids such as coloured water, vegetable oil and syrup; a large jar; a range of objects such as a cork, a grape and a small wooden block; a straw and a piece of modelling clay.

This activity is to explore the properties of different liquids. Mix the three liquids in the jar and ask the children what they think will happen once the liquids have settled. When the liquids have settled into their separate layers, try dropping the different objects into them one at a time. Ask the children what they think will happen before you drop each one in. Push the straw into the modelling clay so that it stands vertically next to the jar. Mark the level on the straw at which each object floats.

Free play
Tactile play.

Set the table and tidy up
Refreshments
Washing-up and story time
Choose a book to use for tomorrow's drama session. Read it to the children.

Ending ritual — Our Day is Nearly Over *(see page 46)*

Thursday

Greeting — Clap and Call *(see page 24)*
Circle game — Walking a Tightrope *(see page 37)*
Circle activity — Spot the Additions *(see page 64)*
Activity of the week — Drama
Assign the children to different roles in the story you read yesterday. Read it through a few times with them, exploring how they can best act out the story's events. If the children wish, they can script some words for their character too. Use any costumes or props that you have available.

Free play
Set the table and tidy up
Refreshments
Washing-up and story time
Ending ritual — Our Day is Nearly Over *(see page 46)*

Week 6

 Monday

As it is the start of a new week, remind the children of the group's rules and the progress of the Trees of Kindness.

Greeting — Bean and Gone (*see page 24*)

Circle game — Spin the Bottle (*see page 37*)

Circle activity — My dream garden
As this is a day for gardening, ask the children to think about what they would like the group's garden to look like, using the sentence stem 'In my dream garden, I would have . . .'.

Activity of the day — Gardening
You will need potting compost, winter pansies and some trowels.

In two groups, plant out the winter pansies in the school tubs and planters.

Free play
Set the table and tidy up
Refreshments
Washing-up and story time
Ending ritual — Roll your Hands (*see page 47*)

 Tuesday

Greeting — Bean and Gone (*see page 24*)
Play Hunt the Toy (*see page 27*).

Circle game — Button and Key (*see page 29*)

Circle activity — Skill selection
Ask the children what skills they used during this game – staying quiet, listening carefully, disguising their voices. Ask the children to think of other occasions when they need to stay quiet and listen. Make a list, exploring why they made their choices.

Activity of the day — Art
You will need collage materials such as scraps of materials, coloured paper and feathers.

The children create flowers from the collage materials provided. They could write statements on the leaves about what makes the group good. The flowers could be used as part of the Trees of Kindness display.

Free play
Set the table and tidy up
Refreshments
Washing-up and story time
Ending ritual — Roll your Hands (see page 47)

Wednesday

Greeting — Go and Greet (see page 25)

Circle game — Fishes in the Sea (see page 31)

Circle activity — Reflection

Use the following sentence stem to help the children reflect on the past six weeks: 'I have enjoyed doing . . . in our group.'

Activity of the day — PSHE

Ask the children to model the expression a child might have if they were starting at a new school. Explore how they think such a child would be feeling.

Discuss what they could do to help a child who was new to their school.

Free play
Tactile play.

Set the table and tidy up equipment
Refreshments
Washing-up and story time
Ending ritual — Roll your Hands (see page 47)

Thursday

Greeting — Go and Greet (see page 25)

Circle game — Ring on a String (see page 36)

Circle activity 1 — A good player

Ask the children what skills they needed to use in the ring on a string game. Suggestions might include looking carefully, working together, moving their hands slowly. Ask the children to think of other occasions when they might need to look or watch carefully. Make a list of their suggestions, exploring why they put them forward.

Circle activity 2 — Spot the Additions (*see page 64*)

Activity of the day — Group game

You will need three beanbags and a box.

Play the following group game with the children. Divide the children into two teams of roughly equal ability. The children each have a turn to try to throw three beanbags, one at a time, into the box. They score one point per beanbag. Record the scores for each team.

Free play

Set the table and tidy up

Refreshments

Washing-up and story time

Ending ritual — Roll your Hands (*see page 47*)

Week 7

 **Monday**

As it is the start of a new week, remind children of the group's rules and the Trees of Kindness display. Ask the children to describe how they behave when they keep the rules and when they don't keep them. As this may be the start of a new half-term too, you may want to introduce a new incentive scheme.

Greeting — Shaky Circle (*see page 25*)

Circle game — Tone of My Voice (*see page 37*)

Circle activity — Feeling happy

Ask the children to complete the sentence stem: 'I feel happy when . . .'.

Activity of the day — Cooking

Making biscuits using shape cutters – see page 112 for the recipe.

Free play

Set the table and tidy up

Refreshments

Washing-up and story time

Clapping rhyme or song

'One man went to mow' (*see page 121*).

Ending ritual — Calming Rhyme (*see page 46*)

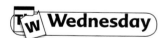

Tuesday

Greeting — Shaky Circle (*see page 25*)
Play Hunt the Toy (*see page 27*).

Circle game — In the Driving Seat (*see page 32*)
Circle activity — Fireworks
In preparation for the artwork that follows, ask each child to complete the following sentence stem: 'If I were a firework, I would be . . . because . . .'.

Activity of the day — Art
You will need black paper, coloured chalk, glitter and glue.

Ask the children to illustrate fireworks using coloured chalks, glitter and glue on black paper. Display the compositions in a prominent place in your room. It works well if you stick it on a black background.

Each child can write out the sentence they said in the circle activity, with help if needed. These can then be displayed alongside their pictures.

Free play
Set the table and tidy up
Refreshments
Washing-up and story time
Clapping rhyme or song
'At the bottom of the sea' (*see page 123*).

Ending ritual — Calming Rhyme (*see page 46*)

Wednesday

Greeting — Speak from the Centre (*see page 25*)
Circle game — What am I? (*see page 38*)
Circle activity — My gift to you
Ask the children to think of a gift they would like to give to someone else in the group. They may choose an object, a skill or a feeling. Make sure everyone in the group gets at least one imagined gift.

Activity of the day — Science
You will need five freshly cut white carnations, five vases and four or five different food colourings.

Show the children the flowers and explain that they need water, which they draw up through their stems, to keep them alive. Fill each of the vases with water, mixing in drops of different food colouring in each. With the children's help, put one of the carnations into each of the vases. Watch what happens to the flowers over the next week.

Free play
Tactile play.

Set the table and tidy up

Refreshments

Washing-up and story time

Clapping rhyme or song
'Michael Finnigan' (*see page 120*).

Ending ritual — Calming Rhyme (*see page 46*)

 **Thursday**

Greeting — Speak from the Centre (*see page 25*)

Circle game — Magician's Cloak (*see page 33*)

Circle activity — How Would You Feel?
Put the children in pairs and give each pair a card from page 126. Ask them to think of a situation that might give rise to their word. They report their findings to the group, who then discuss ways in which the situation might be improved, if it is a negative one.

Circle activity 2 — Spot the Additions (*see page 64*)

Activity of the day — Group activity
Use construction materials, such as building bricks or Lego®, to build a site for a specific purpose – a farm, a safari park, and so on. Ask the children to explain their model to you or the other children.

Free play

Set the table and tidy up

Refreshments

Washing-up and story time

Clapping rhyme or song
'Aye diddle aye' (*see page 123*).

Ending ritual — Calming Rhyme (*see page 46*)

Week 8

 **Monday**

As it is the start of a new week, remind children of the group's rules and the incentive scheme you are currently using.

Greeting — Bean and Gone *(see page 24)*
Circle game — Send a Squeeze *(see page 36)*
Circle activity — Pizza Parlour *(see page 35)*
Activity of the day — Cooking
Make pizzas with the children. You could use mini-pizza bases or large pizza bases cut into segments. The children choose their own toppings from a selection, such as tomato puree, grated cheese, sweetcorn, ham. You will need to cook these pizzas just before refreshment time so that they are warm for the children to eat.

Free play
Set the table and tidy up
Refreshments
Washing-up and story time
Clapping rhyme or song
'She'll be coming round the mountain' *(see page 121)*.

Ending ritual — We are Ready to Go *(see page 47)*

 **Tuesday**

Greeting — Bean and Gone *(see page 24)*
Play Hunt the Toy *(see page 27)*.

Circle game — Send a Smile *(see page 36)*
Circle activity — Smile, please
Discuss with the children why smiling is a positive thing. They may say it makes other people feel happier, it encourages goodwill, it makes them feel better themselves, and so on.

Activity of the day — Art
You will need glue, a digital photo of each child, some pot pourri, and a photo frame made of thick, coloured card that fits the digital photo for each child.

The children use the glue and pot pourri to decorate their photo frame. Once the glue has dried, fix the photo in the centre of the frame. These can be taken home as gifts by the children for their families.

Free play

Set the table and tidy up

Refreshments

Washing-up and story time

Clapping rhyme or song
'On Noah's ark' (*see page 125*).

Ending ritual — We are Ready to Go (*see page 47*)

Wednesday

Greeting — Mingle (*see page 25*)

Circle game — Button and Key (*see page 29*)

Circle activity — Who Can Think of Something . . .? (*see page 38*)

Activity of the day — PSHE
You will need two glove puppets.

This is how we incorporated the small-group activities from the SEAL booklet 'Getting On and Falling Out' into our PSHE activities during the second half-term.

Place a puppet on each of your hands. The children take turns to say 'Hello' to the puppets. Use the puppets to talk to the children about how well they listen and take turns. Ask the children through the puppets what helps them to work well together. Ask your co-worker to write the children's responses on a large sheet of paper to display in the room.

Free play
Tactile play.

Set the table and tidy up

Refreshments

Washing-up and story time

Clapping rhyme or song
'Aiken Drum' (*see page 119*).

Ending ritual — We are Ready to Go (*see page 47*)

Thursday

Greeting — Mingle *(see page 25)*

Circle game — Walking a Tightrope *(see page 37)*

Circle activity 1 — How we walk

Explain to the children that walking often indicates how a person is feeling. Ask for volunteers to show how someone might walk if they were happy, sad, angry, frightened, and so on. Play walking charades. The children have to guess the emotion being depicted by a walk.

Circle activity 2 — Spot the Additions *(see page 64)*

Activity of the day — Group game

You will need the skittles you made previously (see page 61), and three balls.

Allow each child in turn to knock down as many skittles as they can. We allow three throws per turn. Make a note of each child's score. Play a second game.

Free play

Set the table and tidy up

Refreshments

Washing-up and story time

Clapping rhyme or song

'The long-legged sailor' (*see page 125*).

Ending ritual — We are Ready to Go *(see page 47)*

Week 9

Monday

As it is the start of a new week, remind children of the group's rules and the incentive scheme you are currently using.

Greeting — Who's Calling? *(see page 26)*

Circle game — Dice game *(see page 30)*

Circle activity — My object

You will need a box with a lid and a selection of small objects.

Put one of the objects in the box and ask a child to look at it without anyone else seeing. This child then describes the object to the other children without naming it. The children have to try to guess what it is. Repeat this procedure with different children and the other items.

Activity of the day — Gardening

You will need some hyacinth bulbs, flower pots, gardening equipment, soil and labels.

Show the children a hyacinth bulb and explain that it contains food for the flower that will grow out of it.

Use the following sentence stem with the children: 'If I were a tree/flower I would be a . . . because . . .'.

The children take turns to plant a hyacinth bulb in a container. If you can't obtain any flower pots, plastic containers will do. Each child writes their name on a label before sticking it on their pot.

Free play
Set the table and tidy up
Refreshments
Washing-up and story time
Clapping rhyme or song
'This old man' (*see page 122*).

Ending ritual — Spoken round

Sitting in a circle, each child in turn completes the following sentence stem: 'One thing I enjoyed today was . . .'.

 ## Tuesday

Greeting — Who's Calling? (*see page 26*)
Play Hunt the Toy (*see page 27*).

Circle game — Remote Control (*see page 35*)
Circle activity — What can I keep in a treasure box?

Ask the children to think of things they would put in a special box. Tell them they can be as creative as they want, including experiences, things too big to fit in a box, feelings, and so on.

Activity of the day — Art

You will need some old shoe boxes or other boxes with lids, a range of art materials, glue and scissors.

Give each child a box and ask them to decorate it in any way that shows it's their special box. The children can keep work, rewards or anything else special from the group in it.

Free play

Set the table and tidy up

Refreshments

Washing-up and story time

Clapping rhyme or song

'Happy feeling, happy beat' (*see page 124*).

Ending ritual — Spoken round

Sitting in a circle, each child in turn completes the following sentence stem: 'One thing I learnt today was . . .'.

Wednesday

Greeting — High-five Circle (*see* **Shaky Circle**, *page 25*)

Circle game — Musical Mimes (*see page 34*)

Circle activity — Listening

Discuss the importance of listening in the game you have played and what constitutes successful listening – such as looking carefully, thinking about what you hear, asking questions.

Activity of the day — Science

You will need a bowl of water, some Plasticine® and some paper clips.

Place a ball of Plasticine on the surface of the water and watch it sink. Ask the children why they think it did not float. Ask the children to try to make a shape out of the Plasticine that they think will float. Let them experiment. If they produce a successful shape, ask them why they think it floats.

Choose two designs that float successfully, a small one and a large one. Ask the children to guess what they think is the maximum number of paper clips each 'boat' will hold before it sinks. Note down their responses and test the boats.

Free play

Tactile play.

Set the table and tidy up equipment

Refreshments

Washing-up and story time

Clapping rhyme or song

'Mr McGilligan' (*see page 120*).

Ending ritual — Spoken round

Sitting in a circle, each child in turn completes the following sentence stem: 'One thing I learnt today was . . .'.

 **Thursday**

Greeting — High-five Circle *(see **Shaky Circle**, page 25)*

Circle game — Wiggle and Shake *(see page 38)*

Circle activity 1 — Puppets at play

You will need two glove puppets.

Use the puppets to act out playing a game in a friendly manner. Ask the children how they knew the puppets were both enjoying the game. They may mention the polite way they spoke, the language they used, their tone of voice. Write down their responses to display in the room.

Circle activity 2 — Spot the Additions *(see page 64)*

Activity of the day — Board games

Play a range of board games.

Free play

Set the table and tidy up

Refreshments

Washing-up and story time

Clapping rhyme or song

'Copy the leader' (*see page 124*).

Ending ritual — Spoken round

Sitting in a circle, each child in turn completes the following sentence stem: 'One thing I enjoyed this week was . . .'.

Week 10

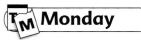 **Monday**

As it is the start of a new week, remind children of the group's rules and the incentive scheme you are currently using.

Greeting — Clap and Greet *(see page 24)*

Circle game — Body Watch *(see page 29)*

Circle activity — Co-operation skills

Ask the children what helped them to work well together in Body Watch. They may say looking carefully, concentrating, and so on.

Activity of the day — Cooking

Making sandwiches using fillings, such as cheese, chocolate spread, jam.

Free play

Set the table and tidy up

Refreshments

Washing-up and story time

Clapping rhyme or song

'Starlight' (*see page 122*).

Ending ritual — Our Day is Nearly Over (*see page 46*)

 ## Tuesday

Greeting — Clap and Greet (*see page 24*)

Play Hunt the Toy (*see page 27*).

Circle game — Baked Beans (*see page 28*)

Circle activity — Talk about the weather

Use the two sentence stems as preparation for the art activity to follow:

- 'I like hot weather because . . .'
- 'I like cold weather because . . .'.

Activity of the day — Art

You will need some rolls of paper or large pieces of card, paints, glitter, sponges and brushes.

Working as a group, the children paint an icy scene to be used as a backdrop for the drama session on Thursday. This is based on the story 'The Snow Queen', which may be found on pages 116–18.

We painted a large piece of card blue and then sponge-painted white paint on top, adding sprinkles of silver glitter. The children painted and then cut out flowers and leaves to lay on the floor to represent the forest.

Free play

Set the table and tidy up

Refreshments

Washing-up and story time

Clapping rhyme or song

'Lazy Laura' (*see page 125*).

Ending ritual — Our Day is Nearly Over (*see page 46*)

 **Wednesday**

Greeting — Whom are you Calling? (*see page 26*)

Circle game — Giant's Garden (*see page 32*)

Circle activity — Friendships matter

You will need two glove puppets.

Remind the children what they considered being friendly means. Ask them to tell you what friends do for each other. Explain that being friendly includes saying nice things to each other. This is called giving compliments. Model this, using the two puppets to give a compliment to each child round the circle. Choose a child to start the round, and ask the children to say something nice to the child on their left. Ask the children how they feel when someone says something nice to them.

Activity of the day — Making invitations

You need paper and felt-tip pens.

Each child prepares an invitation to take home, inviting their family to join them for refreshments and activities at 3 p.m. on Thursday of the following week. You may need to provide the children with a photocopy of an invitation that already has the text filled in. They can then decorate this.

Free play

Set the table and tidy up

Refreshments

Washing-up and story time

Read 'The Snow Queen' story on pages 116–18.

Clapping rhyme or song

'If you're happy and you know it' (*see page 120*).

Ending ritual — Our Day is Nearly Over (*see page 46*)

 **Thursday**

Greeting — Whom are you Calling? (*see page 26*)

Circle game — Express Yourself (*see page 30*)

Circle activity — Spot the Additions (*see page 64*)

Activity of the day — Drama

Practise acting 'The Snow Queen', using any props that you have available. If it has gone well, think about whom you could perform it to at a later date.

Free play

Set the table and tidy up

Refreshments

Washing-up and story time

Clapping rhyme or song

'Clap out, clap in' (*see page 123*)

Ending ritual — Our Day is Nearly Over (*see page 46*)

Week 11

 **Monday**

As it is the start of a new week, remind children of the group's rules and the incentive scheme you are currently using.

Greeting — Free choice

Now that the children have practised all the greetings, place their names, along with the adults' names, in a container. Pull out a name each day and allow that person to choose the greeting. Put their name in another container. This continues until everyone has had a turn. All the names are then replaced in the original container.

Circle game — Get Packing (*see page 32*)

Circle activity — Soft ball challenge

You will need a soft ball.

Explain to the children that you are going to use the following sentence stem in this activity: 'One word to describe *[name of child]* is . . .'.

Ask the children to stand in a circle. Give one child the ball. They pick a child, complete the sentence stem for them, bounce the ball to them, and sit down. The child who receives the ball does the same to another child. This continues until the last child sits down, holding the ball.

Activity of the day — Cooking

Making flapjacks – see page 114 for the recipe.

Free play

Set the table and tidy up

Refreshments

Washing-up and story time

Clapping rhyme or song
'Ten green bottles' (*see page 122*).

Ending ritual — Sing Goodbye (*see page 47*)

 **Tuesday**

Greeting — Free choice
Play Hunt the Toy (*see page 27*).

Circle game — Fishes in the Sea (*see page 31*)

Circle activity — You make me laugh
Ask the children why it is good to laugh; for example, it makes us feel happy, it makes us feel friendly to other people, it chases away sad thoughts.

Activity of the day — Art
You will need coloured paper, felt-tip pens, scissors, glue and glitter. It may be helpful to prepare a template of a star and a Christmas tree for the children to draw round.

In preparation for the Christmas period, we used this session to make some Christmas tree decorations. The children drew round some simple card templates we had prepared, decorated them and cut them out when they were dry.

Be aware of the make-up of your group when you approach this activity. You may decide that it would be better to use an art activity that does not have religious connections.

Free play

Set the table and tidy up

Refreshments

Washing-up and story time

Clapping rhyme or song
'Fee, fi, fo, fum' (*see page 124*).

Ending ritual — Sing Goodbye (*see page 47*)

 **Wednesday**

Greeting — Free choice

Circle game — All Change (*see page 28*)

Circle activity — Skills base

Ask the children to describe what skills they needed to play the game safely so that everyone enjoyed themselves.

Activity of the day — PSHE

You will need two glove puppets.

Act out a quarrel using the puppets. Ask the children to describe how the puppets are feeling after the argument. Emphasise the negative feelings, such as anger, worry, sadness. Ask the children to show you facial expressions that relate to such feelings.

Ask the children to suggest ways in which the puppets might be friends again. Act out their suggestions using the puppets.

Free play

Tactile play.

Set the table and tidy up

Refreshments

Washing-up and story time

Clapping rhyme or song

'Head and shoulders' (*see page 119*).

Ending ritual — Sing Goodbye (*see page 47*)

 **Thursday**

Greeting — Free choice

Circle game — Musical Islands (*see page 34*)

Circle activity — Spot the Additions (*see page 64*)

Activity of the day — Group game

Play some parachute games, ending with a quiet one.

Free play

Set the table and tidy up

Refreshments

Family members join the group.

Washing-up and story time

Clapping rhyme or song

'Clap in, clap out' (*see page 123*).

Ending ritual — Sing Goodbye (*see page 47*)

Week 12

 ## Monday

As it is the start of a new week, remind children of the group's rules and the incentive scheme you are currently using.

Greeting — Free choice

Circle game — Look at the Dragon (*see page 33*)

Circle activity — Back to back

You will need a small whiteboard and pen for each child. Use paper if whiteboards are not available.

In pairs, the children sit back to back. One child in each pair draws a simple pattern. As they do so, they describe each stage to their partner, who tries to replicate the pattern. At the end the children compare drawings and then swap roles.

It will help if you model this activity with your co-worker.

Activity of the day — Cooking

Baking seasonal biscuits using the basic biscuit recipe on page 112. Crush boiled sweets and add these to the mixture to create an attractive stained-glass effect.

Free play

Set the table and tidy up

Refreshments

Washing-up and story time

Clapping rhyme or song

'One man went to mow' (*see page 121*).

Ending ritual — Roll your Hands (*see page 47*)

 ## Tuesday

Greeting — Free choice

Play Hunt the Toy (*see page 27*).

Circle game — Who Can Think of Something . . .? (*see page 38*)

Circle activity — Soft ball challenge (*see page 85*)

Use the following sentence stem for this activity: 'One word to describe our group is . . .'.

Ask the children to stand in a circle, giving one child the ball. They complete the sentence stem, bounce the ball to another child, and sit down. This continues until every child has had a go.

Activity of the day — Art

You will need sheets of card and art materials, including glue, cotton wool, glitter and black card.

The children work in pairs to make pictures of a snowman, which they can take home as they are, or use to make a Christmas card for their family.

Free play

Set the table and tidy up

Refreshments

Washing-up and story time

Clapping rhyme or song

'The long-legged sailor' (*see page 125*).

Ending ritual — Roll your Hands (*see page 47*)

 # Wednesday

Greeting — Free choice

Circle game — Send a Squeeze (*see page 36*)

Circle activity — Friendships

Ask the children to tell you why friendships sometimes break. Ask them how they felt if it has happened to them. Did they manage to repair the damage and, if so, how?

Activity of the day — PSHE

You need card, scissors and felt pens.

Make friendship tokens with the children in pairs. They will need to decide on the shape, colour and message of their token and note these down on the board.

Free play

Tactile play.

Set the table and tidy up

Refreshments

Washing-up and story time

Clapping rhyme or song

'She'll be coming round the mountain' (*see page 121*).

Ending ritual — Roll your Hands (*see page 47*)

 **Thursday**

This is designed as the last session of the autumn term.

Greeting — Free choice

Circle game — Wiggle and Shake (*see page 38*)

Circle activity — Spot the Additions (*see page 64*)

Activity of the day — Party games

Play party games such as Musical Statues, Musical Chairs, Sleeping Lions.

Free play

Set the table and tidy up

Refreshments

Try to have some party food.

Washing-up and story time

Clapping rhyme or song

'Happy feeling, happy beat' (*see page 124*).

Ending ritual — Roll your Hands (*see page 47*)

6 Assessing the children's progress

The on-going assessment of the children who are part of your group is as important as the detailed process by which you initially select them. It is the means by which you judge individual progress, time of reintegration, the value of your group, and how you demonstrate the effectiveness of the group to others.

Setting targets with the children

In addition to the initial selection assessments of the first half-term, we spent time observing and getting to know the children, allowing them time to settle. We then invited the children to discuss their targets with us and help us to decide what they should be. Each child has one target. Some of the targets we use are these:

- I will listen when someone else is talking.
- I will sit at the table until everyone has finished their refreshments.
- I will play with someone during free play.
- I will be gentle with the toys and equipment.
- I will join in with circle games.
- I will remain calm when an adult says 'No'.
- I will share the toys with others.
- I will sit quietly during story time.

The children were very willing to consider aspects of their behaviour which they thought they could improve, and were honest about assessing their progress. If children have class behaviour targets, you could link yours to those.

Once the targets for the next half-term are agreed, they are displayed in the room. Type them up, attach a photograph of the child, and laminate them. We allow the children to draw a tick next to a target each time they achieve it. When a target has ten ticks, the ticks are wiped off and a new target is agreed.

We often begin a session by asking the children to remind us and themselves of their targets.

The majority of children do improve their target behaviours. The nature of a small group means you can remind each child regularly of their target and provide lots of positive feedback. Sometimes you may have to revisit a target to help a child who has slipped back into old habits.

As we mention targets on a regular basis, the children also know what everybody else's are as well as their own, and they are diligent about reminding others what they should be doing. This shows us that the children are willing to take collective responsibility for behaviour within the group, which is a prime aim of circle time. In fact, as the group progressed the children became very solicitous of each other and were always ready to encourage and praise fellow members.

Assessing children's progress

In addition to the on-going assessment that takes place, we have a formal review of each child's progress every half-term using the table on page 127. At the end of the first term, we use these tables as the basis for discussions between ourselves and relevant class teachers. Copies, along with notes from the meeting, are given to the head teacher and the SENCo.

Towards the end of the second term, we ask teachers to complete a Boxall Profile for those of their children who are in the group. This gives us a clear indication of the progress they are making and in which areas, and where they need to develop. This is a beneficial exercise even if the child has moved on to a different teacher in the intervening period.

The results of a child's profile can be used to decide whether they need to remain in the group or are ready to be reintegrated into the classroom. You can also assess the effectiveness of present strategies and approaches, changing them accordingly.

Reintegrating children

If it has been agreed that a child is ready to be reintegrated, a return to the classroom form is completed by one of the adult workers with the child. This includes information on the child's favourite activities in the group, as well as photographs of them keeping to the rules of the group. These images help to remind the child of what is expected of them in their classroom. They start by spending one or two afternoons in their classroom. In order to help effect a successful reintegration, their class targets need to be designed to guarantee successful outcomes. You do not want their healthy self-esteem to plummet, causing a return of inappropriate behaviour. This continues over half a term until a child is fully integrated in their class. This is not a fixed period and we have varied it depending on the child involved. It is important to monitor their progress closely during this phase. We ask them to share what they have been doing in class with the rest of the group during circle time, so that we can encourage them.

Assessing our success

All of the children who have attended our group have shown an improvement in their behaviour. Their Boxall Profiles showed that in over half the children this was carried over to their classroom. The school has not needed to exclude any children since we have been running our nurture group. Our greatest success has been with withdrawn children and those with learning difficulties. The former have been able to contribute more actively in the classroom, while the latter blossomed in an environment where the demands made on them did not exceed their capabilities. They have benefited from enhanced self-esteem.

Of the remaining children in our initial group, all but one had shown improved behaviour, although this was not always observed in the classroom. We felt that one child had made no progress during the first year, but hoped that a further year with us might effect some positive changes. This was, in fact, the case and by the end of his second year his behaviour had improved considerably.

In order to maintain the standard of the group and review its effectiveness, we also produce questionnaires for parents and staff to complete (pages 108 and 128). Our aim is to help children to become capable of functioning at a reasonable level in the classroom. We do not wish to be complacent and assume that we are doing the right thing. By examining the completed questionnaires, we can assess our effectiveness.

Surviving an OFSTED inspection

During the group's fourth year, the school had an Ofsted inspection. Having watched the group in operation and questioned us at length, the inspector concerned acknowledged the good work we were doing. We felt that certain important features contributed to this successful pronouncement. Our advice would be as follows:

- ✪ Keep clear records of the children's progress. Inspectors will give little credence to anecdotal evidence, but they will be reassured about a child's progress by looking at their Boxall Profiles.
- ✪ Be clear about your goals and aims and, if possible, support them with written material.
- ✪ Have clear guidelines for the processes involved in your group, such as selection, evaluation and reintegration.

✪ Keep records of your timetables and curriculum content, making sure you can justify what you do.

✪ Maintain the quality and accountability of your work, regularly asking for feedback from the teaching staff and parents.

✪ Follow good practice at all times so that you will not have to change what you do and unsettle the children.

✪ Have a clear justification to explain why a child's attendance in your group is more suited to their educational entitlement than their being in their usual classroom.

7 Final thoughts

Having conceived and set up the group, we learnt valuable lessons through our experiences. The advice and guidance in this book are a result of what running the group taught us. In summary, we believe that our group is successful because:

- ✪ children receive individual attention;
- ✪ the size of the group encourages withdrawn children to participate;
- ✪ sessions are broken down into small parts;
- ✪ time-out provides a consistent sanction;
- ✪ incentives are chosen with care;
- ✪ children are given unconditional warmth and acceptance;
- ✪ routines provide security;
- ✪ inappropriate behaviour is quickly addressed;

- ✪ activities are selected to guarantee success;
- ✪ activities are engaging and involving;
- ✪ there is a focus on group-building activities;
- ✪ children can shine because of the group's criteria for success;
- ✪ children can be given a different identity from the often negative one they have in the classroom;
- ✪ the definition of acceptable and unacceptable behaviour is clear;
- ✪ there is plenty of humour and fun.

We are very pleased with the progress of the children we have worked with, and we feel that school has become a more enjoyable experience for them. They have gained a reserve of positive experiences and have learnt to co-operate with others. They are no longer daunted by school work, and do not assume they will always fail. We feel that the group has been a satisfying experience for all involved. It has been challenging on occasions – but most worthwhile things are.

We wish you and your children every success with your nurture group.

8 Resources

Useful publications available from LDA

Mosley, J. and H. Sonnet (2002) *101 Games for Self-Esteem*

Mosley, J. and H. Sonnet (2002) *Making Waves*

Mosley, J. and H. Sonnet (2003) *101 Games for Social Skills*

Mosley, J. and H. Sonnet (2005) *Better Behaviour through Golden Time*

Mosley, J. and H. Sonnet (2006) *101 Games for Better Behaviour*

Mosley, J. and H. Sonnet (2006) *Helping Children Deal with Anger*

Mosley, J. and H. Sonnet (2006) *Helping Children Deal with Bullying*

Mosley, J. and H. Sonnet (2007) *Helping Children Deal with Conflict*

All these resources are published by LDA. For information about the full range of Jenny Mosley's books and resources, please contact LDA Customer Services on 0845 120 4776 or visit our website at www.LDAlearning.com

Other publications

Ardley, N. (2006) *101 Great Science Experiments*. Dorling Kindersley: London

Bennathan, M. and M. Boxall (2000) *Effective Intervention in Primary Schools*. David Fulton Publishers: Oxford

Bennathan, M. and M. Boxall (2006) *The Boxall Profile: Handbook for Teachers* (No. 7). Network Group: London

Biddiss, M. (2006) *Dr Mark's Magical Science*. Hands on Publishing: Birmingham

Bishop, S. (2007) *Running a Nurture Group*. Paul Chapman Publishing: London

Boxall, M. (2002) *Nurture Groups in School: Principles and Practice*. Paul Chapman Publishing: London.

Mosley, J. and H. Sonnet (2005) *Clapping Games*. Positive Press: Trowbridge

Mosley, J. and H. Sonnet (2005) *Playground Games*. Positive Press: Trowbridge

Mosley, J. and H. Sonnet (2005) *Singing Games*. Positive Press: Trowbridge

The Nurture Group Network (2006) *Nurture Group Principles and Curriculum Guidelines*. Network Group: London

Simpson, L.-J. (2001) *Into the Garden of Dreams*. Brilliant Publications: Dunstable

Useful organisations

Child Line
Weston House
42 Curtain Road
London
EC2A 3NH
020 7825 2500
www.childline.org.uk

Jenny Mosley Consultancies
28a Gloucester Road
Trowbridge
Wiltshire
BA14 0AA
www.circle-time.co.uk

The Nurture Group Network
004 Spitfire Studios
63–71 Collier Street
London
N1 9BE
020 7833 9603
www.nurturegroups.org

Positive Teaching
11 Delmore Road
Frome
Somerset
BA11 4EG
01373 465708
www.positiveteaching.co.uk

Nurture group policy

Introduction

- ✪ Our nurture group provides a modified curriculum in an environment based on the principles advocated by Marion Bennathan and Marjorie Boxall.

- ✪ The group is an intervention for those children who are unable to access learning successfully in their mainstream classroom. This may be due to fragmented or deprived early childhood experiences, learning difficulties or disorders on the autism spectrum.

- ✪ Our group meets on four afternoons a week, with the children spending the mornings and all day on Friday in their own classes.

- ✪ The group caters for up to twelve children from years 1 to 4.

- ✪ Two experienced members of staff run our group. In the absence of one of these team members, a designated member of staff takes their place.

Our aims

- ✪ To provide a small-scale setting in which children can experience nurturing care from two caring adults, who actively work towards enabling their successful reintegration.

- ✪ To have a predictable, calm and purposeful environment and timetable, free from curriculum pressures.

- ✪ To develop self-esteem and social skills.

- ✪ To develop relationships between adults and children, building trust, confidence and reliability.

- ✪ To develop responsibility for self and others.

- ✪ To help children learn appropriate behaviour.

- ✪ To help children learn to make decisions and wise choices through understanding the consequences of certain ways of behaving.

- ✪ To work in partnership with parents and teachers to achieve consistency of approach at home and school.

- ✪ To provide on-going assessment using the Boxall Profile.

- ✪ To prevent possible exclusion.

Inclusive practice

In the nurture group, we recognise that every child matters and aim to respond to each child's needs, taking into consideration their:

- ✪ cultural background;
- ✪ life experiences;
- ✪ strengths;
- ✪ communication needs;
- ✪ emotional and social needs;
- ✪ developmental needs;
- ✪ physical needs.

Setting

- ✪ The nurture group is a self-contained setting with toilet and kitchen facilities.
- ✪ The room has a homely atmosphere.
- ✪ The room provides space for a formal work area, play areas and a quiet area.
- ✪ A small adjoining room provides a time-out facility for children who need to address emotional or behavioural difficulties.

The role of the adult workers

- ✪ The role of the adult is to sustain nurturing relationships with the children who attend.
- ✪ They should be good role models, demonstrating appropriate and positive behaviour that is consistent and continuous.
- ✪ They need to recognise that it is through a positive and affirming relationship that a child can perceive themselves as worthwhile.

The curriculum

- The nurture group provides a modified curriculum that is suited to the children's needs.
- Mathematics and literacy are covered during the mornings in the child's own classroom.
- The group covers art, science, PSHE, drama and PE. Areas such as cooking and gardening are also included.
- The group sessions are divided into small chunks of time with each activity serving a clear purpose.
- Each session offers the security of a consistent and familiar structure as follows:

  greeting ritual;

  circle-time activities;

  designated activity of the day;

  free play;

  laying table and tidying up equipment;

  refreshments;

  washing-up and story time;

  clapping rhyme or song;

  ending ritual.

- The circle-time activities focus on the following valuable activities:

  turn-taking;

  watching and listening;

  using expressive language;

  learning from others;

  trying something new;

  developing a positive attitude to participation;

  forming positive relationships;

  using agreed codes of behaviour;

  initiating activities with other children;

  learning to respond to sanctions;

  considering the rights and needs of themselves and others.

- All activities are weighted towards the children's PSHE development.
- Activities are designed to offer children criteria for doing well that guarantee success. The aim is to boost a child's self-esteem and sense of identity.

Assessment

✪ Children involved in the group are assessed using the Boxall Profile on a termly basis.

✪ After an assessment findings are discussed with the school's SENCo and linked to a child's targets, both within the group and their classroom.

✪ A written assessment is provided at a child's annual review, if appropriate.

✪ In addition, half-termly records of each child's social and emotional development are kept.

Referral

The following types of children are considered for inclusion in the group:

✪ those who appear to be emotionally insecure, which could present itself as lack of self-acceptance, low self-worth or a lack of trust;

✪ children who are withdrawn and unresponsive;

✪ children with poor social skills, who cannot share or are demanding or uncooperative;

✪ those with a poor attention span;

✪ children who demonstrate immature behaviour;

✪ children who behave aggressively, impulsively, or inappropriately in other ways;

✪ children who find change upsetting;

✪ children who appear unable to integrate into a mainstream classroom.

Referral procedure

✪ When a vacancy arises in the nurture group, class teachers are invited to put forward children whom they feel will benefit from the group.

✪ These children are assessed using the Boxall Profile to determine their eligibility.

✪ If a decision is made to invite a child to join the group, a letter is sent home to inform their parents/carers of the offer of a place. They are invited to a consultation to discuss this.

✪ Following agreement in this meeting, the child is invited to join the group.

Partnership with parents and carers

- ✪ We recognise the importance of involving the parents/carers of a child in their education.
- ✪ Each parent receives a copy of our leaflet explaining the group and detailing who we are and what we do.
- ✪ We aim to keep parents/carers informed of their child's progress and provide them with support and advice.
- ✪ Parents/carers are invited to tea and refreshments once a term to see what their children have been doing and to join in some activities.
- ✪ The nurture group staff are available after school on Thursday to discuss any concerns or issues that parents/carers may have.

Reintegration

- ✪ The period of reintegration is generally carried out over a period of a half-term, during which a child's responses are carefully monitored.
- ✪ The point at which a child is reintegrated into their classroom full-time is based on the results of the Boxall Profile, the nurture group workers' assessments and the class teacher's observations.
- ✪ When a child is thought ready to return to the classroom, a programme of gradual reintegration is initiated, usually beginning with one or two sessions a week.
- ✪ One of the nurture group workers will complete a return to the classroom form with the child to help them to understand what will happen and what will be expected of them.
- ✪ The child's class teacher speaks about a child's nurture group experiences in a class circle time that includes the child in question.

Success criteria

We shall be a successful nurture group if:

- ✪ we provide affirming, positive and manageable sessions;
- ✪ time-out is seen as an effective sanction;
- ✪ the incentives used are seen as desirable by the children;
- ✪ what is acceptable and unacceptable behaviour is made clear;
- ✪ any inappropriate behaviour is spotted quickly and dealt with;
- ✪ a session's routines provide security;
- ✪ the activities are tailored to guarantee success;
- ✪ the children are given unconditional warmth and acceptance;
- ✪ there is a focus on group-building activities;
- ✪ the children have greater attention in class;
- ✪ the children can gain a more positive identity than the one they have 'learnt' elsewhere;
- ✪ the children gain confidence and are more willing to take on new challenges;
- ✪ the sense of success enables the children to put more effort into their work;
- ✪ there is plenty of humour and fun.

Our nurture group aims

Our group aims are:

- ➔ to provide a small-scale setting in which children can experience nurturing care from two caring adults, who actively work towards enabling their successful reintegration;

- ➔ to have a predictable, calm and purposeful environment and timetable, free from curriculum pressures;

- ➔ to develop self-esteem and social skills;

- ➔ to develop relationships between adults and children, building trust, confidence and reliability;

- ➔ to develop responsibility for self and others;

- ➔ to help children learn appropriate behaviour;

- ➔ to help children learn to make decisions and wise choices through understanding the consequences of certain ways of behaving;

- ➔ to work in partnership with parents and teachers to achieve consistency of approach at home and school;

- ➔ to provide on-going assessment using the Boxall Profile;

- ➔ to prevent possible exclusion.

Criteria for attending our nurture group

We have our own criteria to help us assess if it is appropriate to refer a child for inclusion in our nurture group. We consider the following children:

➔ children who appear to be emotionally insecure — which may present as lack of self-acceptance, low self-worth or a lack of trust;

➔ children who are withdrawn and unresponsive;

➔ children with poor social skills, who cannot share, are demanding or uncooperative;

➔ children with a poor attention span;

➔ children who demonstrate immature behaviour;

➔ children who behave aggressively, impulsively or inappropriately in other ways;

➔ children who find change upsetting;

➔ children who appear unable to integrate into a mainstream classroom.

Dear

We run a small group on four afternoons each week for a number of children from years 1 to 4. The group is designed to help those children who have difficulty accessing the curriculum in their mainstream classroom. It helps these children to develop the skills needed for learning. Its aims are to improve the children's looking, listening and concentrating skills, and to use activities that promote use of spoken language and willingness to join in.

Children who attend this group are selected using carefully considered criteria. They benefit greatly from working in a group of no more than twelve children. Your child has been chosen as someone who would gain a great deal from joining this group for a while. This is not a permanent move. Your child will return to their mainstream class for afternoon sessions in due course.

We hope that you will support the work that is carried out in the group. The adults who run the group will be in contact shortly through your child's class teacher to arrange a convenient time to talk to you about the work your child will be involved in and to answer any queries that you might have.

Yours sincerely

Parent/carer interview form

Name of child: .... Date: ....

Name of parent/carer: ....

1   Briefly describe the character of your child.

....

2   How do you feel they get on at school?

....

3   What do you think are their main difficulties at present?

....

4   Has your child had difficulties in the past?

....

5   Have they previously had any help with their difficulties? If so, what?

....

6   How do you feel about your child attending our nurture group?

....

7   Is there anything else you would like to tell us about your child?

....

Dear parents/carers

Your views on our nurture group are vital to its continuing success. In order to help us make the most of what you think, please take a short time to complete the questionnaire below. Please circle the number that relates to how you feel about the related statement, with '0' standing for 'strongly disagree' and '5' for 'strongly agree'. If you have any further comments, please use the space at the bottom of the page.

Many thanks.

Name of child:						
My child has benefited from their time in the nurture group.	0	1	2	3	4	5
I have been kept informed about the group.	0	1	2	3	4	5
I have been kept up to date about my child's progress.	0	1	2	3	4	5
I have found the group's co-workers approachable and helpful.	0	1	2	3	4	5
The group has had a positive effect on my child at home.	0	1	2	3	4	5
The group has had a positive effect on my child at school.	0	1	2	3	4	5
My child gets on better in their own class now.	0	1	2	3	4	5

Any further comments about our group:

Visual timetable cards

Greeting

Circle activity

Activity of the day

Free play

Art

Drink and snack

Washing-up

Story time

Clapping rhyme

Team games

Gardening

Cooking

Singing

Drama

Group game

Toys and games

Cards for a visual timetable: Greetings

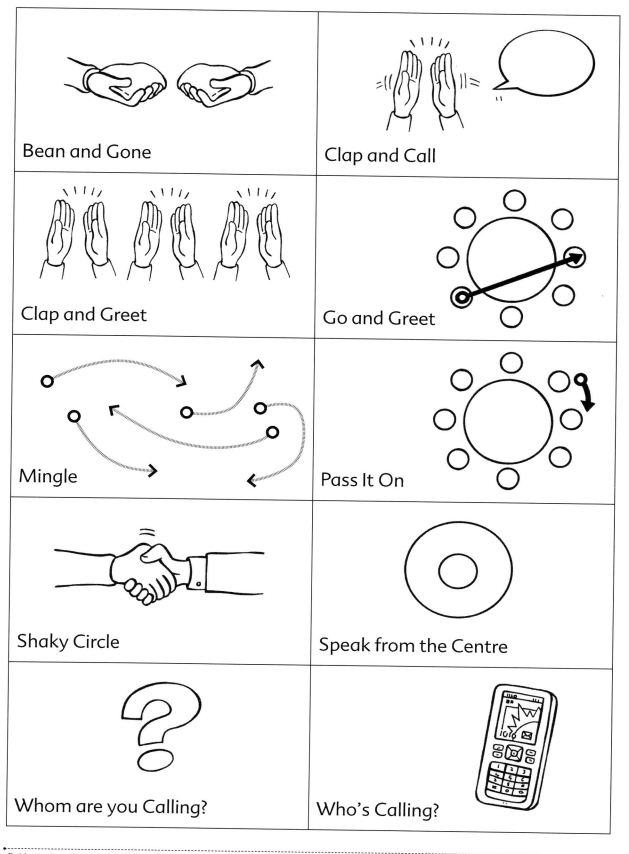

Bean and Gone	Clap and Call
Clap and Greet	Go and Greet
Mingle	Pass It On
Shaky Circle	Speak from the Centre
Whom are you Calling?	Who's Calling?

Useful recipes

Basic biscuits

100g butter
100g caster sugar

1 medium egg
200g plain flour

Cream the butter and sugar together in a mixing bowl. Add the egg and slowly beat it into the mixture. Fold in the flour in small batches. When everything is combined, roll out the biscuit mix on a floured surface and cut the biscuits out with a cutter of your choice. Bake at gas mark 5, 190 °C (375 °F) for 10 minutes, or until the biscuits are pale brown in colour. Allow the biscuits to cool on a wire rack.

Cheese straws

75g Cheddar cheese
100g plain flour
1 teaspoon baking powder

50g butter
1 medium egg

Grate the cheese into a mixing bowl. Add the flour and baking powder. Cut the butter into small pieces and add them to the bowl, combining the ingredients by rubbing the mixture together using your fingertips.

Separate the egg yolk and white into different containers (it may be better for an adult to do this). Add the yolk to the mixture and mix to a stiff dough using a wooden spoon. Divide the dough in half and pat each half into a rectangular shape about 23cm long by 8cm wide. Make short blocks of dough by cutting the blocks across the width of the rectangles. Cut into straws, with each straw about the width of an adult's index finger. Place the straws on a baking tray, which you do not need to grease. Bake in the oven at gas mark 7, 220 °C (425 °F) for 8 to 12 minutes, or until golden brown. Allow the straws to cool on a wire rack.

Chocolate chip cookies

100g butter at room temperature
100g light Muscovado sugar
1 tablespoon golden syrup

150g self-raising flour
85g chocolate chips

Beat the butter and sugar together in a bowl until light and creamy.
Mix in the golden syrup. Fold in half the flour. Stir in the chocolate chips
and the remaining flour. Work the dough together with your fingertips.

When combined, divide the dough into 14 small balls and place them
well apart on baking trays. Do not flatten the balls. Bake the cookies
in the oven at gas mark 4, 180 °C (350 °F) for 10 to 12 minutes until
golden at the edges. Allow the cookies to cool on a wire rack.

Chocolate muffins

175g butter at room temperature
175g Demerara sugar
3 medium eggs
1 teaspoon vanilla essence
250g self-raising flour

1 teaspoon baking powder
50g cocoa
100g chocolate chips
150ml milk

Cream the butter and sugar together until the mixture is pale and
creamy. Beat in the eggs one at a time. Add the vanilla essence.
Stir in the flour, baking powder and cocoa, and fold in the chocolate
chips. Finally, stir in the milk.

Divide the mixture between 12 paper muffin cases. Bake in the oven
at gas mark 6, 200 °C (400 °F) for 15 minutes. Allow the muffins to
cool on a wire rack.

Useful recipes

Flapjacks

100g butter	60g oats
1 tablespoon golden syrup	15g self-raising flour
100g Demerara sugar	75g crushed cornflakes

Melt the butter and syrup gently in a pan. Remove from the heat and stir in the sugar, oats, flour and cornflakes. Spread the mixture in a greased baking tray at least 2cm deep. Bake in the oven at gas mark 5, 190 °C (375 °F) for 15 to 20 minutes. Cut into rectangles and cool on a wire rack.

Rice Krispie cakes

A bar of cooking chocolate   A box of Rice Krispies

Break the chocolate into bits and place them in a heatproof bowl. Carefully place the bowl over a saucepan of recently boiled water held by an adult. Stir the chocolate until it has melted. Remove the bowl from the saucepan. Add Rice Krispies until a stiff mixture is created. Spoon the mixture into cake cases and leave to cool.

Chocolate birds' nests

A bar of cooking chocolate   A packet of mini chocolate eggs
A box of Shredded Wheat

Break the chocolate into pieces and place them in a heatproof bowl. Break up several Shredded Wheats. Carefully place the bowl over a saucepan of recently boiled water held by an adult. Stir the chocolate until it has melted. Remove the bowl from the saucepan. Add the strands of Shredded Wheat and mix until all is combined as a stiff mixture. Spoon the mixture into cake cases. Make a small indentation in the top of each nest. Leave to cool and decorate with a couple of mini chocolate eggs.

Useful recipes

Small sponge cakes

100g butter at room temperature   2 medium eggs
100g caster sugar   150g self-raising flour

Cream the butter and sugar together until pale and creamy. Beat in the eggs one at a time, mixing well. Fold in the flour. When combined, spoon the mixture into 12 cake cases and bake in the oven at gas mark 6, 200 °C (400 °F) for 10 to 15 minutes. Allow the cakes to cool on a wire rack.

These small cakes can be iced with butter icing. For this you will need:

140g butter at room temperature   1—2 tablespoons milk
280g icing sugar

Beat the butter together with half of the icing sugar. Add the rest of the icing sugar with one tablespoon of milk. Combine until creamy. You may need more milk or icing sugar to get the consistency right. Spread the icing on top of the cakes.

Alternatively, you can use the icing to create butterfly cakes. Cut the top off a cake and cut this piece in half. Put butter icing on top of the cake and insert the two smaller pieces of cake into the butter icing, creating butterfly wings.

Useful recipes

The Snow Queen

Cast

Anna
Tom
Their mother (one of the adults)
The Snow Queen
Two guards
Two birds

Two mice
Toby the dog
Wizard
Wizard's apprentice
Narrator (one of the adults)

You may adapt the number of characters to suit the size of your group.

There were once a brother and sister named Anna and Tom who lived with their mother in a cosy little cottage at the edge of a forest. The children played happily all day while their mother was busy. The children were allowed to play in the garden, but their mother told them that they should never go into the forest as it was dangerous. One day, the little girl saw some beautiful flowers at the edge of the forest. 'Mum would be so pleased with those flowers. They would look very pretty on the windowsill. I will go and pick them for her.'

Tom was worried and said, 'But we're not allowed to go into the forest, Anna.'

'I'm not going into the forest, Tom. The flowers are just at the edge.'

Tom was worried but as he could see Anna, he thought everything would be all right. The problem was that when Anna had picked the first flowers, she saw some better ones a little further on, and when she had picked those she saw some more. Before long, she had wandered into the forest.

Tom saw Anna disappear. He was very worried and didn't know what to do. If he told his mother, Anna would get into trouble. He decided to run after her and tell her to come back before their mother noticed. Tom slipped into the forest and began to call Anna's name. Eventually Anna appeared and said, 'Here I am. Look at my lovely bunch of flowers.'

'Very nice,' said Tom, 'but we must get back quickly before Mum misses us.' Unfortunately, try as they might, they couldn't find their way back. They were lost, and it was getting darker and colder. Then in the middle of the forest, they saw a large white palace.

'Oh good!' said Anna, 'There is sure to be someone there who can help us, and we can warm up before they show us the way home.' But what the children did not know was that this was the palace of the wicked Snow Queen. Before they knocked on the gates of the palace, they swung open. Tom and Anna went nervously inside.

They saw a large hall and in it a beautiful woman dressed in white seated on a throne. On either side of her stood a tall, strong guard. 'What are you two strangers doing in my palace?' she asked.

'We were picking flowers in the forest and we lost our way,' Anna explained. 'Please could you help us to get back home? Our mum will be very worried about us.'

The Snow Queen said that she had always wanted a little girl to be her ice princess, so she was going to keep Anna. She didn't want Tom and told the guards to throw him out. He wandered in the gloomy forest until he was so exhausted that he had to lie down and sleep. Luckily for Tom, a pair of kindly birds found him and covered his body with dry leaves so that he would not freeze to death. When he awoke the next morning, he was amazed to find his leafy blanket. Soon he heard a squeaking noise near his feet. Two little mice appeared from a hole in the ground. They were holding some nuts and fruit, which they placed on the ground. They did this several times, bringing enough food to satisfy Tom's hunger before disappearing down the hole.

Just as Tom had finished eating, he heard a loud rustling. Out from behind the trees bounded a large dog. It barked loudly as it ran up to Tom. Tom patted the dog gently under its chin. 'I wonder where you've come from,' he said. 'I wish that you could help me rescue my sister and get back home.'

The Snow Queen

The dog walked away a few paces and turned to look at Tom before setting off again. It did this several times, and it seemed to Tom that the dog wanted him to follow. Well, it was better than being on his own, so Tom set off. When they had walked for a while, it began to feel warmer and brighter. Tom could see a little house in the distance and it looked as if that was where the dog was heading. When they reached the house, Tom looked in through one of the windows. He saw an elderly wizard and a young apprentice working together on some potions. The wizard looked up, straight at Tom, and smiled. 'Goodness, my Toby dog! Who have you brought me this time?' he said.

Tom explained to the wizard the terrible thing that had happened to Anna. He begged the wizard to help him rescue her from the Snow Queen. The wizard thought for a while. Then he looked in his cupboard until he found the potion he was after. He gave the bottle to his apprentice to hold, and they all walked out of the cottage with Toby at their heels.

The wizard led Tom back to the palace. When they stood outside the gates, the wizard took the bottle from his apprentice and uncorked it. Green smoke rose from the bottle and the air became warm. The ice palace began to melt. Suddenly, they heard a shriek from inside. The Snow Queen came rushing out. 'What are you doing?' she screamed.

'I know that you cannot stand warmth. If you do not return Anna, I will melt your palace and get her myself,' said the wizard firmly.

The Snow Queen was furious, but she knew that she could not fight the wizard. Reluctantly, she set Anna free and marched back into her palace. Anna hugged Tom tightly. Leaving the apprentice to walk back to the house, the wizard and Toby led the children back to their cottage. They thanked him over and over for his help and promised their mum that they would never go into the forest again.

A selection of songs and clapping rhymes

Songs

Aiken Drum

There was a man lived in the moon, lived in the moon,
    lived in the moon.
There was a man lived in the moon and his name was Aiken Drum.
And he played upon a ladle, a ladle, a ladle,
And he played upon a ladle, and his name was Aiken Drum.

You can create further verses to this song by changing the lines about what he did to what he wore. The items in the song are traditionally made of food, such as these:

- His hat was made of good cream cheese.
- His coat was made of good roast beef.
- His buttons were made of penny loaves.

The children can add their own verses by thinking of other items of clothing made from different foods.

Head and shoulders

Head and shoulders, knees and toes,
Knees and toes.
Head and shoulders, knees and toes,
Knees and toes.
And eyes and ears, and mouth and nose,
Head and shoulders, knees and toes.
Knees and toes.

This lively action song can lift a group if it is flagging. The children touch the relevant part of their body as they say the rhyme.

If you're happy and you know it

If you're happy and you know it, clap your hands. *(Clap twice)*
If you're happy and you know it, clap your hands. *(Clap twice)*
If you're happy and you know it and you really want to show it,
If you're happy and you know it, clap your hands. *(Clap twice)*

There are all sorts of variations on this theme. Try changing 'clap your hands' to 'stamp your feet', or 'shout "I am"'.

Michael Finnigan

There was an old man called Michael Finnigan,
He grew whiskers on his chin-igan.
The wind came out and blew them in-igan,
Poor old Michael Finnigan, begin-again.

There was an old man called Michael Finnigan,
He went fishing with a pin-igan.
Caught a fish then dropped it in-igan,
Poor old Michael Finnigan, begin-again.

There was an old man called Michael Finnigan,
He grew fat and then grew thin-igan.
Then he died and had to begin-again,
Poor old Michael Finnigan!

Mr McGilligan

Mr McGilligan went away
On his annual holiday.
He took a suitcase, tall and wide,
And this is what he packed inside.

The adult leading the song points to one of the children, who says or sings an item that was in the case. The more far-fetched and silly the item is, the better. The verse is then repeated, another child is asked, and so on.

Songs

One man went to mow

One man went to mow
Went to mow a meadow.
One man and his dog *(Woof)*
Went to mow a meadow.

Two men went to mow
Went to mow a meadow.
Two men, one man and his
    dog *(Woof)*
Went to mow a meadow.

Three men went to mow,
Went to mow a meadow.
Three men, two men, one man
    and his dog *(Woof)*
Went to mow a meadow.

Choose one child to be the dog. They shout 'Woof' after every mention of the word 'dog'. Choose three other children to be the men. Number the children from 1 to 3. When you begin a verse, the relevant number of children must stand up. The children numbered 2 and 3 sit down in the latter part of each verse as their number is mentioned, leaving the child numbered '1' standing.

She'll be coming round the mountain

She'll be coming round the mountain when she comes.
She'll be coming round the mountain when she comes.
She'll be coming round the mountain, coming round the mountain,
    coming round the mountain when she comes.

She'll be driving six white horses when she comes.
She'll be driving six white horses when she comes.
She'll be driving six white horses, driving six white horses,
    driving six white horses when she comes.

And we'll all go out to meet her when she comes.
And we'll all go out to meet her when she comes.
And we'll all go out to meet her, we'll all go out to meet her,
    we'll all go out to meet when she comes.

Songs

Starlight

Starlight, star bright.
First star I see tonight.
Wish I may, wish I might,
Have the wish I wish tonight.

During this song, the children sit in a circle and pass a star made of gold card from one child to another. At the end of the verse, whoever has the star makes a wish.

Ten green bottles

Ten green bottles hanging on the wall.
Ten green bottles hanging on the wall.
And if one green bottle should accidentally fall,
There'd be nine green bottles hanging on the wall.

The verses continue, the number of bottles reducing by I each time, until the final verse for one green bottle. It ends with the line 'There'd be no green bottles hanging on the wall.'

The children in our group painted pictures of green bottles, which we laminated. When we sing this song, they stand in a line, each holding their bottle. One of the adults points at one of the children at the appropriate point of the verse, and that child 'falls down'.

This old man

This old man, he played one.
He played knick-knack on my drum.
With a knick-knack, paddy whack,
Give a dog a bone.
This old man came rolling home.

This basic verse format may be adapted by substituting a different line relating to each number up to 10. For example:

2 He played knick-knack on my shoe.
3 He played knick-knack on my knee.
4 He played knick-knack on my door.
5 He played knick-knack on my hive.
6 He played knick-knack on my sticks.

7 He played knick-knack down in Devon.
8 He played knick-knack on my gate.
9 He played knick-knack on my line.
10 He played knick-knack on my hen.

Songs

Rhymes to clap along to

A sailor went to sea

A sailor went to sea, sea, sea,
To see what he could see, see, see.
And all that he could see, see, see,
Was the bottom of the deep blue sea, sea, sea.

At the bottom of the sea

At the bottom of the sea, so blue and green,
Is the biggest, fattest whale you have ever seen.
He opens his mouth from nose to chin
And all the little silver fish swim right in.

Aye diddle aye

Aye diddle aye, clap high.
Yo diddle doh, clap low.
First to this side, then to that.
Aye diddle aye, clap high.
Yo diddle doh, clap low.

Clap out, clap in

Clap out. *(Stretch arms out in front and clap)*
Clap in. *(Clap with arms close to body)*
Repeat both lines.
Clap under, clap over. *(Clap under and over one leg)*
Clap under, clap over. *(Clap under and over the other leg)*
Clap above here, clap above there. *(Clap high to the right and
    then the left)*
Repeat.
Clap, clap, clap around. *(Clap and turn round on the spot)*

Copy the leader

We'll copy the leader, copy the leader, copy the leader,
    whatever they do.
Who will be our leader, our leader, our leader?
Who will be our leader and show us what to do?

At this point, a child volunteers to show an action for the others to copy.

Fee, fi, fo, fum

Fee fi fo fum, I spy Giant Glum,
Giant Glum fast asleep. I spy Bo Peep,
Bo Peep round the corner. I spy Jack Horner,
Jack Horner up a pole. I spy King Cole,
King Cole drinking juice. I spy Mother Goose,
Mother Goose being nice. I spy blind mice,
Blind mice eating tarts. I spy Queen of Hearts.

Happy feeling, happy beat

Clap your hands, stamp your feet.
Happy feeling, happy beat.
Clap your hands, stamp your feet
To chase your cares away.
If you're feeling sad,
If you're feeling down,
Take that feeling, wrap it up
And send it out of town.
Clap your hands, stamp your feet,
Happy feeling, happy beat.
Clap your hands, stamp your feet
To chase your cares away.

Clapping rhymes

Lazy Laura

Lazy Laura, sleepy head, likes to spend all day in bed.
> *(Say and clap slowly)*

Tiny Tina, tippy toes, quietly comes and quietly goes.
> *(Whisper and clap quietly)*

Busy Boris, brisk and bright, strides along with all his might.
> *(Say in a loud voice and clap loudly)*

Rapid Ryan racing past — like the wind he's really fast.
> *(Say and clap as quickly as you can)*

On Noah's ark

There's a chimpanzee and a crocodile.

There's a spotted cheetah with a cheeky smile.

There's a white rhino and a hippo too,

With wrinkled skin, and there's a kangaroo.

There's a wiggly snake and a small, brown mouse,

And an elephant that's as big as a house.

There's a friendly dog with a noisy bark

And they all live together on Noah's ark.

The long-legged sailor

Did you ever, ever, ever in your long-legged life

See a long-legged sailor with a long-legged wife?

No I never, never, never in my long-legged life

Saw a long-legged sailor with a long-legged wife.

Clapping rhymes

Expressions

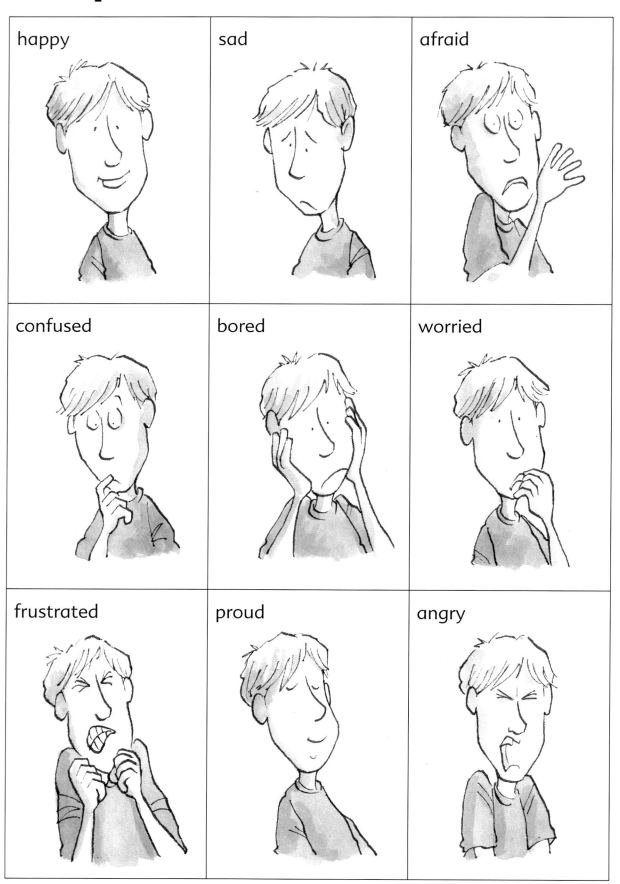

happy

sad

afraid

confused

bored

worried

frustrated

proud

angry

Half-termly review

Name of child: .... Date: ....

Skills	Consistently achieved	Occasionally achieved	Not achieved
Social skills			
1 Has a good relationship with adults.	☐	☐	☐
2 Shares toys and equipment.	☐	☐	☐
3 Plays co-operatively with a partner.	☐	☐	☐
4 Play co-operatively with a group.	☐	☐	☐
5 Loses graciously.	☐	☐	☐
6 Waits and takes turns.	☐	☐	☐
7 Lines up without interfering with others.	☐	☐	☐
Listening			
1 Listens without interrupting.	☐	☐	☐
2 Follows instructions.	☐	☐	☐
3 Asks a question about what has been said.	☐	☐	☐
4 Sits still, listens and looks.	☐	☐	☐
Emotional literacy			
1 Identifies and models facial expressions.	☐	☐	☐
2 Identifies and models body postures.	☐	☐	☐
3 Attributes appropriate feelings to characters in stories.	☐	☐	☐
4 Responds to questions, such as 'How would you feel?'	☐	☐	☐
5 Recognises how their body feels when calm/upset/angry.	☐	☐	☐
6 Articulates their feelings appropriately.	☐	☐	☐
7 Understands the needs and views of others.	☐	☐	☐
8 Expresses wishes/dissatisfaction without negative verbal or physical behaviour.	☐	☐	☐
9 Accepts responsibility for actions.	☐	☐	☐
Denial acceptance			
1 Can accept a clear choice.	☐	☐	☐
2 Can accept a 'No' answer.	☐	☐	☐
3 Can do as asked without argument.	☐	☐	☐
Understands the rules of the group.	☐	☐	☐
Accepts the rules of the group.	☐	☐	☐

Teacher questionnaire

Please circle the number that relates to how you feel about the related statement, with '0' standing for 'strongly disagree' and '5' for 'strongly agree'. If you have any further comments, please use the space at the bottom of the page.

The group has had a positive effect on all the children in the school.	0	1	2	3	4	5
The group has had a positive effect on the adults in the school.	0	1	2	3	4	5
Having a child from my class in the group has benefited the other children in my class.	0	1	2	3	4	5
Having a child from my class in the group has been a positive experience for me.	0	1	2	3	4	5
I have been able to discuss any problems that have arisen with the group's facilitators.	0	1	2	3	4	5
I would have liked more opportunities to discuss issues and problems with the group's facilitators.	0	1	2	3	4	5
I would like more opportunities to visit the group.	0	1	2	3	4	5
I feel that I have a good understanding of what a nurture group is and how the children are helped.	0	1	2	3	4	5
I feel that the children who have attended the group have made good progress in functioning in the school.	0	1	2	3	4	5
I feel that the children who have attended the group have made good academic progress.	0	1	2	3	4	5
The group helps to prevent children failing at school.	0	1	2	3	4	5

Any further comments: